White Male Nostalgia in Contemporary North American Literature

Tim Engles

White Male Nostalgia in Contemporary North American Literature

Tim Engles
Eastern Illinois University
Charleston, IL, USA

ISBN 978-3-319-90459-7   ISBN 978-3-319-90460-3   (eBook)
https://doi.org/10.1007/978-3-319-90460-3

Library of Congress Control Number: 2018940732

This Palgrave Macmillan imprint is published by the registered company Springer International Publishing AG part of Springer Nature
The registered company address is: Gewerbestrasse 11, 6330 Cham, Switzerland

PREFACE

Fig. 1 Everett T.C. Engles surveys another spectacular view

About twelve years ago, I traveled to Alaska with my father, Everett Matisse Engles. He passed away while I was finishing this book, although much more than inopportune timing prompts me to dedicate it to him. I've been studying white American masculinity for over a decade now, and considering literary novels in the ways that I do in this book has helped me see anew my father and myself, that trip we took together, and how we felt about it.

We rented a car in Anchorage, and over the course of two weeks we drove nearly 4,000 miles, mostly in pursuit of ever-better trout and salmon fishing. We continually marveled as we moved through what struck us as vast, open, untrammeled territory. We made time for hiking trails, especially those that took us upwards, high enough so that we could survey what struck us as spectacular views. Outside of its cities and towns, Alaska mostly registered for us an especially glorious example of unspoiled "wilderness" and almost never as a place where indigenous people had preceded us. I didn't realize it at the time, but our status as white American men encouraged us to see it all in certain ways—to feel entirely free and welcome to travel there, for example, and to enjoy the "spectacular" views and to feel perfectly entitled to the reaping of its riverine resources. Our unwitting social status also helped us feel a certain wistfulness, a sort of longing for an earlier time, when more of the earth had been similarly "unspoiled." Unspoiled by what, we might have asked, but didn't.

"Fishy" resources now seems a better way to describe what we reaped and then had freeze-dried and shipped back home. Something disconcerting was tugging at me during that trip, and perhaps at my father too, although we never talked about it. When we heard while there that the place we'd long known as Mt. McKinley was commonly referred to by an indigenous name, Denali, we nodded and did our best to remember and use this other name, but our acknowledgement of an indigenous past ended there. We made no effort to learn about the people who had used that name for the mountain, nor whether any of their descendants were alive. I had a nagging feeling that there was something off about our presence in Alaska—our relation to the place and how that relation encouraged us to see it. Analyzing for this study the deeply interiorized portraits of white American male protagonists provided by six novelists has helped me view those feelings as particularly common white American male ones.

My father was born and raised in Goodman, a small, northern Wisconsin lumber town surrounded by what we'd both long been encouraged by our social order to think of as "wilderness," although vast tracts of it are basically privately owned tree farms, crisscrossed with logging roads. He and my mother, Lynette Adell (Giere) Engles, moved to the city of Milwaukee after high school, where they raised me and my sister, Kimberlyn. My parents moved back home to Goodman in the 1980s to run the town's single grocery store, and Dad spent as much time as he could hunting and fishing and then, as he grew older, more and more evenings just driving through "the woods." When I rode along with him, he often reminisced about his own remembered past, the days when Goodman was a vibrant, teeming town, and the waters held so many more fish. And the fish themselves were "native," meaning they hadn't been farmed and then planted in the lakes, streams, and rivers by the state government. My father's favorite activity was fly-fishing for trout, in places like the Pike River, the Peshtigo, and a place I can't find on any maps that he called the Kedger. He often waxed nostalgic in particular about brown trout, which used to be so much bigger and more plentiful than those few that one might be lucky enough to catch in those places now. These were the days of his youth, the 1940s and 1950s, times that are usually looked back on quite so fondly in the United States only by other white men who grew up then. I learned something later about this particular fish that I never had the heart to point out to him: that brown trout were not native to Wisconsin, having been imported in the late 1800s from Germany.

My father may well have known that fact. If not, he would have immediately understood my implication had I stated it: that his longing for a pure unspoiled past, a feeling and perspective that also had both of us in its grips in Alaska, was a fallacy. Had I pushed the point, he might have acknowledged how his nostalgia, for the good old days of a bustling lumber town, but also for a prelapsarian "wilderness" and for a relatively active and autonomous way of being that we both imagined was more possible back then—was more likely to be felt by white American men like us. He would have acknowledged such corrections to his sense of the past, but I know he wouldn't have especially appreciated it. He knew, of course, about previous indigenous peoples in northern Wisconsin— the Potowatami, the Menominee, the Oneida—and about the "reservations" where their descendants live. He might have even known that the Oneida were not native to the place that white Americans dubbed with an appropriated indigenous word, Wisconsin, that they'd been forcibly relocated from what is now called New York. We both knew some of these kinds of facts about others, though vaguely, and in ways that we suppressed in favor of more nostalgic conceptions of times and places where men like ourselves seemed less encumbered, less constrained.

I now know that the mountain name, Denali, likely derives from the Denaakk'e language, also known as Koyukon, and that people who speak it still live in the area. I also know more about what discouraged me (while traveling) from acknowledging the significance of such knowledge and the presence of such peoples. I'd been trained in certain ways, ways that I'm still learning about, to think and act like an ordinary white American man, albeit a man who could afford to fulfill a common, nostalgia-tinged dream by traveling to Alaska. Thanks to academic training in creative literature and related studies in history, psychology, philosophy, theology, and other fields, I can now argue, as I demonstrate in this book, that because literary authors often depict in their characters such complex interior depths, many novels offer effective case studies of common white American male feelings, dispositions, attitudes, pathologies, and more. Their protagonists often reveal that as with my father and myself, a common white male response to the challenges of changing times is to resort to nostalgic reveries for supposedly simpler times and supposedly open spaces, where it seemed that people like us had more freedom to move and act. And, sometimes, to conquer and even kill, though had it been us, in ways that would've always been justified or at least excusable. Such reveries are, of course, disturbed by facts, such as those that reveal the lack of freedom and resources that others had, the suffering they often endured, and the resistance with which they often fought back, and still do, precisely because they were subject to the same white supremacist patriarchal ideology that still benefits and infects us white male nostalgics.

Urbana, IL, USA   Tim Engles

ACKNOWLEDGEMENTS

Over the past six years, many people have helped with this project. I am indebted to Eastern Illinois University for a sabbatical leave and course releases and to its Council on Faculty Research for generous summer grant funds. I would also like to note innumerable forms of help from those who serve at Eastern's Booth Library, especially Karen Whisler, Jana Aydt, and Sue Yocum. I learned much from the perspectives, insights, and camaraderie provided by Eastern Illinois graduate students in two related seminars: "African American Whiteness" and "Race, Ethnicity and Masculinity in Contemporary American Literature." I am grateful, for their consistently meticulous and provocative suggestions, to members of the Chambana writing group, Jeff Magee, Gayle Sherwood Magee, and Christina Bashford; to my colleague, Jeannie Ludlow, for careful reading of an especially thorny chapter; and to three other colleagues, Linda Coleman, Melissa Ames and Melissa Caldwell, for further help, commiseration, and inspiration.

I appreciate and applaud the patient guidance and advice of my Palgrave editor, Allie Bochicchio, as well as editorial experts of various kinds at two other places, which published early versions of two chapters: Cambridge University Press ("White Male Nostalgia in Don DeLillo's *Underworld*," which appeared in Len Platt and Sara Upstone's 2015 book, *Postmodern Fiction and Race*) and University Press of Mississippi ("About Schmidt's Whiteness: The Emotional Landscapes of WASP Masculinity," which appeared in Stephen Middleton, David R. Roediger, and Donald M. Shaffer's 2016 book, *The Construction of Whiteness: An*

Interdisciplinary Analysis of Race Formation and the Meaning of a White Identity). I am also grateful to those at the University of Huddersfield who so graciously hosted my trying out of early thoughts on DeLillo's meditations on white male nostalgia, especially Sarah Falcus, as well as Merrick Burrow, David Rudrum, and Todd Andrew Borlik.

I also owe unpayable debts to my greatest joy, my daughter Zavi Kang Engles, for among many other gifts, her careful editing and proofreading prowess, for reading novels along with me, and for lengthy walks devoted to discussing them. Finally, for more than I can ever describe in terms of help, support, and inspiration, thank you Christina, light of my life, song of my heart.

CONTENTS

1 **Introduction: Making America White Male Again**   1
   Common White Male Dispositions   3
   Forms of White Male Nostalgia   9
   Bibliography   21

2 **Ethnicized White Male Nostalgia: Sloan Wilson's**
   The Man in the Gray Flannel Suit   25
   White Anglo-Saxonism   26
   Resurgent White Anglo-Saxonism   32
   Empathetic Black Male Embodiment and White Male
   Emotional Constipation   35
   The Ethnicist Presence   41
   Pseudo-Feudal Nostalgia   47
   Bibliography   65

3 **Moralizing White Male Nostalgia: Richard Wright's**
   Savage Holiday   69
   White Male Histories   72
   Purified White Male Bodies   81
   The White Male Death Drive   89
   Bibliography   105

4   Spatialized White Male Nostalgia: Carol Shields's
    Happenstance   109
    Contexts for Happenstance   110
    An Unwittingly White Male Historian   114
    Communally Cognizant Reflective Nostalgia   124
    Dehistoricized Land   132
    Geographical Space and White Male Mobility   135
    Bibliography   144

5   Denying White Male Nostalgia: Don DeLillo's
    Underworld   147
    The Relational Underpinnings of Cold War White Masculinity   149
    Reflective Nostalgia and Communal Art   160
    White-Male Pattern Deafness   164
    Masculinized Isolation and Feminized Community   169
    Bibliography   180

6   Possessive White Male Nostalgia: Louis Begley's *About
    Schmidt*   185
    Entitled White Masculinity   188
    Sovereign WASP Masculinity   197
    Nostalgic White World-Traveling   202
    The White Manchild   205
    Repressed White Male Shame   209
    Bibliography   219

7   Epilogue: Margaret Atwood's *The Heart Goes Last*
    and the Futures of Domineering White Masculinity   223
    Bibliography   237

Index   239

CHAPTER 1

Introduction: Making America White Male Again

When a candidate who had been caught bragging about sexually assaulting women ran during the 2016 presidential election with the full-throated support of the Ku Klux Klan, all while repeatedly promising to "Make America Great Again," he both embodied and deployed a form of nostalgia that was particularly appealing to white men. Indeed, as a discrete demographic, white American men were the group who supported Donald Trump far more than any other did.[1] Since the election, simmering resentment has surged into the open as "alt-right" support for what amounts to a form of fascism grounded in white nationalism, and the vast majority of its adherents have been disgruntled men who mourn the way things supposedly used to be. What many clearly miss in particular is unchallenged white male dominance, which Trump helped them locate in a fantasized past, where ethnoracial minorities and women cowered in the background, except when summoned into service by their white male betters.

As those who reject such a reactionary vision struggle to find effective ways of doing so, one way that has arisen is to fight back. One such example is "Punch a Nazi," a revived form of World War II–style sloganeering that constitutes a left-leaning form of nostalgia promulgated primarily by, again, white American men. Another, potentially more productive way of countering the new wave of overt nationalism is to examine how such illusory fears of disempowerment function inside white men and where such feelings come from. In addition to the important work of understanding the contexts that produce such fears, what

© The Author(s) 2018
T. Engles, *White Male Nostalgia in Contemporary North American Literature*, https://doi.org/10.1007/978-3-319-90460-3_1

1

interior psychological and emotional responses do they produce? How does what amounts to a collective delusion—entitled, domineering white masculinity—work at the individual level, and what part is played by the contrary notion, common among the white American male collective, that they are not a collective and are instead atomized, free-floating individuals? Although nostalgia is often thought of as an emotion felt by individuals, how does it work within them to shore up entrenched collective power? Where has this misguided sentiment come from historically?

Twentieth-century literary fiction often includes intricate portrayals of common psychological and emotional states, and the novels examined here provide adept analysis of representative white American male psyches. In addition, as Frederik Tygstrup points out in his study of literary representations of affect as a function of mapped geographical space, if we understand the self as socially situated in such a way that discernible structures such as whiteness and masculinity tend to provoke common emotional responses, then literary fiction can help us "study the self in different historical situations and chart different historically contextualized emotions." With its often deeply examined portrayals of personal interiority, literary fiction can help to trace "how subjectively felt emotions taint the perception of outer stimuli ..."[2] Common proclivities and reactions are, of course, prompted and shaped by the particulars of any person's social situatedness; a crucial yet overlooked feature of the ironically collective white American male mindset that the novelists considered here illuminate is the forms of nostalgia often provoked in white American men by those who resist their dominance. Perceiving this emotion as common to a particular collectivity calls for explanatory context, especially that of the actual history denied by what appears to be a common white male nostalgic reflex. Writing from various identities positioned outside of normalized middle-class white masculinity, these authors dramatize how complex and widespread such longings among the dominant have been. Such feelings surface nowadays among white men of the sort who would likely never consider voting for a demagogue like Trump. Since the mid-1990s, scholars have extensively examined literary depictions of reactionary forms of white male backlash, but the personally felt and imagined forms of backwardness signaled by the term "reactionary" have received little attention.[3] This study conducts such an endeavor, finding in analytic case studies a preliminary taxonomy of particular forms that white American male nostalgia has recently tended to take.

COMMON WHITE MALE DISPOSITIONS

A working understanding of this study is that the perspective of the subordinated outsider can induce a keen understanding of the dominant white male psyche. The novels considered here are by authors socially categorized in ethnoracial and national terms as African American (Richard Wright), Italian American (Don DeLillo), Jewish American (Louis Begley), and Canadian (Carol Shields and Margaret Atwood, who focus extensively as well on patriarchal inclinations). The sixth author, Sloan Wilson, is commonly regarded as a more or less "ordinary" American man of his time, but his zeitgeist-capturing novel, *The Man in the Gray Flannel Suit* (1955), betrays both him and his protagonist, Tom Rath, as another sort of outsider, the bearer of a largely unconscious White Anglo-Saxon Protestant (WASP) heritage. This positionality is largely hidden from Tom and apparently even from Wilson himself. Nostalgic feelings repeatedly arise for these novels' white male protagonists, usually when faced with heightened expectations of egalitarian treatment and opportunity by women and subordinated ethnoracial minorities. The protagonists often evoke elements of selectively conceived pasts, illustrating not only an illusory sense of unfair treatment of themselves but also a broader failure of the social order that has long favored and exalted them. This failure springs from a collective refusal to acknowledge, let alone attempt to reconcile, a lurking contrast between the brutal realities of the nation's past and its mythical, vainglorious representations of both itself and its archetypal white male leaders, a contrast that to this day continues to haunt the nation's sociopolitical landscape.

With their sustained method of sociohistorically situated interior portraiture, these novelists demonstrate that, in terms of self-conception, white men in the United States are not what they are more likely than others to think and feel they are—free-floating individuals without significantly raced and gendered identities. As legal scholar Ian Haney López reminds us about the history of racial formations in the United States, all identities are socially formed and thus ineluctably relational: "Fathoming the content of white identity requires a shift from thinking about races as categories toward conceptualizing races in terms of relationships. [...] It is in the elaboration of these relationships—invariably of domination and subordination, normativity and marginality, privilege and disadvantage—that white identity is given content."[4] A grounding presumption of this study is that in a putatively meritocratic, egalitarian social order, dominance is continually normalized into commonsense ideology. The largely unexamined social water in which we all swim inculcates in individuals a discernible array of suppositions, feelings, prejudices, and inducements toward seemingly appropriate action; this array generally functions, as social theorist Pierre Bourdieu succinctly puts it, as that which "goes without saying because it comes without saying."[5] Race, gender, sexuality, and other categorizing forces have intertwined coterminously in favoring and disfavoring ways, and those least aware of the resultant hierarchical social order tend to be those most marked, yet unmarked, as the norm—heterosexual middle-class white men. Their greater ignorance of such social forces and their results constitutes a mass delusion, a psychological and emotional state produced by a history of often brutal dominance within a culture that denies such history and such dominance.

As the chapters here demonstrate, understanding white male dominance in the hopes of countering it calls for elucidation of both its historical context and the inner workings of those who enact it. As Joel Kovel put it in his groundbreaking "psychohistory" of white racism, "It is the average man, with his 'normal' racism and fantasies, whose behavior will give the key to the deeper meanings of racism. For, if personality and culture are congruent, then it is the 'normal' man's personality which most accurately mirrors the psychohistory of his culture."[6] I have drawn heavily from both critical whiteness studies and critical masculinity studies for theoretical help, but I do see in each a common lack: what is posited in critical whiteness studies as true of white people is often especially true of white men, and what is posited in masculinity studies as true of men is also often especially true of white men. I hope that my project will help to flesh out this rarely acknowledged conceptual overlap.[7]

Additionally, as historians of the United States continually remind us, stark contrasts have always existed between the way the nation presents itself to both its citizens and the rest of the world and the reality of its often brutal ways; indeed, the obliteration of other "Americas" in its other, well-fondled name effectively emblematizes the erasure that is endemic to the nation's self-presentation. Although any nation functions as such on the necessary grounding of a narrated, shared past, the truths of which often get glossed over, in the United States, certain obscured truths exist at an especially grotesque level and scale. The harsh realities of genocide, stolen lands, stolen lives, enforced labor, and more continue to go largely unspoken (especially by the dominant) and—when spoken—largely unheard. When the subordinated speak historical truth and resist its ongoing results, they increasingly do so in ways that must be heard by the dominant, because they make the contrast between putative meritocratic egalitarianism and ongoing subjugation and expropriation too obvious to deny. Common white male reactions, both individually and (ironically enough) collectively, are to deny national truths that strike others as obvious and to seek reassertion and bolstering of white male dominance. Hearkening back nostalgically to earlier eras, in which the subordinated are cast as less restive, and the settings more enabling of unfettered white male action and self-staging, can seem to provide such reassertion—or at least, an assuaging, compensatory reassurance.

As the novels studied here effectively dramatize, white men who engage in such self-bolstering denial and nostalgia are not only those who display white supremacist tattoos and haircuts while marching for recognition of the supposedly threatened white race, but "ordinary" men as well, members of the normalized middle-class—a group in which the majority of men also voted for Donald Trump and his revanchist agenda. The desired return to previous eras of seemingly unchallenged eminence commonly animates even those white American men who do not recognize the dominance of their collective or, if they do, would not consciously seek reassertion of such dominance. Nevertheless, such men often react negatively to progressive change that highlights and challenges their ascendancy, resulting in feelings that they struggle to understand. These feelings in turn often result in emotionally saturated returns to fantasized earlier social arrangements and settings that seem more congenial to the performance of unfettered white masculinity.

Extended studies of white male nostalgia per se do not yet exist, although studies of white masculinity do, within and across numerous fields.[8] A common assertion in such work is that although collective white male dominance persists, overt declarations of its presumptions and assertions receded during the late twentieth century, largely in response to feminist and civil rights agitation. One result of this recent seemingly unmarked status (an unmarkedness less perceived as such by others) has been confusion for many white men over what feels like an undeserved loss of status. In terms of literary cultural production, scholars have increasingly pointed out that most vaunted American novels with white male protagonists have been written by authors who are themselves white men, and a scholarly consensus has emerged that white male American authors have unwittingly tended to reproduce the same egregious common tendencies enacted by their beleaguered, primarily middle-class protagonists. Such authors did so by complaining via their novels about supposed attacks on people like themselves, attacks launched merely because they were white men. In her landmark study, *Marked Men: White Masculinity in Crisis*, Sally Robinson labels such novels white male "liberationist" narratives, and she traces in them an "identity politics of the dominant" and a common plot, that of a white man who finds freedom from the social circumstances that supposedly oppress him.[9] Like subsequent scholars, Robinson demonstrates how such novelists gave voice to a conviction held by many white men that the rise of identity politics among disempowered groups, and the consequent highlighting of empowered white masculinity, resulted not in justified calls for restitution and opportunity but rather in a supposed attack on white men merely for being white and male. This common, blinkered claim of white male victimhood, which has also been prevalent in American politics and popular culture, ironically echoes minority struggles for liberation from oppression, reformulating as it does a privileged social status into a supposed set of disadvantages.

In contrast, the authors gathered here, positioned as they are outside of normalized middle-class white masculinity, can largely be credited with providing more insightful and potentially recuperative assessments of common late-twentieth-century forms of white-male malaise. They do so, whether with apparent intention or not, by acknowledging the contextual backdrop of the influential history and ongoing reality of American white supremacist patriarchal domination. In particular, these novels repeatedly register the more brutal realities of American history as well as a common white American male orientation toward the past, thereby demonstrating the nostalgic thrust of their protagonists' representative conceptions of earlier and supposedly better times. When read in light of their white male characters' particular forms of temporal backwardness, these novels demonstrate that such common white-male emotions are often better understood as a consequence of new pressures and expectations in a newly consumer-driven and hyper-individualistic era, rather than of supposedly unfair demands or encroachments made by women and ethnoracial minorities. As signaled by the terms that begin each of my chapter titles, they also demonstrate that white male nostalgia tends to take particular forms, resulting in actions that spring from dispositions commonly inculcated among the often unwittingly dominant.

Ultimately, these authors provide insight into a tripartite and hitherto unexamined topic: the vexed feelings that financially stable, middle-class white American men have often experienced about their challenged social status; their consequent turn at times to compensatory and seemingly restorative nostalgia; and the wide-ranging repercussions and implications of this turn. These authors thereby manage to sidestep that which has appeared all too often in the white male–dominated literary field: the predictable and melodramatic narrative pattern of white male despair and rejuvenation. As Nina Baym pointed out in 1981, a (white) male critical consensus had produced a revered literary canon, a constructed tradition amenable to and exclusively occupied by (white) male authors. Baym labeled this tradition "melodramas of beset manhood."[10] As Baym explained, that which supposedly beset men—who were cast in the form of male protagonists and of male authors themselves—was conventional society, which alienated these authors and their protagonists by constraining them from pursuit of unfettered action as the expression of a genuine self. In such a tradition, womanhood existed primarily in projected, phantasmagorical guises, as constraining antagonist, or as a perpetually feminized "virgin" landscape, and by the rules of such a masculine-oriented and -constructed literary tradition, women were disregarded as serious literary artists. Any positive outcome in such narratives, whether realized or merely desired, was cast as the rejuvenation of the liberated male protagonist. As Sally Robinson and others have since demonstrated, such a solipsistic tradition persists, despite the heightened recognition and ascent of other (women's, ethnoracial, and LGBTQ+) identity-marked literatures.

With the notable exception of Wilson's *Grey Flannel*, which recapitulates many of its era's blinkered white male anxieties and complaints, the novels considered here cast a more discerning gaze on the dilemmas of supposedly beset white manhood, recognizing it as a form of character casting that continues to exist in reality. Ordinary white men often cast themselves melodramatically (and, in Robinson's terms, hysterically) as struggling protagonists of their own lives, unjustly besieged by the status-threatening demands of women and ethnoracial minorities. As a current meme of apparently indeterminate origin puts it in describing such emotions, "When you're accustomed to privilege, equality feels like oppression."[11] In regard to history and nostalgia, narratives that reiterate the weary plot of "melodramas of beset manhood" rarely address or assess the national past judiciously, as most of the novels considered here do. Such acknowledgement of the broader, actual sociohistorical context helps to explain just how such melodramas fail in their depictions of white male entrapment and rejuvenation. They do so by in effect re-inscribing white male hegemony, an entrenched form of collective control and entitlement that such individualized narratives typically fail to even acknowledge, let alone challenge.

Thus, the novels considered here, ranging from those written and set in the 1950s to Margaret Atwood's recent depiction of a possible near-future, constitute a literary counter-history of the era's anxious white masculinity, functioning as case studies of an empowered social positionality. This positionality—that of a white American man widely depicted and seen as ordinary—commonly induces what I will label restorative nostalgia. Here, I follow Svetlana Boym's landmark study, *The Future of Nostalgia*, in which she identifies two primary modes of nostalgia that reflect national contexts and resonate within them. "Restorative nostalgia" is a desire (an *algia*, or aching) to return to a previous time and place (a *nostos*, or a home), and thus to an idealized set of conditions, ultimately as a way of securing dominance in the present. As Boym explains, attendant to restorative nostalgia is an effort "to patch up the memory gaps," a replacement of historical unknowns with fabricated memories that serve a fabricated present.[12] As many historians of memory and nostalgia have noted, conceptions of this complex feeling have moved from its origins in the late seventeenth century, when the term diagnosed a supposedly physical illness among European soldiers literally longing to go home, to the current meaning of a seemingly personal and emotionally laden desire, that of retrieving hazily remembered elements of some previous time.[13] Of course, though illusory and often wielded in suspect ways, nostalgia is not a necessarily negative condition. As several authors considered here demonstrate, its forms and uses can be constructive, including a form that Boym distinguishes as "reflective nostalgia." Unlike restorative nostalgia, this form "acknowledges the imperfect process of remembrance" and, more significantly, uses conceptions of the past, often playfully, toward the building of a more relationally cognizant and communally oriented present, and future.[14] Conversely, as insightfully dramatized in most of the novels examined here, ordinary white men often resort to nostalgic feelings in a solipsistic mode as a form of compensation, for a felt diminution in the present of their circumstances and status and as an attempt to restore conditions that supposedly fostered a less encumbered state of being.

In these terms, the gathering of authors here stages a confrontation of sorts between how white men commonly understand themselves and how women and members of subordinated ethnoracial groups often understand them differently. Given the starkly binarized social frameworks in which these authors necessarily write, conceptions of the past that frame it in positive "reflective" terms are sometimes cast as the resistant work of characters who are women, and, at least in DeLillo's *Underworld* (1997), of such ethnoracially marked artists as Simon/ Sabato Rodia and the fictional Ismael Muñoz.

FORMS OF WHITE MALE NOSTALGIA

As an initial foray into analysis of white male nostalgia, this study identifies in these novels the extensive depiction of five different socially inflected forms that contemporary white male nostalgia can take in the United States: ethnicized, moralizing, spatialized, possessive, and denying. In all cases, these forms constitute an illusory and backwards temporal orientation, including a longing for the restoration of a romanticized past. These novelists thus provide insight into a common emotional reflex felt and acted upon by many white American men when confronted with threats to their status, prerogatives, and control over others.

In the postwar setting of the first two novels considered here, Sloan Wilson's *The Man in the Gray Flannel Suit* and Richard Wright's *Savage Holiday* (1954), a newly declared racial and ethnic tolerance in the United States made ignoring uglier parts of a national past less tenable. Nevertheless, maintenance of a superior positionality for white men continued, in part by casting women and ethnoracial minorities in familiar terms and as unsuitable for full-fledged participatory citizenship. Conceptions of the national past remained useful in this regard, as national self-declarations and sentiment framed those unsettling elements of the past that could not be ignored *merely* in the past and thus of no concern to those living in the shiny new, consumerist present. As postwar America launched itself into an obstinately segregated, male-dominated future, conceptions of the national past instead consisted primarily of fantasies about foundational American strength, innocence, and goodness, fantasies promulgated by popular culture and clung to by many white men as a bulwark against changing social mores and growing demands for equality. In her analysis of nostalgic fictional paeans during the 1950s to romanticized indigeneity and the early American "frontier,"

Sara L. Schwebel writes that middle-class white men who suffered from the "Organization Man's malaise," a condition induced by anxiety-inducing change, commonly turned to popular culture in order to gaze backward: "Frontier tales on television and in popular literature celebrated American dominance while simultaneously idolizing [white male] individuality, open land, and freedom from social constraints—precisely what the era of consensus, conformity, and anticommunism denied."[15] As middle-class white masculinity shifted further toward a status of heightened individualism that was purportedly unremarkable in ethnic, raced, and gendered terms, all while the nation professed a commitment to increased ethnoracial and gendered inclusion, the dominance, exclusion, and abuse committed at the hands of a de facto white male collective persisted.

Sloan Wilson's portrait of a disaffected corporate climber in *Grey Flannel* struck a popular chord at the time as a sympathetic exposé of the new trials inflicted on the era's everyman, especially when the eponymous film version starring Gregory Peck quickly appeared. The novel follows the melodramatic liberationist plot codified by Baym and Robinson, with protagonist Tom Rath struggling through his malaise as a lackluster corporate climber and his personal guilt about his own wartime actions, toward release from having to sell his laboring self to others. However, what accounts more specifically for this flagging hero's eventual rejuvenation is the material and psychological inheritance of white Anglo-Saxon ethnicity, which I term a "dominant hidden ethnicity." In addition, Tom Rath's status as archetypal, white 1950s everyman is challenged by Wilson's usage of overtly ethnic characters as foils for Tom's coolheadedness. These caricatured types, which I identify as examples of a narrative "ethnicist presence," closely resemble the Africanist presence delineated by Toni Morrison in her landmark study, *Playing in the Dark: Whiteness in the Literary Imagination*. As elements of Wilson's own background and of his other writings reveal, while he apparently strove to write more broadly about the travails of ordinary but anxious American manhood in a new, supposedly more egalitarian era, the resurgence of his protagonist's privileged northeastern background ultimately betrays Wilson's own nostalgia for the days of more overtly eminent and securely ensconced WASP male dominance.

When Richard Wright also chose an office worker, Erskine Fowler, as the protagonist of *Savage Holiday*, he depicted more overtly violent undercurrents in his protagonist's psyche. Given Wright's stated choice of a representatively white protagonist, the novel explores a fundamental conflict between common white male assumptions of moral superiority, and thus of deserved ascendancy, and their collective's horrifically abusive past and present. As a lifelong and necessarily keen observer of the dominant white masculine mindset, Richard Wright told an interviewer in 1956 that "the most important problem white people have to face [is] their moral dilemma. This is why I have chosen this white New Yorker as a protagonist."[16] Wright invited readers to move beyond the novel's conventional potboiler trappings to consider his protagonist as a representative, though satirically presented, white man and, more specifically, to interpret his tortured interior machinations in terms of a gendered, raced, and Christian-oriented moral context. The novel's overtly Freudian clues to the underpinnings of Fowler's tormented behavior, long dismissed as artlessly heavy-handed, also illuminate a broader context. I argue that, when read allegorically, such clues suggest that, as social theorist Ross Honeywill puts it, "the root of destructive masculinity lies deep in the psychoanalytic symbology of the Western cultural imaginary."[17] Thus, in this novel, Wright elaborates on a probing observation offered by James Baldwin in his 1965 essay "White Man's Guilt": "One can measure very easily the white American's distance from his conscience—from himself—by observing the distance between white America and black America. One has only to ask oneself who established this distance, who is this distance designed to protect, and from what is this distance designed to offer protection?"[18] With his focus on the interior machinations of a white male protagonist, Wright's *Savage Holiday* allegorizes hegemonic white masculine dominance in the United States by exposing its veneer of morality, and its consequent projection onto gendered and racialized others of the charge of immorality, as a self-protective refusal to acknowledge the stark contrast between the white male collectivity's abusiveness and its claim to moral superiority. Even today, given dominant white masculinity's continued mistreatment of its racialized and gendered others, not only is the insistence of such men on the adherence of others to their group's moral codes and on their own supposedly superior capacity to follow them ironic and hypocritical, such an insistence is also often propped up by memories or reminders of eras and settings in which white masculine dominance seemed more natural (especially to white men themselves). Wright's protagonist dramatizes through his actions, and through his overtly Freudian dreams, the compensatory nostalgia commonly resorted to by men who miss times in which perceived inferiors—women and ethnoracial minorities—were more securely under control, a control they supposedly deserved and needed as moral inferiors. The horrific violence enacted by Wright's protagonist both allegorizes the era's pent-up white male anxiety and warns about the potentially lethal effects of the refusal to acknowledge the contrast between an actual history of theft and carnage that lives in the present and the nation's broader, obliviously nostalgic framings of its past.

In these ways, *Savage Holiday* serves as a remarkably prophetic touchstone for later formations of white masculinity, including the forms dramatized in novels by Shields, Begley, DeLillo, and Atwood. All of the protagonists considered here respond emotionally to egalitarian calls from the subordinated, and all respond at times with frustration and anger as well as bouts of restorative or compensatory nostalgia, or both. As these novelists demonstrate, these particularly socially inculcated moments of white male emotion are *necessarily* nostalgic, a deeply psychic homesickness for a nationally situated structure of uncontested, self-assured, and unchallenged eminence that never really existed. As *Savage Holiday* ultimately suggests, assessing the national past more honestly would help to expose the hypocritical morality that has long buttressed both mythologizing white male presumptions about their vaunted collectivity and selves and the denial of their abuses of subordinated others, all within an imagined, selectively populated geographical space long configured in terms suited to the staging of properly performed white masculinity.

In another of the relatively neglected and only recently revived novels considered here, Canadian author Carol Shields offers a conjoined pair of novellas that together portray a late 1970s marriage in transition. Set in Chicago and published together as *Happenstance*,[19] this two-part novel contrasts what amount to masculine and feminine versions of emotion-driven, nostalgic constructions of history. Although the novel depicts a week in the lives of the Bowman family, Shields repeatedly registers a national context in geospatial terms; one half is told from the perspective of wife Brenda as she travels to the foundational city of Philadelphia for a quilting convention, and the other is told from that of husband Jack as he deals, in the carefully delineated city of Chicago, with their two children, other people's troubled marriages, and his own efforts to literally write history, in the form of a stalled book about "Indian trading practices." Jack Bowman's difficulties with his book stem from the sudden and representative expectation that he assume traditionally feminine domestic responsibilities and from the professional challenge posed by a woman who is apparently poised to publish her own book on the same topic as that of Jack's project.

While trying to write about "trading practices" between various Native American nations, Jack is clearly not driven by any sense of a moral imperative, one that could take the form of a more critical stance that he might attain by writing about more direct connections between Native Americans and people like himself. The extant legacy of white masculine abuse of others, and of his own collectivity's relational self-construction in terms of them, completely escapes Jack, but it does not escape Carol Shields. She depicts Jack's perception of "history"—a topic which he discusses with a male friend during weekly lunches—as distanced, abstract, and self-servingly nostalgic. This mode of white male nostalgia takes on a more "restorative" form when he visits a Chicago park with his father; this is a space he remembers playing in as a child, but also a space he remembers in particularly besieged white male ways. The self-staging that he practiced as a child in this sequestered and seemingly natural and empty space foreshadows his more overtly nostalgic figuration of conceptually cleansed natural space in what I read as the climax of Jack's half of the novel, a scene in which he takes an absurdly long walk home by himself through snow-filled city streets. Jack's emotional and ultimately solipsistic conception of this setting is again unwittingly inflected by a history of white male conceptions of selectively populated geographical space, which is configured in certain ways that seem suited to idealized white American male action. Shields thereby demonstrates that, as social geographers Owen J. Dwyer and John Paul Jones III write, identities are *"contingent* both historically and geographically" and, more specifically, that white masculinity tends to inculcate in its bearers an identity-bound and literally self-serving relation to geographical space.[20] The ultimately domineering psychic state that Shields illuminates is a conjoined spatialized epistemology and ontology, a state and perspective convincingly depicted in *Happenstance* as exacerbated by nostalgic masculine desire for seemingly open yet selectively populated space.

Here, as in other novels, Shields counters such a hyper-individualized white male perspective with community-oriented constructions of history, which she casts in feminine terms, and with female characters who conceive of and use geographical space toward their own ends and in resistance to masculine control. Scholars have recently delineated what amounts to Shields's depictions of feminist histories in knowingly nostalgic terms, which constitute a "reflective" form of nostalgia. Critics have yet to credit Shields with insightfully dismantling in her fiction a traditionally self-serving and morally blinkered masculine conception of history, nor with critically examining the emotions that have commonly led men to resort to such illusions. Like the other novels examined here, *Happenstance* shows that common white male conceptions of history constitute a retreat from contemporary realities, a retreat prompted by a set of entrenched sociohistorical inducements toward conceiving of oneself and of one's geographically bound relations to others in self-serving, damaging, and finally life-denying ways.

Jewish American Louis Begley is a Holocaust survivor who emigrated from Poland to the United States in 1947. Begley worked his way through anti-Semitic barriers toward a successful career in New York City as a corporate lawyer. A late-life publishing phenomenon, Begley has since produced over a dozen critically successful works of fiction and non-fiction, including his most renowned novel, *About Schmidt* (1996). We can easily imagine that while attending Harvard and then working as a lawyer, Begley studied the ways and mores of the northeastern white elite. In this novel he dramatizes the subtle feelings, nostalgic inclinations, and possessiveness among men descended, in terms of both ancestral lineage and cultural inheritance, from the same northeastern elite illustrated in a more unconscious manner by Sloan Wilson. Begley portrays in Albert Schmidt, also a recently retired lawyer, the lingering effects in the late twentieth century of white Anglo-Saxon proclivities, including both a resentment of feminine and ethnoracial incursions into previously WASP-male enclaves and an irrational sense of possessiveness in response. Begley thereby exposes what amounts to a localized and embodied form of "patriarchal white possessive logic," indigenous scholar Aileen Moreton-Robinson's term in the Australian context for "a mode of rationalization [...] that is underpinned by an excessive desire to invest in reproducing and reaffirming the nation state's ownership, control, and domination."[21] This possessive modality operates at both national and personal levels, in which white male subjects absorb and deploy historically constituted possessive logics to impinge on the sovereign subjectivity of others, often while pining for earlier times in which such dominance seemed to face less resistance.

As Schmidt confronts not only his adult daughter's new emotional and financial independence but also her plans to marry a Jewish American lawyer, his sexist and bigoted responses to these changes reveal that as the self-declared "last of the Wasps," he is emotionally mired in a calcified set of elite WASP dispositions and emotions.[22] *About Schmidt* acknowledges that these dispositions and their attendant emotional reactions occupy an ever-smaller place in an increasingly tolerant and egalitarian social order. However, Begley goes much further, offering as well a convincing demonstration of the destructive effects that white male nostalgia can have when prompted by the perceived incursions of subordinated groups and by the reenactment of an entitled sense of possessiveness. An unfortunate tendency among the empowered raced and gendered elite has been to pine obstinately for a past in which people like themselves enjoyed a less overtly challenged wealth, eminence, and attendant dominance over others. Schmidt's outmoded reactions, especially to his daughter's independence and her choice of a Jewish fiancé (both of which he construes as personal losses), also demonstrate the potential destructiveness of such backwards-oriented stubbornness. In the end, as in the concluding pages of *Savage Holiday* and Jack Bowman's half of *Happenstance*, Begley rewrites the traditional plot trajectory of the melodrama of beset white manhood, severely undercutting Schmidt's ostensibly affirmative sense of rejuvenation by reminding readers of the costs to him and others of an obstinately possessive white patriarchal mindset.

Often considered the most significant novel by the prolific and award-winning Italian American author Don DeLillo, *Underworld* is a massive, roving attempt to capture the psychic and emotional states of dozens of characters during and immediately after the Cold War. The sprawling narrative returns continually to Nick Shay, an ostensibly successful middle-aged corporate executive who, while living in 1992 with his family in an Arizona suburb, feels a gnawing sense of loneliness and loss. Like DeLillo, Nick grew up in the Italian section of the Bronx, and his memories of that time constitute the attempts of a spiritually deadened and de-ethnicized white man to restore vigor to his life, all while denying the deeper sources of his feelings and various facts surrounding them. Like many men, Nick longs for a younger version of himself that he remembers as reckless and impetuously masculine, and he figures his faded ethnicity in terms that rely nearly as much on media-generated stereotypes as on actual memories. Nick currently works as a waste management specialist, and garbage and its containment become multipronged metaphors, representing in part historical realities and, more specifically, the collective white male refusal to acknowledge them. As with Wright's protagonist Erskine Fowler, the expectation that men contain their emotions also provokes Nick's nostalgia, and his representative white masculine solipsism provokes not only his despair over the lost, overtly ethnic version of himself but also the denial of more genuine, potentially recuperative connections with others, including family, friends, and coworkers, and more broadly with the members of groups still denigrated by an ongoing legacy of domineering white masculinity.

In terms of race, ethnicity, and masculinity, DeLillo had depicted such topics with compelling insight earlier, but he is at his most aware and probing in this novel, in part because the authorial perspective is more explicitly Italian American. *Underworld* highlights not only the racially specific artificiality of the ideal 1950s suburban setting but also that of later common white memories of this supposedly better decade, as well as more accurate memories by those who did not match its whitened ideal. DeLillo also works to demythologize such modes of collective white male nostalgia as the complex lore surrounding professional baseball, which he begins undercutting by opening the novel with a spectacular prologue, set in 1951 at Yankee Stadium, and portraying a famous game that included "the shot heard round the world," the game's winning home run. DeLillo was also intrigued by the *New York Times* notice the next day on its front page of another "shot," that of the Soviet Union testing an atomic bomb. The newspaper's front-page subordination of the latter, momentously historic moment to news about a baseball game foreshadows the eclipsing in the collective American imagination of legitimate fear about nuclear Armageddon by entertaining spectacle, a recurrent motif represented perhaps most suggestively in Nick's nostalgic purchasing for a great deal of money of what he wants to believe is the famous home-run ball. *Underworld* includes significant male and female characters from several races and ethnicities, many of whom function agentially to expose common white male denial of the uses and abuses of others. DeLillo's interweaving of fictional characters and events with actual historical ones does much to puncture common modes of restorative white male nostalgia, as when he exposes the racialized delusions underlying much of baseball fandom, and at the novel's end, where he effectively swaps his solipsistic male protagonist for a communally oriented female one. Like other *Underworld* characters from socially subordinated groups, this woman, a nun named Sister Edgar, dramatizes a more reflective, recuperative nostalgia when she dies and her spirit enters the internet. While floating in cyberspace, Sister Edgar connects with others, including J. Edgar Hoover and the Japanese victims of atomic bombs. In this way, writing as a circumspect, re-ethnicized outsider to normative white masculinity, DeLillo echoes Carol Shields's proffered feminized conception of both usefully reflective nostalgia and more accurate conceptions of the relations throughout U.S. history of its gendered and ethnoracial groupings.

This study's epilogue is grounded in a briefer reading of Margaret Atwood's most recent work of "speculative fiction," *The Heart Goes Last* (2015). Author of a widely acknowledged classic in this genre, *The Handmaid's Tale* (1985), and of the similarly dystopian and well-received MaddAddam series, Atwood crafts plausible, politically trenchant novels that often warn about the potential outcomes of what amounts to unchecked white masculine dominance. In *The Heart Goes Last*, Atwood depicts a social landscape in which the social contract, nearly broken, is sustained by nostalgic figurations of a past that is cast in thinly veiled patriarchal, white supremacist terms.

Stan and Charmaine (whose last names we never learn) are a married white couple who live in their car in an economically blasted, near-future United States landscape. They both work chronically underpaid jobs and worry about falling prey to roving bands of the unemployed. Nostalgia has become thoroughly commodified and its value for the distant elites who seek ever more gain via neoliberal privatization is figured in the form of Consilience, a gated, simulated 1950s-suburban neighborhood that actually functions as a prison. By way of satirizing the contemporary white masculine insistence on corporeal, ideological, and emotional containment, Atwood depicts inmates who become residents of this prison town voluntarily, and for life, by agreeing to spend alternate months in a surrounding faux-1950s suburb, and then inside a factory, as laboring prisoners. Nostalgia for a homebound version of "the way we never were," as Stephanie Coontz has put it, lures Stan and Charmaine into selling themselves by buying into a specifically raced, classed, and gendered version of the American Dream.[23] Although Atwood's satire often verges on farcical comedy, her urgent message is a warning not unlike the influential conceptions of late capitalism offered by philosopher Giorgio Agamben. Both observers raise the question of whether, as Agamben puts it, we should reconsider the concept and realities of the concentration camp as the "biopolitical paradigm of the West," that is, "the hidden matrix and *nomos* of the political space in which we are living."[24]

While the titular notion of the heart going "last" has a grisly literal meaning in Atwood's novel, the notion also engages in several metaphorical ways the traditional Western idea of the heart as the seat of emotions. *The Heart Goes Last* offers extensive satiric commentary on what can happen when emotions in the romantic realm become both commodified and intertwined with technological advances wrapped in an alluring package of nostalgia; for example, Stan escapes from the prison, which sells products made by prison labor, by disguising himself as one of its products, an Elvis Presley sex robot. Common white American longings for the 1950s often cast the era as a time of sunlit optimism. In this sense, this novel's vision of something more than the stark misery of Agamben's "bare life," a version of which Stan and Charmaine had nearly been living before, amounts to nostalgia for a particular future—for a time when a stable, everlasting national future seemed not only possible but imminent. Yet the greatness of this American Dream seemed so mostly to white middle-class Americans, whose men were most effectively served by it.

Atwood's broader message, effectively anticipated in the work of the other five novelists considered here, is a warning: unless those subjected to increasingly precarious conditions gather together somehow to resist the dominant longing for the self-aggrandizing control and material gain that was once allotted more readily, and indeed more exclusively, to white men, the economic elite really could leave the rest of us to a *Mad Max*-like social order while they live luxuriously, as the elite in Atwood's novel do, in slave-built offshore fortresses. Atwood warns her readers about logical consequences of the unleashed, murderous white male dominance that Wright presciently allegorized sixty years earlier in *Savage Holiday*—a hyper-individualized, chronically stress-inducing, and "already dead" social order that ignores the necessity of communal values at the same time that it sells nostalgic versions of them.[25]

NOTES

1. Contrary to common misperceptions, support for candidate Donald Trump was not primarily a working-class white male phenomenon. Working with exit poll results, statistician Nate Silver reported that the median household income of a Trump voter was "about $72,000. ... well above the national median household income of about $56,000." As Ta-Nehisi Coates wrote in an *Atlantic* piece on the whiteness of the Trump phenomenon,

Trump's white support was not determined by income. According to Edison Research, Trump won whites making less than $50,000 by 20 points, whites making $50,000 to $99,999 by 28 points, and whites making $100,000 or more by 14 points. This shows that Trump assembled a broad white coalition that ran the gamut from Joe the Dishwasher to Joe the Plumber to Joe the Banker. [...] He won white people with college degrees (+3) and white people without them (+37). He won whites ages 18–29 (+4), 30–44 (+17), 45–64 (+28), and 65 and older (+19). [...] According to *Mother Jones*, based on preelection polling data, if you tallied the popular vote of only white America to derive 2016 electoral votes, Trump would have defeated Clinton 389 to 81, with the remaining 68 votes either a toss-up or unknown.

    Among the many commonly gauged identity-bound variables, whiteness and masculinity consistently emerged as the most salient combination for support of Trump. Shortly after the election, CNN exit polls showed Republican support among all white men at 62% (and at 52% for white women despite the potential of the first female president).

2. Tygstrup, 195.
3. In the past two decades or so, a distinct realm of literary scholarship has arisen that examines depictions of white-male characters. Foundational works repeatedly referred to in such recent work include Sally Robinson's *Marked Men: White Masculinity in Crisis* and Catherine Jurca's *White Diaspora: The Suburb and the Twentieth Century*. A less cited though useful study is Nina Baym's early analysis of canonicity, "Melodramas of Beset Manhood." More recent work in this area includes Josep Armengol, *Masculinities in Black and White: Manliness and Whiteness in (African) American Literature*; Josef Benson, *Hypermasculinities in the Contemporary Novel*; Suzanne Clark, *Cold Warriors: Manliness on Trial in the Rhetoric of the West*; Alice Ferrebe, *Masculinity in Male-authored Fiction, 1950–2000*; Joshua David Gonsalves, *Bio-Politicizing Cary Grant: Pressing Race, Class and Ethnicity into Service in "Amerika"*; Alex Hobbs, *Aging Masculinity in the American Novel*; Andrew Hoborek, *Twilight of the Middle Class: Post-World War II Fiction and White Collar Work*; Horlacher and Floyd (eds.), *Post-World War II Masculinities in British and American Literature and Culture: Towards Comparative Masculinity Studies*; Kathy Knapp, *American Unexceptionalism: The Everyman and the Suburban Novel after 9/11*; Levmore and Nussbaum (eds.), *American Guy: Masculinity in American Law and Literature*; Stephany Rose, *Abolishing White Masculinity from Mark Twain to Hiphop*; Graham Thompson, *Male Sexuality Under Surveillance: The*

Office in American Literature; and Daniel S. Traber, *Whiteness, Otherness, and the Individualism Paradox from Huck to Punk.*

4. Haney López, 116.
5. Bourdieu, 167.
6. Kovel, 45.
7. I would add that distinct national contexts often merit more direct attention as well. Thus, I follow R. W. Connell's reminder that gender is "unavoidably involved with other social structures. It is now common to say that gender 'intersects'—better, interacts—with race and class. We might add that it constantly interacts with nationality or position in the world order" (75).
8. Foundational works on white masculinity include Dana D. Nelson, *National Manhood: Capitalist Citizenship and the Imagined Fraternity of White Men*; Fred Pfeil, *White Guys: Studies in Postmodern Domination and Difference*; David Savran, *Taking It Like a Man: White Masculinity, Masochism, and Contemporary American Culture*; Harry Stecopoulos (ed.), *Race and the Subject of Masculinities*. Recent extensive studies include Hamilton Carroll, *Affirmative Reaction: New Formations of White Masculinity*; Cederström and Fleming, *Dead Man Working*; Christopher Forth, *Masculinity in the Modern West: Gender, Civilization and the Body*; Michael Kimmel, *Angry White Men: American Masculinity at the End of an Era* and *Misframing Men: The Politics of Contemporary Masculinities*; Jason E. Pierce, *Making the White Man's West: Whiteness and the Creation of the American West*; and Nicola Rehling, *Extra-Ordinary Men: White Heterosexual Masculinity and Contemporary Popular Cinema.*
9. Robinson, 29.
10. Baym, 123.
11. O'Toole, n.p. As Garson O'Toole notes on his popular website Quote Investigator, this concept, which has appeared in many places and in several phrasings, seems to have grown on its own through repeated usage. Like other investigators, O'Toole has not been able to trace it to a single definitive source.
12. Boym, 41.
13. Studies of nostalgia that have especially informed my project include Zygmunt Bauman, *Retrotopia*; Alistair Bonnett, *The Geography of Nostalgia: Global and Local Perspectives on Modernity and Loss*; Svetlana Boym, *The Future of Nostalgia*; Helmut Illbruck, *Nostalgia: Origins and Ends of an Unenlightened Disease*; Jennifer Ladino, *Reclaiming Nostalgia: Longing for Nature in American Literature*; David Lowenthal, *The Past is a Foreign Country*; and Susan J. Matt, *Homesickness: An American History.*
14. Boym, 41.

15. Schwebel, 38.
16. Interview with Raymond Barthes, in Kinnamon and Fabre, 167.
17. Honeywill, 87.
18. Baldwin, 48.
19. Jack Bowman's story was initially published in 1980 as *Happenstance* (McGraw-Hill Ryerson), and Brenda Bowman's in 1982 as *A Fairly Conventional Woman* (Macmillan). In 1994, Harper Collins-Flamingo published the two novellas together under the title *Happenstance*, with two sections, "The Husband's Story" and "The Wife's Story."
20. Dwyer and Jones, 212, emphasis in original.
21. Moreton-Robinson, xii.
22. Begley, 143.
23. As Coontz writes, common white American nostalgia for an idealized 1950s family life is an "idea that combines some characteristics of the white, middle-class family in the mid-nineteenth century and some of a rival family ideal first articulated in the 1920s" (9).
24. Agamben, 166, 181.
25. I refer with the term "already dead" to Eric Cazdyn's metaphorical diagnosis of emotional responses induced by late capitalism's enforced economic precarity, a general, suspended condition between life and near-death that he usefully labels "the new chronic": "The new chronic extends the present into the future, burying in the process the force of the terminal, making it seem as if the present will never end" (7–8).

Bibliography

Agamben, Giorgio. *Homo Sacer: Sovereign Power and Bare Life*. Stanford: Stanford University Press, 1998.

Armengol, Josep M. *Masculinities in Black and White: Manliness and Whiteness in (African) American Literature*. New York: Palgrave Macmillan, 2014.

Atwood, Margaret. *The Heart Goes Last*. New York: Doubleday, 2015.

Baldwin, James. "The White Man's Guilt." *Ebony* 20, No. 10 (August 1965): 47–48.

Bauman, Zygmunt. *Retrotopia*. Cambridge: Polity, 2017.

Baym, Nina. "Melodramas of Beset Manhood: How Theories of American Fiction Exclude Women Authors." *American Quarterly* 33, No. 2 (1981): 123–39.

Begley, Louis. *About Schmidt*. New York: Alfred A. Knopf, 1996.

Benson, Josef. *Hypermasculinities in the Contemporary Novel: Cormac McCarthy, Toni Morrison, and James Baldwin*. Lanham, MD: Rowman & Littlefield, 2014.

Bonnett, Alistair. *The Geography of Nostalgia: Global and Local Perspectives on Modernity and Loss.* Abingdon, UK: Routledge, 2015.

Bourdieu, Pierre. *Outline of a Theory of Practice.* Cambridge: Cambridge University Press, 1977.

Boym, Svetlana. *The Future of Nostalgia.* New York: Basic Books, 2002.

Carroll, Hamilton. *Affirmative Reaction: New Formations of White Masculinity.* Durham and London: Duke University Press, 2011.

Cazdyn, Eric. *The Already Dead: The New Time of Politics, Culture, and Illness.* Durham and London: Duke University Press, 2012.

Cederström, Carl, and Peter Fleming. *Dead Man Working.* Alresford, UK: Zero Books, 2012.

Clark, Suzanne. *Cold Warriors: Manliness on Trial in the Rhetoric of the West.* Carbondale and Edwardsville: Southern Illinois University Press, 2000.

CNN Politics. "Exit Polls." *CNN,* November 23, 2016. http://www.cnn.com/election/results/exit-polls. Accessed 10.5.2017.

Coates, Ta-Nehisi. "The First White President." *The Atlantic,* October 2017. https://www.theatlantic.com/magazine/archive/2017/10/the-first-white-president-ta-nehisi-coates/537909/. Accessed 10.5.2017.

Connell, R. W. *Masculinities.* Berkeley, CA: University of California Press, 2005.

Coontz, Stephanie. *The Way We Never Were: American Families and the Nostalgia Trap.* New York: Basic Books, 1992.

DeLillo, Don. *Underworld.* New York: Scribner, 1997.

Dwyer, Owen J., and John Paul Jones III. "White Socio-spatial Epistemology." *Social & Cultural Geography* 1, No. 2 (2000): 209–22.

Ferrebe, Alice. *Masculinity in Male-Authored Fiction, 1950–2000: Keeping It Up.* Basingstoke: Palgrave Macmillan, 2005.

Forth, Christopher E. *Masculinity in the Modern West: Gender, Civilization and the Body.* Basingstoke: Palgrave Macmillan, 2008.

Gonsalves, Joshua David. *Bio-politicizing Cary Grant: Pressing Race, Class and Ethnicity into Service in "Amerika."* Alresford, UK: Zero Books, 2015.

Haney López, Ian. *White by Law: The Legal Construction of Race.* New York and London: New York University Press, 2006.

Hobbs, Alex. *Aging Masculinity in the American Novel.* Lanham, MD: Rowman and Littlefield, 2016.

Hoberek, Andrew. *Twilight of the Middle Class: Post-World War II Fiction and White-Collar Work.* Princeton, NJ: Princeton University Press, 2005.

Honeywill, Ross. *The Man Problem: Destructive Masculinity in Western Culture.* Basingstoke: Palgrave Macmillan, 2016.

Horlacher, Stefan, and Kevin Floyd (eds.). *Post-World War II Masculinities in British and American Literature and Culture: Towards Comparative Masculinity Studies.* Farnham, UK: Ashgate, 2013.

Illbruck, Helmut. *Nostalgia: Origins and Ends of an Unenlightened Disease.* Evanston, IL: Northwestern University Press, 2012.

Jurca, Catherine. *White Diaspora: The Suburb and the Twentieth-Century American Novel.* Princeton, NJ: Princeton University Press, 2001.

Kimmel, Michael. *Misframing Men: The Politics of Contemporary Masculinities.* New Brunswick, NJ: Rutgers University Press, 2010.

———. *Angry White Men: American Masculinity at the End of an Era.* New York: Nation Books, 2013.

Kinnamon, Kenneth, and Michel Fabre. *Conversations with Richard Wright.* Jackson, MS: University Press of Mississippi, 1993.

Knapp, Kathy. *American Unexceptionalism: The Everyman and the Suburban Novel after 9/11.* Iowa City, IA: University of Iowa Press, 2014.

Kovel, Joel. *White Racism: A Psychohistory.* 1970. New York: Columbia University Press, 1985.

Ladino, Jennifer. *Reclaiming Nostalgia: Longing for Nature in American Literature.* Charlottesville and London: University of Virginia Press, 2012.

Levmore, Saul, and Martha C. Nussbaum (eds.). *American Guy: Masculinity in American Law and Literature.* New York: Oxford University Press, 2014.

Lowenthal, David. *The Past Is a Foreign Country.* Cambridge: Cambridge University Press, 1985.

Matt, Susan J. *Homesickness: An American History.* New York: Oxford University Press, 2011.

Moreton-Robinson, Aileen. *The White Possessive: Property, Power, and Indigenous Sovereignty.* Minneapolis: University of Minnesota Press, 2015.

Nelson, Dana D. *National Manhood: Capitalist Citizenship and the Imagined Fraternity of White Men.* Durham and London: Duke University Press, 1998.

O'Toole, Garson. "When You're Accustomed to Privilege, Equality Feels Like Oppression." *Quote Investigator,* October 24, 2016. https://quoteinvestigator.com/2016/10/24/privilege/. Accessed 1.24.2018.

Pfeil, Fred. *White Guys: Studies in Postmodern Domination and Difference.* London and New York: Verso, 1995.

Pierce, Jason E. *Making the White Man's West: Whiteness and the Creation of the American West.* Boulder, CO: University Press of Colorado, 2016.

Rehling, Nicola. *Extra-Ordinary Men: White Heterosexual Masculinity and Contemporary Popular Cinema.* Lanham, MD: Lexington Books, 2009.

Robinson, Sally. *Marked Men: White Masculinity in Crisis.* New York: Columbia University Press, 2000.

Rose, Stephany. *Abolishing White Masculinity from Mark Twain to Hiphop: Crises in Whiteness.* Lanham, MD: Lexington Books, 2014.

Savran, David. *Taking It Like a Man: White Masculinity, Masochism, and Contemporary American Culture.* Princeton, NJ: Princeton University Press, 1998.

Schwebel, Sara L. *Child-Sized History: Fictions of the Past in U.S. Classrooms.* Nashville: Vanderbilt University Press, 2011.

Shields, Carol. *Happenstance: Two Novels in One About a Marriage in Transition.* 1980, 1982. New York: Open Road Integrated Media, 2010.

Silver, Nate. "The Mythology of Trump's 'Working Class' Support." *FiveThirtyEight*, May 3, 2016. https://fivethirtyeight.com/features/the-mythology-of-trumps-working-class-support/. Accessed 5.21.2018.

Stecopoulos, Harry (ed.). *Race and the Subject of Masculinities.* Durham and London: Duke University Press, 1997.

Thompson, Graham. *Male Sexuality Under Surveillance: The Office in American Literature.* Iowa City, IA: University of Iowa Press, 2003.

Traber, Daniel S. *Whiteness, Otherness, and the Individualism Paradox from Huck to Punk.* New York: Palgrave Macmillan, 2007.

Tygstrup, Frederik. "Affective Spaces." In *Panic and Mourning: The Cultural Work of Trauma*, edited by Daniela Agostinho, Elisa Antz, and Cátia Ferreira. Berlin and Boston: Walter de Gruytcr GmbH, 2012, 195–210.

Wilson, Sloan. *The Man in the Gray Flannel Suit.* 1955. Cambridge, MA: Da Capo, 2002.

Wright, Richard. *Savage Holiday.* 1954. Jackson, MS: University Press of Mississippi, 1994.

CHAPTER 2

Ethnicized White Male Nostalgia: Sloan Wilson's *The Man in the Gray Flannel Suit*

To the extent that *The Man in the Gray Flannel Suit* endures in American consciousness, it does so mostly in the figuration of its protagonist as a rather bland, angst-ridden "everyman," especially as played in a 1956 Hollywood version by Gregory Peck. At the time, Sloan Wilson's eponymous and recently published novel was nearly as well known, a middle-brow literary success that seemed to capture and articulate simmering middle-class white male anxieties about the demands of a new social order, including domestic and workplace expectations that many found constraining, conformist, and inauthentic. Wilson's narrative depicts the postwar civilian resituating of a World War II veteran, Tom Rath, who has returned to his wife Betsy and to life in a house that strikes them both as too small, particularly when an opportunity for enrichening corporate success arises for Tom. Another option arrives when Tom's grandmother dies, leaving him her house and its extensive landholdings. Owing to Tom's uneasiness with the enforced cheerfulness, kowtowing, and other demands of corporate work, he and Betsy eventually decide to move into the inherited house and sell off its land as plots for suburban development. Tensions flare when, among other familial and property-related problems, Tom's hidden wartime liaison with an Italian woman resurfaces. Tom struggles to maintain a morally appeasing sense of himself both at home and in the workplace, and he longs to come clean, which he thinks he could do by quitting his soul-destroying job and by telling Betsy about his affair.

© The Author(s) 2018
T. Engles, *White Male Nostalgia in Contemporary North American Literature*, https://doi.org/10.1007/978-3-319-90460-3_2

In retrospect, it seems strange that few observers of the time perceived either Wilson or his protagonist as far from the all-American everyman that Tom Rath came so quickly to represent. Although both were white, and World War II veterans as well, each also had roots in established northeastern, "old money" families, a highly privileged demographic that Wilson later labeled in the title of another novel, *All the Best People* (1970). That Wilson and his gray-flannelled protagonist Tom Rath were far from ordinary white American men, and instead fit a group sometimes labeled (though rarely by its members themselves) as "WASPs," seems to have escaped most observers, including even recent scholars of the film and novel. The regional and familial roots that Wilson evinces in his novel were actually and more specifically "Anglo-Saxon," a once commonly overt affiliation that by the 1950s had largely faded from national consciousness, and apparently even from that of Wilson himself. Nevertheless, both Wilson and his protagonist demonstrate the remnants of white American Anglo-Saxonism, including certain nostalgic leanings that betray not only their ethnoracial lineage and attendant dispositions but also those inspired by their class background and gender. Indeed, the backward-leaning proclivities of both Tom and Betsy Rath evince the largely unconscious machinations of white American male hegemony, especially the ostensibly liberal usage of more overtly ethnic characters. Explaining how the novel manifests the submerged dispositions of what I will label a dominant hidden ethnicity calls for some preliminary review of a history largely lost to popular consciousness, that of white Anglo-Saxon racial formation.

WHITE ANGLO-SAXONISM

Although popular notions of the founding of the United States in indignant claims of abuse at the hands of English rule have long existed, standard accounts of subsequent national identity formation have failed to account adequately for the countervailing nostalgia felt by many Americans for the England that once supposedly was. The Anglophilia currently expressed in the common, largely white American enthusiasm for English-heritage novels, films, and television shows has a lengthy and continuous lineage of precedents, even among those with no actual ancestral ties to England. In the past, those with such an interest often chose an oddly ancient affiliation: "Anglo-Saxon." By the nineteenth century, as Reginald Horsman writes in his groundbreaking study of the origins of this largely fantasized ethnic grouping, the belief of most white Americans in their inherent racial superiority had become overt, and their seemingly legitimate sources for such a belief multiple:

> [From] the English they had learned that the Anglo-Saxons had always been particularly gifted in the arts of government; from the scientists and ethnologists they were learning they were of a distinct Caucasian race, innately endowed with abilities that placed them above other races; from the philologists, often through literary sources, they were learning that they were the descendants of those Aryans who followed the sun to carry civilization to the whole world.[1]

As numerous historians of race and ethnicity have subsequently explained, a dominant sector within the relatively new white American race found a variety of reasons to look back to England more existentially. By the mid-1800s, these Americans, who "had long believed that they were a chosen people... also believed that they were a chosen people with an impeccable ancestry"; this was a lineage they widely proclaimed *both* white and Anglo-Saxon.[2] One impetus for declarations of racial superiority was a felt need to address in some way the moral and existential contradiction posed by a budding empire's claims to exceptionalist roots in anticolonialism; such morality-challenging extortions as the theft of land and labor were justified as natural results of membership in an inherently superior subset of the dominant white race. As for the more specific Anglophilia marked by the term Anglo-Saxon, it became less a sign of adoration for all things English and more one of distaste for things and people *not* English. Self-declared white Anglo-Saxons held fast to their imagined notions of superiority to all peoples they deemed "darker," including not only those of indigenous and African descent but also immigrants from other parts of Europe.

By the late 1800s, as industrialization brought further waves of disparate immigrants from Europe (while owing in part to the "free white" portion of the 1790 Naturalization Act, non-European immigration to the United States waned), many filled the increasingly crowded cities, a general urban growth that countered a lingering feudal ideal. One result was that the nation's multinational and multiracial origins came to strike many instead as a purely English beginning. Nostalgic white Anglo-Saxon identity gained salience, taking on as well a more overtly elitist tinge. As David Lowenthal writes, "The 1880s and 1890s saw the birth of scores of Sons, Daughters, Dames and other commemorative genealogical societies, with Anglo-Saxon origins a sine qua non of membership."[3] In the early twentieth century, the concept of "ethnicity" gained currency as a way to differentiate provisionally white immigrants from putatively full-fledged white Anglo-Saxon Americans.[4] Those perceived as Anglo-Saxons were not labeled "ethnic Americans," yet many continued to anoint themselves members both of the dominant race and of an ethnic group within it. In this way, white Anglo-Saxons viewed themselves as both being distinct from the "melting pot" of the United States and singularly embodying the signature ideals of American progress and achievement.

As intermarriage and the passage of time and geographical distance from England gradually rendered claims to Anglo-Saxon purity (let alone superiority) ever more specious, a further irony arose when Anglo-Saxon adherents found more evidence for non-English inferiority in the supposedly pathological nostalgic tendencies of new immigrants. As Susan J. Matt points out in her historical account of American manifestations of homesickness, "Nativists believed Anglo-Saxons to be the best race and worked assiduously to limit the in-migrations of southern and eastern Europeans, Asians, and Africans. Immigrants' perceived mental instability and vulnerability to the ravages of nostalgia provided them with ammunition, for they could point to the newcomers filling America's asylums as a threat to national strength and racial purity."[5] Because this sort of homesickness still carried nostalgia's original stigma of mental illness, pointing hypocritically to inevitable immigrant pinings for lost homelands served to bolster white Anglo-Saxon claims to racial superiority and, by morality-assuaging implication, to their own greater material access and accumulation. Nevertheless, when push came to shove in legal terms, as when people from various countries applied for citizenship, both Anglo-Saxon Americans and others from Europe fell under the racial heading of "white." Finally, by the 1950s, those who fit the characteristics of white Anglo-Saxons had come to eschew both the term and the increasingly disparaged acronym that had come to describe them, "WASP" (White Anglo-Saxon Protestant). Yet, as Wilson in effect demonstrates in *The Man in the Gray Flannel Suit*, with both his protagonist and his own authorial methods, some still felt what amounts to a lingering Anglo-Saxon nostalgia, a nagging sense of lost eminence that perhaps was felt more keenly by many men, who perceived threats from a more openly egalitarian social order to the formerly stable status, material assets, and prerogatives of people like themselves.[6]

As both Wilson and his protagonist Tom Rath demonstrate, the new social forces that seemed vaguely threatening to many Anglo-Saxon descendants included the heightened ethnoracial integration that had arisen during the Second World War, the defeat of more blatantly racist enemies, further waves of eastern and southern European immigration, and domestic demands from the still ethnoracially and religiously subjugated for greater sociopolitical inclusion. Again, and almost as if in response, self-identification in explicitly ethnoracial terms among the descendants of the Anglo-Saxon elite had largely faded. The era's new liberal pluralism positioned a more general and less explicitly marked form of whiteness at the center of U.S. institutions, politics, and culture, and along with other groups, descendants of those who had once proudly and often defensively declared themselves Anglo-Saxons were assimilating into it. Within the white race, greater opportunities for religious and ethnic others arose, while awareness declined of the genuine relations and connections between the extant ethnoracially dominant—that is, those whose ancestors had most overtly and tenaciously clung to Anglo-Saxon heritage—and more recent immigrants, the "inbetween peoples" and their descendants. These were the technically white people, as represented in Wilson's novel by Italian and Jewish American characters, who still experienced their American-ness as provisional and whose work toward inclusion and equal treatment had nevertheless become impossible to ignore.[7]

Of course, such mid-century changes in white racial formation also took place in response to heightened demands from Americans who were neither firmly nor provisionally white, an increasingly restive racial force that produced further tensions for the white men who navigated suddenly less familiar social and workplace landscapes. Although Wilson never labels the racial status of Tom Rath, he does mark him early in the novel in such terms, as an ordinary (white) man of his time, in large part by repeatedly depicting Tom's encounters with overtly ethnic and racial others. A more subtle (and likely unintentional) marking of Tom as an ultimately nostalgic Anglo-Saxon scion arises only gradually. Tom's status as a more ordinary white man first becomes implicitly apparent during a crucial early scene. As the protagonist whom many (at the time) read as the embodiment of an archetypal new everyman, Tom pensively rides a commuter train back home from another day of trying to embody the era's newly minted corporate masculine ideal. When he looks out the window as the train passes through Harlem, Tom enacts both the era's new racial liberalism and its particularly white oblivion. Scanning the "littered streets and squalid brick tenements," Tom gazes on what amounts to a figuratively invisible woman, a female cohort of sorts to the titular character in Ralph Ellison's epochal novel *Invisible Man*, published three years earlier.[8] This "aged colored woman with sunken cheeks," leaning out of a window to water some flowers, starkly contrasts with a more manufactured figure positioned just a few feet above the older woman, on "a huge billboard showing a beautiful girl thirty feet long lying under a palm tree. 'Fly to Miami,' the sign said" (*M*, 45). Of course, the literally and ideologically enlarged woman can only be a white woman; however, like Tom's whiteness and that of the author and of his presumed readers, her racial status is the hegemonic norm that, as such, goes without saying.[9]

Nevertheless, given as well the fundamentally relational nature of racial demarcations in all modes of American culture, the marking of this woman's blackness here functions to imply something about whiteness as well. *Gray Flannel* has been chiefly read as an individualistic and ultimately reactionary *cri de coeur* against its era's hypocritical, emasculating conformity, as figured in representative corporate and suburban settings.[10] As Jonathan Vincent writes in a standard interpretation of that which Wilson depicts as thwarting Tom's efforts to become his own man, "the novel's politics, indicative of the political mood of its time, are concerned solely with personal redemption through the pursuit of a clean conscience, the acceptance of the responsibilities of fatherhood, and the longing for contentment in the security of the middle-class suburban ideal."[11] That the ideal threatened by creeping corporate conformity is specifically white is signaled by Wilson's use in this scene of a romanticized Africanist presence. This briefly glimpsed woman registers in no particularly significant way for Tom, and thus in a way that also signals his lack of overt racial prejudice. In addition, her impoverished blackness imbues the moment for white middle-class readers with a nostalgic earthiness, and thus with a contrasting sense of seemingly noncorporatized authenticity. This paradoxically stereotypical dash of seemingly genuine humanity contrasts with, and thus highlights, the sanitized corporate sterility that threatens Tom and his family, as represented by the billboard and the white woman garishly splayed across it. In sum, that the ideal threatened by a looming conformity is a specifically white one is registered by Wilson's authorial use, here and elsewhere, of a romanticized Africanist presence.[12] While Wilson might seem unconcerned with situating his protagonist amidst his era's ethnoracial structures in any terms other than those of individualized liberal tolerance, he repeatedly figures both racial and ethnic otherness in ways that evince a particularly situated white-male nostalgia. This markedly "WASP" male sense of lingering, wistful inclinations undergirds and helps to justify the eminence enjoyed by members of what had become a paradoxically hidden dominant ethnicity.

As in the interactions between white characters and Ralph Ellison's "invisible" protagonist, the brief appearance of this anonymous black woman registers in no self-aware or contextually insightful manner for Wilson's white character. Although Tom does briefly perceive her difference from himself, he fails to see his own relation to her, that is, *both* of their relative positions in a classed, gendered, and raced geospatial network. In his analysis of the commuting motif in suburban fiction, Christian Long writes regarding this scene, "Tom is not interested in his environment qua environment; it says nothing to him about other people. ... Tom sees not the condition particular to the urban tenements ... but still another reflection of himself."[13] Wilson depicts in this scene, no doubt inadvertently, a trained white ignorance to such matters that belies not only the era's illogically collective vaunting of "American" individualism but also the broader white culture's heightened racial tolerance. Both Wilson and Tom demonstrate what Charles Mills describes as "racial erasure: the retrospective whitening, the whitewashing, of the racial past in order to construct an alternative narrative that severs the past from any legacy of racial domination."[14] And, given this novel's particular socio-geographic setting and choice of characters, what Tom also enacts in this cross-racial moment is the erasure in the dominant sector of not only the era's liberal white consciousness of communal relations that remained obstinately fixed in terms of race and ethnicity, and thus of social class, but also the manifestations at the individual level of a selectively whitened historical memory.

In terms then of ethnicity, neither Tom nor his restive wife Betsy, nor apparently Sloan Wilson, explicitly identifies as a descendant of a social set that once widely declared itself Anglo-Saxon. Yet all three exhibit what amounts to the psycho-emotional symptoms and inherited cultural capital of what had become, in Ashley W. Doane's terms, a "hidden ethnicity."[15] Because this dominant group identity had lost salience by the time of *Gray Flannel's* setting and because the group nevertheless continued to favor its de-ethnicized members and disfavor those marked more explicitly as "outsiders," I will label the group which Tom and Betsy evince most acutely in their nostalgic longings hidden Anglo-Saxons. Although the Raths exhibit financial and existential problems widely read as typical for middle-class white suburbanites of their era, they also bear the traces of a dominant-yet-ethnic lineage, inherited dispositions that provide anxiety-relieving solutions that they falsely believe they arrive at solely through their own skill, hard work, and good-heartedness.

RESURGENT WHITE ANGLO-SAXONISM

Wilson opens *Gray Flannel* with a portrait of familial suburban angst, as felt by Tom and Betsy. Aside from uncertainty about whether Tom's efforts to advance in corporate life will result in a satisfying salary, a primary source of discontent is their house. Their suburban location marks them as people who seemed (especially to white readers) naturally suited to domestic conditions far preferable to those endured by people like the relatively impoverished African American woman whom Tom briefly considers from the train. Yet, while the Raths' suburban house is much easier to live in than a Harlem tenement, it strikes them as "too small, ugly, and almost precisely like the houses on all sides of it" (*M*, 3). Murkier troubles fester as well, as suggested by an unrepaired plaster crack in the shape of a symbolic question mark, the result of Tom's having hurled a vase during a heated argument about their strained finances. The house's unkempt state is also suggestive; Tom would be the appointed one to do household repairs and maintenance, but as with the rest of his current life, he has no enthusiasm for such masculine duties and, given the privileged upbringing that we learn about later, little practice as well. A certain nagging vagueness in this couple's general discontent is summed up at one point by Betsy: "I don't know what's the matter with us. ... Your job is plenty good enough. We've got three nice kids, and lots of people would be glad to have a house like this. We shouldn't be so *discontented* all the time." Although Tom emphatically agrees, the true source of their agitation remains elusive: "Their words sounded hollow" (*M*, 3). The couple's emotions, both surface-level and submerged, are the novel's immediate, primary focus, and the particulars of their house have become the site onto which they project their muddled feelings. Such a projection is symptomatic of how they generally see leaving this residential area as the solution, making them, as Catherine Jurca puts it in her study of this novel, "sanctimonious suburbanites," individualists who resemble their neighbors most fully and ironically in their conviction that they don't belong among them because they somehow fundamentally differ from them.[16]

While the Raths seek individuation, they also clearly long to embody their era's newly minted notion of a better domestic future, a familial happiness manifested by a bigger, better house and the higher income it would take to sustain such a domestically centered life. Yet consideration of their particular socio-geographic positioning demonstrates that a certain remembered and felt past remains resonant for them as well, albeit in more unconscious ways. Greentree Avenue seems an ironically named location for their suburban house, nestled as it is amidst little more than similar houses and thus removed entirely from "nature." Indeed, part of Tom's discontent with new suburban areas, such as those encroaching on his hometown of South Bay, Connecticut, is their falsely touted connection to an older, supposedly pure landscape: "Brightly painted one-story houses filled the fields where Tom had hunted rabbits as a boy, and even the old nine-hole golf course had miraculously become something called 'Shoreline Estates,' in spite of the fact that it was a good two miles inland" (*M*, 16). South Bay itself, however, is depicted as resistant to change and thus eventually as a more suitable residential locale for the Raths; it has not only larger houses and wider unhoused spaces but also a social hierarchy in which members of established wealthy families like themselves reside at the top. Resettling in South Bay soon arises as a possibility for the Raths when Tom's grandmother dies, leaving him as the sole descendant and apparent heir to her country estate.

While specific causes of Tom and Betsy's gnawing restlessness are not particularly evident to either one of them, they persist with a general belief that more money would solve all of their problems. The Raths' neighbors also imagine more money as the main solution to their discontent, but Tom's thoughts exhibit an additional temporal orientation:

[He] thought wryly of the days when he and Betsy had assured each other that money didn't matter. They had told each other that when they were married, before the war, and during the war they had repeated it in long letters. "The important thing is to find a kind of work you really like, and something that is useful," Betsy had written him. "The money doesn't matter." (*M*, 7)

Any adult could have such a memory, of a stage in life when a coherent sense of personal finances had yet to develop, but what Tom actually misses, here and elsewhere, is a time when money didn't matter because his family had plenty of it. More to my point in this chapter, Tom's ancestors had plenty because they occupied the upper reaches of a localized ethnoracial hierarchy, which included not only others who were more clearly subjugated in classed, raced, and ethnicized terms but also their own consciously named dominant group.

In the 1920s and 1930s northeastern United States locale of Tom's youth, self-proclaimed Anglo-Saxons were in an earlier stage of their gradual fade into the "ever-expanding boundaries of whiteness," which gradually incorporated not only European immigrants marked as other in terms of "ethnicity" but also an "Anglo-Saxon" or, more rarely, "Nordic" or "Caucasian" elite.[17] Regarding the occasional usage of such terms in the early twentieth century to describe those who were considered the whitest white Americans, historian Kevin M. Schultz writes of the more common use of "Anglo-Saxon" for assertions of racial superiority, and thus for seemingly justified dominance, by an ethnic (yet putatively non-ethnic) minority: "[At] the beginning of the 20th century, there was a need in America for a term that would differentiate the social elite from all others. Anglo-Saxon served that need. ... Anglo-Saxonism became a badge of social acceptance; in many ways, it was the most important social demarcation one could possess in the late 19th and early 20th centuries."[18] Reading *Gray Flannel* in these terms suggests that Tom's longing for a less troubled past is actually a certain hidden Anglo-Saxon male nostalgia—male because his backward orientation is in part a response to new configurations of the masculine burden of bread-winner expectations, and hidden Anglo-Saxon because, in this novel's setting, to have lived while feeling unconcerned with financial security generally meant having come from family wealth accumulated over generations. For the most part, those families that had long occupied such positions were descendants (or claimed descendants) of those who more explicitly and proudly traced their lineage to England and who also saw the increasing presence of "ethnic" European immigrants in their social, institutional, and work-related settings as something like an invasion.

As noted earlier, by the 1950s, a person like Tom would have been unlikely to bear his ethnoracial identity consciously and, if he did so at all, to think of it instead as simply "white." Indeed, that Tom never self-identifies with that word (let alone as Anglo-Saxon) indicates that he assumes and enacts an unremarkable, "simply American" identity, one in which whiteness has a hidden quality similar to that of his ancestral ethnic heritage. As Tom briefly misses his wealthy past while displaying no awareness of its undergirding ethnoracial privilege, he rejects such nostalgia immediately, reasoning that "a man with three children has no damn right to say that money doesn't matter" (*M*, 7). Tom and Betsy fall into a money-grubbing rut throughout most of the novel, forgetting their earlier disdain for the act of monitoring personal finances, and failing to recognize how the wealthy background that they each once enjoyed had allowed the cavalier financial disregard they now miss in their adult lives. By novel's end, readers are encouraged to believe, as the Raths do, that Tom has managed merely to stay honest to himself, rejecting the money-focused, family-sacrificing life of the man he was in danger of replicating, his robotically work-obsessed boss at the United Broadcasting Company (UBC), Ralph Hopkins. A happy resolution eventually arrives for the Raths, not only because they believe that Tom has regained his integrity but also because they have found a path back to relationally marked, socially elevating wealth. As the novel closes, the Raths have moved into an inherited estate and begun the process of selling portions of their landholdings, on which houses suggestively similar to their old home will be built, thereby providing an array of smaller, feudally arranged homes located in sight of and below their quasi-baronial manor. The Raths' ancestral comfort and status will more or less return, and ethnic, racial, and class-specific others will also clearly continue to be available, as hired hands and minds, and as subordinated human markers of the Raths' social elevation.

EMPATHETIC BLACK MALE EMBODIMENT AND WHITE MALE EMOTIONAL CONSTIPATION

While the social order in the United States has long equated money with happiness, Tom and Betsy's fiscal hunger is thus more pointedly markable in terms of a hidden ethnicity. Part of what indicates an Anglo-Saxon influence on their nostalgia for a wealthier past is the gradual emergence of their sense that they are, or should be, rightful occupants of a heightened stature relative to others. In earlier times, this status had been contraindicated by more explicit recognition of subordinated ethnic and racial others. In the earlier generations of their families, this recognition occurred in part because those who had declared themselves Anglo-Saxon highlighted the differences of others in response to such exclusionary social currents as scientific racism, which helped to suggest the others' supposed "eugenic" inferiority and thus their dubious potential for fully contributory citizenship. These intraracial dynamics also had spatial and temporal dimensions; Irish, Italian, Polish, Jewish, Catholic, and so on were variably salient markers of "ethnic" difference in different times and places in the United States. Those deemed inferior to white Anglo-Saxons included both racial and ethnic groups; the latter were accorded fully white status only in certain regional, cultural, or social contexts. As Matthew Frye Jacobson points out in regard to ethnoracial formations in the early twentieth century, when Tom and Betsy's parents would have been coming of age, both the extant clause of the 1790 Naturalization Act that limited citizenship to "free white persons" (a clause that lasted until 1952) and the influx of European immigrants created a "political crisis" of exacerbated nativism, which arose in response to a perceived "over-inclusivity of the category 'white persons.'"[19] "Anglo-Saxon" favoritism was both fading and changing, sometimes into broader forms of supposedly pure whiteness, as racial preference moved toward simply "white" favoritism. By the 1950s, Sloan Wilson, himself the scion of a by-then subdued Anglo-Saxon heritage, gave his novel an ostensibly liberal tinge of inclusion by peppering both racially and ethnically othered characters throughout *Gray Flannel*, several of whom have extensive speaking roles. Ultimately, a closer look at both Wilson's and Tom Rath's perception of, and *use of*, these explicitly raced and ethnicized characters also identifies both men as reactionary inheritors of a fading Anglo-Saxon legacy.

Although neither Tom nor any other character identifies him as a member of what was once more directly labeled the white Anglo-Saxon elite, Wilson's protagonist clearly is one, to the extent that this by-then amorphous group can be discerned. By 1953, the time of this novel's setting, one evident marker of this dominant group was its very lack of self-definition as a group. As George Lipsitz has pointed out in an oft-quoted clarification of how this phenomenon worked more generally in terms of late-twentieth-century racial domination, "As the unmarked category against which difference is constructed, whiteness never has to speak its name, never has to acknowledge its role as an organizing principle in social and cultural relations."[20] By the 1950s, Anglo-Saxon dominance had lost its overtly declarative status while the concept of "ethnicity" lingered as a marker for those who were not quite white, that is, not quite full-fledged members of the dominant group that "Anglo-Saxon" contained but less and less directly described. As noted earlier, when this dominant northeastern grouping was labeled in this era, "Anglo-Saxon" (often including the word "white") had moved toward "white Anglo-Saxon Protestant" (or "WASP") and its occasional usage remained an oddly illogical concept, a marker not only of racial and class-based dominance but also of that which racial dominance ostensibly excluded—ethnicity.[21] In a later novel, *All the Best People* (1970), Wilson revisited the postwar era by depicting the travails of Dana and Caroline Campbell, a couple who strongly resemble the Raths, and indeed Wilson himself, and he handled the concept of the protagonists' hidden ethnicity less subtly than he had in his depiction of the Raths.

Like both Wilson and Tom Rath, Dana Campbell has graduated from Harvard and served in the war, and he too bears discernible traces of a white Anglo-Saxon heritage. During a conversation about the future between Dana and Caroline while both are in their mid-twenties, such roots become more explicit than they ever do in *Gray Flannel*. As this couple discusses what sort of life each would like to pursue, various perquisites emerge that were generally limited to those not only of their race but also of their elevated, geographically situated class. These include the expectation of a "veterans' loan" (which were largely limited to white male veterans), family connections to a beginning position on Wall Street, and a steady confidence that nothing is holding them back.[22] As Dana announces his intention to "make a lot of money," he adds, "Have briefcase, will travel. ... Mobility is one of my assets."[23] He means a willingness to physically relocate for a lucrative job, but the phrase also references his fealty to the era's expectations of educated young white men—that they be ambitious, especially in financial terms, and thus upwardly aspirant in terms of social status. However, the more specifically white Anglo-Saxon underpinnings that both buttress and propel Dana become more apparent when he recalls both of their upbringings and an exclusive inn that people they knew had frequented: "Do you remember how they kept saying 'all the best people' went up there? ... people who had all the power and wealth they wanted."[24] Like Tom, Dana has a family that pushes him in a particularly status-conscious way, hoping that he will be the one to "Restore the family glory!"[25] Significantly, given the postwar setting and the fading of explicit white Anglo-Saxon affiliation, their background becomes labeled as such not through Dana's own self-declaration but rather through his recognition that the label indicates how *others* see them: "They call people like us WASPS, Caroline, white Anglo-Saxon Protestants." When Caroline says she'd rather not claw their way to the wealthy status that WASP glory has largely been boiled down to for Dana, and instead "Just [be] Caroline and Dana," Dana jokes about how poor they would be, left with little more than "a few good books from the library and a visit to an art museum now and then."[26] Although Dana recognizes such cultural capital and the propelling relevance to his future of his privileged ethnic background much more fully than does Tom, he too fails to fully acknowledge its direct ties to his most fervent desire, that of making a great deal of money. While doing so was a common postwar desire among middle-class white aspirants, the relative ease with which Dana could do so and his expectation that he will arc especially attributable to his status as a vaguely self-aware WASP.[27] More generally then, while actual people thusly situated may not have embraced their WASP status, others did see them in such terms, marking what amounted to a dominant (yet often hidden, especially to themselves) ethnicity, as well as an inherited habitus that shaped their conceptions of others and, as Wilson's authorial methods exemplify, their usages of them.

Among *Gray Flannel*'s markedly black and ethnic characters, the former mostly function in a manner similar to Toni Morrison's delineation of an instrumentalized Africanist presence, "traditionally used constructs of blackness" that register in white-authored literature mainly in order to highlight features of the central white characters.[28] As with the woman who briefly catches Tom's eye as he passes through Harlem, a minor black character typically works this way by evoking stereotypical elements or connotations of blackness that reside in the collective white imagination. Although some of Tom's current malaise seems attributable to what we now label post-traumatic stress disorder, he also rather fondly remembers a soldierly version of himself, a more confident participant within restorative memories that compensate for the bland, seemingly emasculating roles of corporate drone and responsible family man that he is trying to embody. Aside from Tom's brief encounter with the woman in Harlem, he consciously registers the racial status of black soldiers during one of his wartime flashbacks. When Tom is thrown into shock by his own killing of a fellow white soldier and friend, Hank Mahoney, with a poorly thrown hand grenade, he picks up the corpse and searches for medical help. A group of implicitly white medics tell him that Hank is already dead, so he obstinately wanders off in search of different medics, only to encounter a segregated group of "Negro" soldiers disembarking from a landing barge. In the scene that follows, Wilson's inclusion of a black sergeant reflects a 1950s-era white liberal ideal of heightened individualized racial cooperation, rather than recognition of the ongoing systemic racist realities of wartime and postwar segregation.[29] Tom's interaction with this unnamed black sergeant also works in a contradictory way, with the individualizing effect of having this character speak countered by Wilson's stereotypical depiction of him as more emotional and bodily than Tom and the white medics, that is, as remarkably empathetic and conspicuously large.

Recognizing quickly that Tom is in a state of crazed denial about Hank's death, the "gigantic" sergeant rests a "big hand" on Tom's shoulder and "one great arm around Hank's body." When the sergeant quickly perceives Tom's state of shocked denial, he suggests that Tom sit down and rest and then places the body with "gentle and respectful hands ... a hundred yards" from the other collected dead (*M*, 94). While Wilson depicts this man interacting purposefully with Tom and speaking with apparent agency and even goes so far as having this black sergeant issue orders to Tom, a white captain, the overall effect is that of a presence rendered racially typical, in ways likely to register as such for Wilson's white readers. As Morrison points out, the Africanist presence has been widely used by white American authors in certain codifiable ways; two deployed here include the repeated metonymic emphasis on black hands that function for white purposes and his open display of emotion. Dialectically constituted racial formation has long encouraged white people to repress emotional display in their own demeanor and to project a conception of excessive and often uncontrolled display onto racial others. In literary terms, this tendency has, of course, been exacerbated when the central character is performing ordinary white masculinity as well; secondary female characters have been commonly depicted, as Nirmal Purwar writes, as "lacking rationality and all that the abstract male type exemplified ..." and instead represent "emotion, bodies, nature, particularity and affectivity."[30] Wilson's black soldier becomes a superficially positive character in terms of marked racial inclusion because he speaks and acts with apparent agency and because he is more helpful than the white medics whom Tom has previously encountered. However, this unnamed character exists solely in order to labor willingly for the sake of the white male protagonist's well-being, and he does so in the emotional and physical (rather than intellectual) modes deemed appropriate for members of his race in most of the era's white-authored, white-centered cultural production. Liberal-minded white readers could thereby feel good both about the inclusion of a black (albeit very minor) character and about the positive effect that his heightened emotionality and physicality has in resuscitating Tom's soldierly capacities. Overlooked in this process was the countervailing reinforcement of common white stereotypes about black people.

Thus, Tom's memory of the sergeant as black, and also as someone not only toward whom he felt no racial animus but also from whom he accepted help in an especially vulnerable state, conveys raced and gendered significance in a novel that would seem largely unconcerned with such matters. Tom's recollection ultimately signals nothing significant about this sergeant or about black soldiers or people more generally, but rather something in particular about Tom—that he is a good (that is, tolerant) white man, one able and willing to look beyond the mask unfairly imposed on black people by centuries of racism. In addition, the scene's emotional resonance—which, as racially gendered norms dictate, cannot be depicted as pouring forth from the scene's white male and thus emotionally restrained protagonist—is registered by the highly empathetic, caring black character. By portraying Tom's memory this way, Wilson responded, perhaps intentionally, to his era's newly configured demographic relations. The war's highlighting of xenophobic fascist regimes had exposed racism, ethnocentrism, and religious intolerance as hypocritically pernicious elements of the United States' vaunted "democracy" and thus as national characteristics that its leadership recognized as a deterrent to the country's global reputation and ambitions.[31] Wilson's liberal-hearted narrative reflects the era's resultant, ostensibly tolerant white middle-class acceptance of racial and ethnic difference. The doubled irony is that a racist mask remains on this character's face; a black foil appears in this highly white-centered narrative as a bit more than a metonymic set of working muscles and hands, but only as a way of suggesting that racism against blackness is rightfully in decline, because white individuals were becoming less racist toward black individuals, as exemplified by tolerant Tom being ahead of the times in the then rigidly segregated military. Although the moment evokes feel-good white liberal tolerance, no recognition, let alone concern, is conveyed for the fact that most African Americans continued to live in highly segregated, subordinated conditions.[32]

THE ETHNICIST PRESENCE

While the scene in which an anonymous black soldier helps Tom deal with a friend's accidental death lends a racially liberal tinge to Tom's compensatory reveries about a more vividly alive version of himself, a more extensive suggestion of ethnoracial tolerance arises from his wartime affair with an Italian woman, Maria Lapa. This episode becomes another plot-driving existential dilemma when Tom agonizes over whether to reveal the affair to Betsy. Maria and three other markedly ethnic characters constitute what amounts to (paralleling Morrison's Africanist presence) an ethnicist presence in the novel, and Wilson uses these characters for more complex and submerged purposes than he does the black sergeant and the briefly glimpsed Harlem resident. In *Gray Flannel*'s narrative present, Tom's numerous encounters with explicitly ethnic characters begin when he visits the United Broadcasting Company for a job interview. As he enters an elevator, he notices not only something familiar about the elevator operator, who turns out to be his wartime comrade Caesar Gardella, but also his ethnic difference. Like those of other ethnically marked characters, Caesar's differences from Tom are signaled in both linguistic and bodily terms. Not only does the elevator operator have a "slight Italian accent," he is also described as "a stout, dark-complexioned man ... with thick black hair," a "deep voice," a "fat, almost round" face, "black and unblinking eyes," and a "thick neck" which bears "a long, thin white scar" (*M*, 25). Feeling "oddly flustered" by this brief first encounter, Tom finds a men's room to wash his face and comb his hair before proceeding to his job interview. As the novel progresses, this act of ablution clearly signals Tom's unconscious rejection of discomfiting memories conjured up by Caesar, and particularly of his wartime version of himself, one blemished by his hidden affair with Maria. The memory he has of a wartime self who indulged in bodily pleasure is a "dirtier" one that counters the dry-cleaned, gray-flannelled man he is trying to embody. Caesar's corporeal, closely described masculine excess functions *as* excess because it contrasts with, and thus helps to define, the relatively disembodied white masculinity that Tom is rather paradoxically trying to embody. Suppressing reminders of the wartime version of himself becomes in part an effort to achieve that more whitened manhood by washing away, as it were, the Italian-stained identity that Tom had slid into during the war, especially by engaging in a prolonged affair with Maria.

When Tom realizes that the elevator man is Caesar Gardella, whom he remembers as a fellow soldier and "a thin boy of Italian ancestry," stirrings of guilt and shame arise, coupled with thoughts that indicate how his current struggles trigger nostalgic visions of a former, more conventionally masculine self:

> How curious it was that apparently nothing was ever really forgotten, that the past was never really gone, that it was always lurking, ready to destroy the present, or at least to make the present seem absurd, or if not that, to make Tom himself seem absurd, the perpetuator of an endless and rather hideous masquerade. I am a good man, he thought, and I have never done anything of which I am truly ashamed. Curiously, he seemed to be mimicking himself. "I am a good man," he seemed to be saying in a high, effeminate, prissy voice, "and I have never done anything of which I am truly ashamed." A gust of ghostly and derisive laughter seemed to ring out in reply. (*M*, 77)

As Tom struggles to contain himself here, a complex array of other feelings also arise, including frustration, humor, alienation, and the anger suggested by Tom's last name.[33] At a more unconscious level, what also appear are haunting echoes from Tom's own ancestral past of a denigrated form of elite masculinity. Wilson's depiction of Tom's angst here might seem squarely in line with his era's general anxieties about the supposed decline of (white) masculine virtues. In an analysis of elite American masculinity during the mid-twentieth century, during which numerous renowned cultural critics "bewailed the 'softness' of men setting their compass by the collective whims and demands of bureaucratic life…", historian Robert Dean notes that while such critiques struck a chord with many (white) Americans of the day, concerns about masculine flaccidity resonated in further, long-standing ways for men in the northeastern leadership class.[34] Quoting John Adams, the revolutionary leader and second U.S. president, Dean writes that "the Revolutionary forefathers had lamented the 'elegance, luxury, and effeminacy' that threatened the 'great, manly, and warlike virtues' of the new republican society," a society created and run, of course, by elite white men.[35]

By establishing his protagonist as an aspirant to the mainstream postwar idealization of self-reliant masculinity, Wilson appealed to middle-class readers who were concerned about such a supposed decline in the state of American manhood; he also implicitly called for sympathetic understanding of men who struggled to resist the era's threats to masculinity, including traumatized war veterans. Less evident is just where the "ghostly and derisive laughter" that Tom hears in that moment comes from and why he oddly feels that he is "mimicking" himself. Given the elite WASP background of both Wilson and his protagonist and the lack of awareness both display of their lingering adherence to the dictates of WASP masculinity, I would argue that part of what Tom feels is an ethnically informed derision for his own impulse to declare to himself, "I am a good man ... and I have never done anything for which I am truly ashamed" (*M*, 77). This derision comes from the part of Tom, and likely of Wilson himself, that has tried to reject the patrician heritage that helps to prompt such a declaration, including the doing so in such stiffly formal terms, which helps to explain why Tom hears himself saying it in "a high, effeminate, prissy voice." Tom's hearing of his own self-declaration of goodness in this tone evokes not only the era's broader anxieties about the new (white) everyman as a feminized, obedient rule follower but also a long-standing tradition of casting aristocratic masculinity in terms of effeminacy. In response to such stereotypes, as Dean explains, many mid-twentieth-century northeastern elite men felt a need to prove their virility, and many tried to do so by performing heroically in war (or, in the case of John F. Kennedy, by managing to seem as if they had done so). Such men felt obligated as society's future leaders to prove their martial mettle, but they also did so in response to common conceptions of the elite class's aloof "anglophilia" and "enervating privilege," and especially of elite masculinity as soft and effeminate.[36] Although Tom's struggles to adapt to the constraints of corporate life echo his era's common anxieties about its threats to self-reliant masculinity, a submerged part of him also perceives within himself, and tries to reject, the remnants of an aristocratic effeminacy associated with his own elite WASP past.[37]

Faced with an array of pressures on both the home and work fronts, Tom's wartime reveries center on a supposedly more alive, assertive, and capable version of himself. The current demands that he perform a highly whitened, less embodied masculinity evoke not only a more marked embodiedness via Caesar's ethnicity but also the version of himself that he became by effectively stepping out of his puritanically and, ironically enough, ethnically confined masculinity via an affair with another markedly ethnic character, Maria. Once Caesar identifies himself and asks Tom to help Maria and the son she has had by Tom, both she and Caesar evoke a heightened emotionality that white middle-class readers would have stereotypically associated with Italian people. The novel's wartime flashbacks thus function as a contrasting backdrop in which Tom remembers an assertive masculinity that he now has trouble enacting. Also, in a pattern that has by now become familiar in white male-authored U.S. literature, darker others, both male and female, help to draw out this otherwise tightly contained protagonist, whom Wilson depicts as gradually developing a masculine courage to resist demands that he fulfill a role unsuited not to the Anglo-Saxon inflected person he has been raised to be but rather to the individualized person he "really" is. Yet, in part because he is a white Anglo-Saxon inflected person, there is no individualized "real" Tom that he eventually becomes.[38]

Despite the confusion and horrors of a war in which Tom killed not only his best friend but also sixteen other people, he also remembers it as a setting imbued with honesty and sincerity. Caesar's presence continues to inspire Tom's guilt, right in the soul-threatening heart of the UBC building, because Caesar embodies the honesty and integrity that Tom misses in his own current self, as an unfaithful husband and a man unsuited to corporate obsequiousness—Caesar married his wartime paramour, Gina, instead of abandoning her as Tom did Maria. Also, Caesar eventually reveals that he struggles to get by on the wages earned by his manual labor; Tom is clearly headed toward more financial success, but—given the particular demands of the corporate world—at the potential expense of his integrity and his current family. When Tom first has lunch with Caesar, his class-based consciousness of the gaze of his gray-flannelled colleagues leads him to think that he shouldn't be seen fraternizing with an elevator operator, so he steers Caesar to a Mexican restaurant. However, the choice of an ethnic restaurant also helps to suggest that Tom's sense of shame for doing so, and for cheating on his wife, is heightened by Caesar's seemingly more authentic ethnic status.[39] While Wilson writes from an even more fundamentally conservative perspective than did such ethnoracial fetishists of his era as Jack Kerouac and Norman Mailer, he too deploys figurations of more vibrant, genuine ethnic otherness to contrast with, and thereby expose as relatively flaccid, the newly minted middle-class white masculinity that Tom is struggling to embody.[40]

Again, the masculine nostalgia triggered in Tom by Caesar is for the better self he supposedly was during the war, a more vigorous and "alive" version of himself triggered in part by his interactions with ethnoracial, and thus supposedly more honest in bodily terms, others.

In racial terms, the wartime setting enabled a psychic evacuation of his white self, whereby Tom imagined that raced and ethnicized people were more genuinely alive and that he could become someone other than his constrained, seemingly flaccid self while interacting with them. Tom remembers, for instance, that Maria's body "was as beautiful as the body of any woman, and much more beautiful than most" and thus his first words to her were, "My name's Bill Brown..." (*M*, 79). Even then, he felt compelled to pretend to be a different person—the Tom Rath that he had been raised to be could not leap spontaneously into doing what he was about to do with Maria, and the current version of himself feels less authentically alive than the person whom he briefly enacted during the war, especially during his idyll with Maria. In this sense, one reason that Tom felt less guilt during his affair with Maria than he likely would about one conducted in the United States (an action that never even tempts him while living with Betsy) was her ethnicity, which made it easier for Tom to slip out of his own straight-laced, contained—and thus inauthentic to what he was really feeling—masculine self and into what seemed like a more authentic mode of being. In terms of race, whiteness thus functions for Wilson as a novelist as it did more generally, as a whitening out, as it were, of that with which people like oneself had been affiliated before. Thus, while Tom may currently be traumatized by wartime atrocities, including those he himself committed, gender, race, and ethnicity functioned together in ways that felt freeing, springing him temporarily from an encaged prior self. And just as Wilson figures more directly the prewhitened authenticity of his era's marked ethnicities, so too does he ultimately figure Tom and Betsy's rejection of the 1950s suburban white ideal as a revival of their former, implicitly white Anglo-Saxon heritage.

Wilson again deploys Italian ethnicity as a contrasting marker of whitened inauthenticity when Tom joins his new boss, Ralph Hopkins, for an elegant lunch. Tom thinks the current version of the speech on mental health that he's been helping others write for Hopkins is horrible, and he considers whether to say so honestly or to temper his opinion in more falsely obsequious terms. Before Tom speaks, another ethnicist presence appears, a nameless waiter who asks for their order "in a thick Italian accent" (*M*, 201). The accent clearly evokes Caesar and Maria, and thus Tom's looming wartime lies, but also an ethnic contrast to the seemingly immaculate racial whiteness of Tom's current setting—the scrubbed corporate executive world—in which men like Tom Rath and

Ralph Hopkins are especially welcome and enabled because they *are* men like them, that is, educated, connected, and "proper"-speaking white men, as well as men who have sacrificed or left behind something in order to be regarded that way. In other words, the waiter's accent again evokes Italian ethnicity as a coalescence in the white imagination of countervailing yet ultimately whiteness-serving authenticity.

Having been subliminally prompted by the waiter's accent to value the honesty and integrity he feels are at risk in his guise as junior executive, Tom decides on frankly criticizing the speech. The lie here is not only the smiling, phony corporate life to which Tom feels he has refused to sacrifice his integrity but also, along with it, the form of white masculinity staged in this scene's setting and embodied most fully by Hopkins. This is a raced and gendered status supposedly stripped of categorical specificity that is inadvertently exposed as such by Wilson's use yet again of romanticized ethnicity. Tom's directness with Hopkins about the speech pays off, and he decides to play it straight from then on in corporate life, a trait that leads to Hopkins's invitation to follow in his wealthy footsteps by becoming his protégé. Tom's countervailing desire to be a good husband and father by spending more time at home quickly intervenes, leading him to reject the sort of all-consuming career that is destroying Hopkins' family, but the point remains—white male nostalgia figures ethnic otherness as sincere and genuine, in part because of guilt inspired by awareness of that to which hegemonic white masculinity has subjected ethnic and racial others.[41] When entitled white men like Sloan Wilson felt pushed to acknowledge subjugated ethnoracial others, they often responded with narcissistic nostalgia, by figuring ethnicity as a trace or echo of something seemingly genuine that they themselves have lost.

Although white authors in the United States have often used racial presences for such purposes, the particular impulse of Wilson (whose own life paralleled that of Tom Rath in many ways) in doing so could well have arisen from his own subliminal white Anglo-Saxon guilt about the mistreatment and erasure of those long excluded from the more original, "purely" white club, that is, members of supposedly lesser races and ethnicities. In Tom's case, these and other internal machinations eventually lead to a compromised rejection of the era's newly manufactured white male ideal in favor of, and in retreat to, the reconstruction of another nostalgic fantasy, that of life as a noble, patrician member of the de facto white Anglo-Saxon landed gentry.

Pseudo-Feudal Nostalgia

Tom's unsettled psyche is not this novel's only site of resurgent white Anglo-Saxon proclivities; a major reviver of such feelings in Tom is his wife Betsy, whose consciousness the narrative briefly occupies. Unlike significant female characters that I will consider in later chapters, Betsy Rath reads primarily as a contented suburban housewife who feels entirely satisfied with her circumscribed role as wife and mother. Betsy does have restless nighttime thoughts about a better life, but they reveal her longing for improvement in terms of domestic and material betterment for her immediate family, rather than for increased independence as a woman in the wider world. Where Betsy differs, like Tom, from suburban typicality is that her current malaise is based less on anything wrong with where they currently live than on memories of previous domestic settings. In the second half of the novel, Betsy springs into action, pushing Tom to win back his grandmother's estate from the threat of loss in a lawsuit and to convert the land into wealth-generating housing plots. For the most part, Betsy's narrative function is entirely secondary—to prod Tom into vigorous, unspokenly WASP masculine activity in the hopes of regaining the wealthy splendor that her family also once enjoyed.

Restless with insomnia, Betsy recalls her childhood in Boston, where her family occupied a "big brick house on Beacon Street ... a cavernous building with a long dark staircase" (*M*, 110). The ongoing salience of Betsy's affluent upbringing in her current disposition is more subtly demonstrated by her weariness regarding parties on Greentree Avenue. Seemingly to the contrary, what bothers her more than the monotonous conversation topics and the heavy drinking is the incessant talk of money. The particular invitation that prompts Betsy's thoughts is for a party being thrown to celebrate a husband's rise in salary; at other gatherings, "Budgets were frankly discussed, and the public celebration of increases in salary was common" (*M*, 109). That last word takes on a suggestive second meaning when paired with a complaint made by Tom's "imperious" grandmother upon being placed in a hospital: "The nurses are so *common!*" (*M*, 49, emphasis in original). Betsy does not explicitly think of her neighbors as common people in this sense, but her memories of early married life with Tom do reflect their decidedly un-"common" beginnings, raised as they were by adults who rarely spoke of money because they had plenty of it. As newlyweds, the Raths had little money of their own, but unlike most people in the United States, they did have savings, "an absurd proportion" of which Tom spent on "her engagement ring and a diamond-sprinkled wedding ring to match" (*M*, 111). A particularly inherited sense of money is reflected in Betsy's current realization that "because diamonds had increased in value a great deal since the war," the rings "had turned out to be the only shrewd investment they had ever made" (*M*, 111). Again, few people had enough extra money when Betsy was a child to think of funneling it into "investments." Like Tom, Betsy does not consciously frame her own discontent with their situation in terms of a wealthy white Anglo-Saxon past, and yet, the "common" desire for movement up the social ladder that they too feel is ultimately distinct. For the Raths, this feeling is driven more by wistful remembrances enabled by ancestral wealth than by excited pursuit of the era's new forms of white masculine fiscal opportunity, as represented by Tom's budding career at the UBC.

Tom's framing of the hopes of moving upwards in terms that amount to moving backward is less overt, as Betsy is the one who, again in the middle of the night, conceives of a way in which they can do so. When it becomes evident after the death of Tom's grandmother that he is the sole heir to her large house upon a hill and its twenty-three attendant acres, but also to high tax and maintenance costs they cannot currently afford, Betsy excitedly awakens him with a new scheme—not only to move into the much bigger house but also to grow wealthy (again) by developing the acreage into small housing plots. When Tom advocates instead staying in their current house and scaling down their ambitions, Betsy accuses him of having lost his manly confidence. Tom counters that he's being "sensible" but then adds, "It's time we forget the Rath family's dreams of glory, and *your* family's dreams of glory too.... Dreams of glory.... I've spent my whole life getting over them" (*M*, 61, 63). Wilson devotes little space to Tom's conflicted feelings about his ancestral past beyond this simple rejection, but by the novel's end, his family's "glory" and the entitled dispositions that go with it have been revived. Tom eventually rejects the self- and family-sacrificing corporate ladder-climbing embodied by Ralph Hopkins. Nevertheless, having adopted Betsy's scheme, Tom uses his inherited cultural capital to pull various strings in South Bay toward making it happen, setting his new family on a path toward growing comfortably rich, in a pseudo-feudal, small-town setting where his resurgent white Anglo-Saxon self will reside, literally and symbolically, above others who are more overtly marked in terms of social class, race, and ethnicity.

One privilege that Wilson depicts for people like the Rath family is a local judicial system tilted in favor of their social class. Despite his marked status as Jewish, and thus as the sort of person normally ostracized by the local, whiter elites, Judge Bernstein acts as a legal servant of sorts by bending the law to help out Tom once he moves back to South Bay. In a chapter that switches to the perspective of this ethnicist presence in order to provide his backstory, his double-barreled full name—Saul Bernstein—appears repeatedly, underlining his ethnic status, which again serves to highlight by reflexive implication the submerged dominant ethnicity of the Raths. Indeed, what Judge Bernstein ultimately helps the Raths with is Tom's masculine pursuit of what amounts to his white Anglo-Saxon heritage, the material marker of which is the inherited ancestral manse. At one point, Betsy comes close to recognizing more explicitly the extent to which Tom's own ancestral legacy remains an integral part of him: "You're spoiled. You've spent most of your life feeling sorry for yourself because you knew Grandmother wasn't going to leave you a lot of money" (*M*, 64). Although Tom's grandmother and his own father have largely spent the remains of the family fortune, she does leave her land and house to him, which also come with Edward, a servant who suddenly refuses to stay in his subordinated place.

Whereas Edward Schultz refers to Tom as Mr. Rath, Tom has to struggle at one point to remember Edward's last name. When a plot-thickener enters in the form of Edward's dubious claim to the Rath estate, Tom and his family lawyer solicit the advice of Judge Bernstein. Despite the "hidebound" customs of a "Connecticut town notorious for its prejudice against Jews" (*M*, 133), a place where the judge and his wife still cannot gain entrance to the country club, Judge Bernstein enjoys dispensing justice here precisely because this is a small-town setting; he believes he can do so more fairly when he is more likely to know the disputants who end up before him.[42] Wilson thus acknowledges in a white liberal fashion the bigotry that lingered in such places—where, after all, the judge is a "respected" man who has been allowed to grow "reasonably rich"—and as a novelist, he seems to have consciously gone one step further, by fleshing out this character with a full chapter and backstory of his own (the book also ends with the image of Judge Bernstein, smiling down benevolently from his office window at Tom and Betsy). Nevertheless, this character ultimately serves as another ethnicist presence who helps to trigger hidden Anglo-Saxon nostalgia, in part by being physically "fleshed out" in explicitly corporeal ways that Tom, Betsy, and other less provisionally white characters are not. That is, as with Caesar, the judge is continually described in corporeal terms. As a motif that also renders comic relief, this "small stout man with a large mole on his left cheek" finds that dispensing justice often gives him a stomachache unless proceedings go smoothly enough that no one but the guilty suffers (*M*, 131). He is also, like the honorably married Caesar, one-dimensionally virtuous.[43] Again, my point is not merely that Wilson limits his explicitly ethnoracial characters to little more than caricature; he also does so in the service of a narrative stance and a pair of central characters that together evince white Anglo-Saxon inclinations, partly in response to the fading into a more general, expanded whiteness of a more explicitly privileged ethnic heritage and partly in response to the era's status-threatening imposition of socially striving, provisionally white men.

It is important to recall here that ideology, including constructions of normality, functions to justify hidden authority, as well as its iniquitous position at the top, where those who embody it reside at the material and social expense of those below them. One reason that it seems natural for Tom to move back to his ancestral grounds is not because life in South Bay would restore him as a white Anglo-Saxon scion but rather because it would grant him much more autonomy—pursuit of the era's vaunted, newly heightened individualism becomes even more attractive, and more available, to a man with a family background and attendant resources like those that Tom has. That his easier achievement of an individualized sense of freedom is actually a white Anglo-Saxon inheritance renders Tom a certain discernible social type, a member of a group, even though it's an unspoken and only indirectly acknowledged group that grants Tom the achievement of his countervailing and illusory sense of individuality. Crucially, the presence of others, who are discernible *as* subordinate others by way of certain defining and denigrated attributes, helped to establish the seemingly natural suitability of white Anglo-Saxon men to their position of dominance. Tom is depicted as a vacillating, ineffectual man throughout much of the novel, and although various troubles and lingering wartime issues help to explain his flaccidity, his eventual rejuvenation is especially enabled by his ancestral setting of South Bay, where he effectively seizes the reins of his heritage despite his earlier rejection of old familial "glory." Tom's seemingly natural membership in the setting's long-dominant group becomes more apparent when he meets with a local contractor about the possibility of regaining his family's wealth by developing his inherited land, in part because the contractor is another ethnicist presence who, accordingly it seems, interacts deferentially with Tom.

Like Judge Bernstein, Antonio Bugala is another character whose overt ethnicity is more than just doubly nominative, and he too is accorded his own chapter. Wilson introduces "Tony" as a person who, as Betsy says, "looks like a man who can get things done," suggesting an emasculating contrast with Tom (*M*, 144). For Betsy, the kinds of "things" that such a man can apparently get done are physical tasks, and as with Caesar and Judge Bernstein as well as the black sergeant, descriptions of Tony are more bodily than are those of Tom: "He was stocky, dark-haired, and had once been told by a girl that he looked like pictures of Napoleon as a young man" (*M*, 144). Also directly countering laconic Tom, Tony is a "man of quick enthusiasms and fast decisions"; he's a smaller man literally, but also figuratively, in terms of the local ethnoracial hierarchy (*M*, 147). Nevertheless, as with Judge Bernstein, South Bay has come to allow ethnic strivers to attain some measure of financial success, and "for the past five years [Tony] had been astonishing everyone by becoming almost as successful as he had always predicted. Already, at the age of twenty-eight, Bugala was a contractor with thirty-four men, including his father, on his payroll" (*M*, 144). As another ethnicist presence who verges on caricature in the service of comic relief, Tony stalks about the Raths' new estate, a big-talking, pushy go-getter who grows so physically agitated by the possibility of becoming rich by building houses for the Raths (and by grossly calculating just how much money he could earn) that he seems about to burst.

While Wilson's novel displays a mild authorial interest in promoting ethnoracial tolerance and respect for circumscribed womanly ambition, his instrumentalizing characterization reflects not only his unexamined masculinity and whiteness but also his more specific white Anglo-Saxon bias. Indeed, although Tony Bugala is not Jewish, his immoderately expressed ambition echoes common conceptions of Jewish students at Wilson's alma mater, Harvard. As anthropologist Karen Brodkin explains, "The Protestant elite complained that Jews were unwashed, uncouth, unrefined, loud, and pushy. Harvard University President A. Lawrence Lowell, who was also a vice president of the Immigration Restriction League, was open about his opposition to Jews at Harvard."[44] Wilson's narrator also refers to Tony engaging in dubious "trade secrets" that undercut his competition, evoking stereotypes of underhanded ethnic cohesion and, given Tony's Italian ethnicity, practices not unrelated to those of the mafia. Nevertheless, Wilson also describes Tony's decision to "play it straight" in his proposal to Tom rather than subjecting him to "small-time cleverness" (*M*, 147), apparently in recognition of the supposedly evenhanded dealings engaged in and expected by his wealthier, whiter potential clients. That an Italian American businessman of his time would have been more likely to engage in aboveboard forms of cooperation with other Italian American business concerns seems to have escaped Wilson, as does the surreptitious, string-pulling nature of Tom's budding entrepreneurial practices when he later uses his cultural capital and expectations of respect, if not exactly deference, while dealing with local citizens and officials about zoning laws. Although Tony is a fictional character, we can also consider another factor that Wilson apparently ignored (or perhaps did not realize): the likelihood that a person such as Tony, who like Tom has served in the Second World War, would have drawn on benefits made available by the GI Bill. The ready access both men would have had to these benefits, which included various forms of low-interest loans that could have helped a person like Tony start his business, makes them more similar to each other than Wilson allows; their whiteness unites them in this respect since returning black veterans were routinely denied such benefits.[45]

As Tony talks to the Raths and as we listen to his often countervailing thoughts, he demonstrates having learned more carefully grammatical and "polite" ways of speaking to his locale's de facto landed gentry. Tony is also more excitable than the Raths, another trait that becomes highly physical; as he looks around at their land and realizes its development possibilities, Tony's "imagination, which was always at a slow simmer, suddenly began to boil over. Why not put up a whole housing project on quarter-acre lots? All right, you'd have to jump over the Zoning Board somehow, but if it could be done—the prospect was fantastic!" (*M*, 145). Tony Bugala is a particularly ethnicized striver and thus readily rendered, from a subsumed elite Anglo-Saxon perspective that draws on common ethnic stereotypes, as comically and almost frantically reaching above his current (and perhaps, in Wilson's estimation, appropriate) station in life. While fantasizing about the future housing project, he begins to "sweat," imagining himself as Tom Rath's full-fledged partner, "complete with all financial details and photographs in national magazines showing what Antonio Bugala, *Mr.* Antonio Bugala, *Esquire*, had done" (*M*, 146, emphasis in original). Wilson also works to provide narrative exposition here about how this housing development could happen, but since he relates the possibilities through Tony's perspective, we gather much about him as well, and thus about how different this Italian American is from the Raths (and also, by contrast, in what ways the Raths are different from him). Comedy is further provided to more securely white middle-class readers by depicting Tony's fervent dream that attaining a level of wealth commensurate with that of people like the Raths could gain for him as well as the feudalistic respect evoked by the term "Esquire."

While he excitedly jumps ahead in his thoughts by foreseeing various specific financial details and opportunities, Tony comes "striding up to Tom, perspiring with excitement. 'Mr. Rath,' he said bluntly, 'I've got a proposition to make'" (*M*, 148). Wilson carefully renders grammar, diction, and exclamation points here that mark Tony as both an overtly ethnic member of the working class and one striving all too mightily to make a good impression on a wealthier, whiter man: "I got a good name! ... Hell, everything's a gamble! It's the guys who take the chances who make the dough!" (*M*, 149). Tony Bugala is rash and emphatically impassioned and since these attributes were stereotypically associated with Italians, his ethnicity helps to suggest as well the opposite in Tom—caution and circumspection (accordingly, he replies in measured tones to Tony's feverish overtures: "There are a lot of wrinkles to be ironed out of your ideas yet" [*M*, 149]). Tom and Tony do briefly bond in a leveling way over the war, with Tom remembering an airstrip that Tony says he built, but they quickly snap back into their relative masculine positions within a hierarchy marked in terms not only of class but also of ethnicity, and the hidden white Anglo-Saxon's supposed lack thereof, when resuming discussion of the housing project.

Wilson's characterization of Tony and other ethnicist characters thus relies heavily on rather cartoonish forms of exaggeration, an effect that Sianne Ngai usefully terms "animatedness." As Ngai writes of this common narrative method as deployed by many white American authors, "Whether marked as Irish, Jewish, Italian, Mexican, or (most prominently in American literature and visual culture) African American, the kind of emotional expressiveness that I call animatedness seems to function as a marker of racial or ethnic otherness in general."[46] This conglomeration of hyperactive, ethnoracially informed "affective qualities" typically includes "liveliness, effusiveness, spontaneity, and zeal..." and tends to operate in ways that suggest both a lack of self-control in the animated character and thus, relationally, self-mastery in those who do not register as overtly ethnoracial.[47] In *Gray Flannel*, this set of familiar associations registers not only for comic effect but also, like Morrison's Africanist presence, as a contrasting ethnic marker for the supposedly calm, reasonable, and self-possessed white (and, at a subdued level, Anglo-Saxon) characters.[48]

In effect, this mode of characterization renders another meaning to Betsy's comment as she listens to the men, a meaning that applies to Wilson as well: "Tom always looks at the dark side of everything!" (*M*, 149). In his revelatory study of Alfred Hitchcock's cinematic handlings of the Americanized English masculinity of Cary Grant, Joshua David Gonsalves reminds us that in the 1950s, "the ethnic and racial category of whiteness" was felt to be "under siege," an anxiety especially felt by men.[49] In *Gray Flannel*, Sloan Wilson betrays a latent nostalgia for times when black and ethnic Americans were more firmly at bay, less intrusively insistent on larger portions of his current decade's sweetened American pie. Thanks to heightened degrees of World War II–era and postwar demands for integration and equal opportunity, these other Americans undeniably demanded more space in the American scene that Wilson more broadly seeks to depict and critique—it seems that they had to be dealt with, yet Wilson does so in ways that are both belittling and vaguely anxious. As Gonsalves pauses to note of Wilson's novel, "If whiteness is threatened by race mobility, or by others passing as *The Man in the Gray Flannel Suit*, fifties-era America also insists on imagining a space free from race anxiety... where the other can be safely contained as a service person."[50] Wilson's narrative registers a specifically positioned white male longing for such a space that was induced not only by the perception of encroaching others but also by a newly felt need to at least seem fair-minded in response. This duality leads to superficially sympathetic narrative inclusion of Africanist and ethnicist presences, which often veer into caricature, a mode of exaggeration that in turn applies as well to the consequent relational depiction of Tom as an ideal, moral, and supposedly individualized man. Gonsalves also notes the era's common mainstream cinematic deployment of "invisible workers," barely glimpsed characters who "are decisively marked as non-white by being denied any semblance of a menacing racial mobility."[51] Although Bernstein and Bugala do enact visible, talkative, and to some degree interiorized autonomy, Wilson renders them less menacing by limiting their economic and social mobility in comparison with those of the Raths. Accordingly, the narrative encourages little more than mild disapproval of South Bay's social rejection of Judge Bernstein and his wife, and by the novel's end, Tony has more or less disappeared, despite the heavy amount of planning that he and Tom have so far done together.[52] Tom's return to his ancestral home, his revivifying within himself of attendant inclinations, and his easy assumption of a well-paying and nearby suburban sinecure all ensure the kind of well-situated future for Tom, Betsy, and their children that resembles the lives of their ancestors in terms of more than just wealth.

The Man in the Gray Flannel Suit is classifiable as yet another white male "liberationist narrative," Sally Robinson's useful label for the slew of late-twentieth-century novels in which white male authors bemoaned what felt like the impending diminution of their raced and gendered privileges.[53] However, this novel also functions more specifically as a reaction by a member of an increasingly unmarked dominant ethnicity to certain postwar changes in ethnoracial relations, especially the perceived need for heightened inclusion of subordinated others. By this time, the dominant white Anglo-Saxon ethnicity had lost the legitimacy and visibility it had conferred upon itself, perhaps most explicitly in the late nineteenth century. Yet, generationally transferred privileges and consequent dispositions persisted, as did subsumed expectations of dominance and masculine enactment of it, resulting in assumptions that a social order that maintained this dominance was right and natural—instead of the understanding that the social order was initially and purposefully constructed to position them as the dominant. Indeed, it would take a willed effort for many descendants of such an Anglo-Saxon heritage not to reproduce such inherited, backward-oriented dispositions. As Doane writes regarding the hierarchical nature of racial and ethnic formations, "The key element here is that dominant group ethnic assertion tends to focus upon the defense of existing social structures and cultural norms ... and the negation of subordinate group claims. Consequently, there is less effort devoted to elevating group identity and cultural practices—as opposed to the cultural or psychological decolonization practiced by subordinate groups—and lower group self-awareness."[54] Tom and Betsy's reassertion of themselves at the top of a feudally reminiscent hierarchy, with ethnically marked servants and residentially positioned subordinates in the form of a future village of sorts literally spread out before

and below them, is not the result of their consciously perceiving themselves as white Anglo-Saxon descendants. Nevertheless, *Gray Flannel* is
less what it has primarily been read as—an individualistic rejection of the
new and stifling corporate conformity inflicted on the era's middle-class
men—and more an ironic and nostalgic longing for the reconstitution of
a patriarchal ethnic identity.

In a sense that again evinces the white Anglo-Saxon male nostalgia
of Sloan Wilson and thus of his protagonist, *Gray Flannel*'s Africanist
and ethnicist presences reflect actual people, those who are perceived, in
Nirmal Puwar's useful terms, as "space invaders." In the United States,
these are the resurgent minorities who seek entry in social spaces and
"'privileged' positions which have not been 'reserved' for them, [and]
for which they are not, in short, the somatic norm."[55] Nevertheless,
they are also a constitutive part of the norm, helping to define it as
such by apparently being that which it is not. As Valerie Babb describes
this process in racial terms, "The very existence of whiteness embodies
an odd duality of distinguishing itself from something nonwhite while
appropriating the nonwhite to justify its being..."[56] As the novel closes,
Tom and Betsy have extracted advice and assistance from marked and
subordinated ethnic presences—indeed, the marked, stereotyped ethnicities of such characters specifically help to position them *as* subordinated—toward the imminent development of inherited land that will
soon place them in the vaunted social position once occupied by their
respective families of origin. Writing in the pre–civil rights era, Wilson
acknowledges in a good-hearted white liberal mode the presence of
darker or darkened bodies or both, but he keeps them outside the borders of an empowered social center in which both entrenched ethnoracial privilege and mainstream hegemonic whiteness enable much greater
upward social mobility, according them little characterization beyond
the familiar racial and ethnic codings commonly used in white-authored,
white-centered cultural production. In terms of ethnicity, Wilson does
convey the ostensibly inclusive message that in his postwar northeastern setting, non–Anglo-Saxon ethnic male strivers have earned more
opportunity than ever before. On the other hand, when such men seek
positions of authority (as a judge) and financial power (as a businessman), positions traditionally occupied by members of the Anglo-Saxon
elite, their presence, merely because of who they are and what they are
thought to be like, and merely because they are not among the "best
people," feels to the male inheritors of white Anglo-Saxonism like an

invasion. Although the equally intra-racial, group-bound, and thus "ethnic" origins of such feelings are hidden from Tom, and apparently from Wilson as well, and because the privileged spaces that seem subject to invasion are those in which men have almost always occupied positions of power, the response is ultimately nostalgic, a reactionary desire to restore hierarchies of old in which white Anglo-Saxon masculine superiority defined itself as such in relation to ethnoracially marked inferiority. Although *Gray Flannel* is often read as a critique of the threats to masculinity imposed by the era's corporatized, commodified conformity, the novel also evinces Sloan Wilson's longing for his own hidden White Anglo-Saxon Protestant masculinity.

NOTES

1. Horsman, 5.
2. Ibid.
3. Lowenthal, 121–22.
4. "Provisionally white" is David R. Roediger's term for the non–Anglo-Saxon European immigrants who eventually worked their way into whiteness. *Working Toward Whiteness*, 243. For overviews of the dialectic that was "Anglo-Saxon" self-assertion and discrimination against ethnic others, see Frye Jacobson, 39–90 and Brodkin, 27–52.
5. Matt, 166.
6. For more on to the waxing and waning of what amount to Anglo-Saxon identity and group cohesion, see Baum, *The Rise and Fall of the Caucasian Race*; Kaufman, "The Decline of the WASP in the United States and Canada"; and Kaufman, *The Rise and Fall of Anglo-America*.
7. James Barrett and David R. Roediger describe "inbetween peoples" as the "millions of Eastern and Southern European immigrants who arrived in the United States between the end of the nineteenth century and the early 1920s." Their relations with settled white Americans and their efforts to assimilate into the dominant racial order were fraught:

> A whole range of evidence—laws; court cases; formal racial ideology; social conventions; popular culture in the form of slang, songs, films, cartoons, ethnic jokes, and popular theater—suggests that the native born and older immigrants often placed these newer immigrants not only above African and Asian Americans ... but also below "white" people. Indeed, many of the older immigrants and particularly the Irish had themselves been perceived as "nonwhite" just a generation earlier. (4)

These inbetween people were the "Polish, Italian, and other European artisans and peasants" whose descendants, and sometimes themselves, eventually became fully white.

8. Sloan Wilson, *The Man in the Gray Flannel Suit*, 45. Hereafter cited as *M*. In his study of (presumably white) middle-class reading tastes, Gordon Hutner also connects *Gray Flannel* and *Invisible Man*, suggesting that they be taught together: "their juxtaposition might be especially productive: surely it would cast a stronger light on the Invisible Man's experience of alienation, given the 'invisible' black characters in Wilson's novel" (333). Hutner does not elaborate, as I do in this chapter, on how this sort of invisibility works in terms not only of race but also of ethnicity. Andrew Hoberek also briefly connects the two novels, seeing in both a reflection of "the typical postwar nostalgia for nineteenth-century American individualism" while crediting Ellison with a nuanced recognition of this ideology's unspoken whiteness (56). My analysis sharpens Hoberek's point by reading *Gray Flannel*'s nostalgic paean to individualism as a more specifically Anglo-Saxon-inflected longing for fading status and property ownership.

9. That which Toni Morrison points out regarding racial assumptions about general readership long applied as well to authors and their characters unless they were labeled (that is, labeled otherwise): "until very recently, and regardless of the race of the author, the readers of virtually all of American fiction have been positioned as white" (xii).

10. As Wilson himself wrote decades later, although the novel includes many themes, conformity stood out to many readers as its sole concern: "To my surprise, my novel, which I had regarded as largely autobiographical, was taken by some serious thinkers as a protest against conformity and the rigors of suburban life," and soon, "Intellectuals, hippies and flower children began to consider [Tom Rath] not a protester against conformity, but an arch example of it, the squarest guy in the world" ("Afterword," n.p.). Jürgen Martschukat provides a representative continuation of this focus in later scholarly treatment of the novel: "In 1955, the archetype of the other-directed, domesticated, conformist man was invented. Tom Rath … perfectly incorporated the 1950s' male dilemma of opposite demands. On the one hand, he lived his life according to the familial imperatives of the postwar world, and yet, on the other hand, he was grayish, conformist, not in control of his own existence, subordinated, and consequently considered 'no man at all'" (16). Among the growing number of studies of the novel, almost none—with the brief exceptions of Catherine Jurca (*White Diaspora*) and Hutner (*What America Read*)—considers its intertwined articulations of race and ethnicity.

11. Vincent, 20.
12. As I will explain in more detail later in this chapter, I refer here to Toni Morrison's central and highly influential concept in *Playing in the Dark*.
13. Long, 205.
14. Mills, 220.
15. Doane explains, "Without the existence of a society where all people belong to the same ethnic group, there is no such thing as 'non-ethnicity,' even though it has been popular to view the dominant group in the United States as lacking any ethnic affiliation. Instead, what exists is a phenomenon best described as *hidden ethnicity*—the lack of awareness of an ethnic identity that is not normally asserted in intergroup interaction" (378, emphasis in original). As I will explain, although Doane refers to whiteness itself as a hidden ethnicity, I find this concept useful for explicating as well the hidden nature in *Gray Flannel* of the Anglo-Saxon habitus in which Wilson and his characters were raised and which still affects them.
16. Jurca, 133–59. As Jurca writes, the Raths distinguish themselves from their neighbors by thinking what people like their neighbors also presumably thought: "Other people belong in a development, not us; everyone else is happy as a corporate drone, except for me. And their fundamental dissatisfaction with the suburb and the corporation proves an engine of mobility that frees them from the constraints of each" (139). Jurca also briefly sees the Raths, as I do, as missing, in particular, the heightened status of their childhoods: "The question that the question mark in the living room raises is how can they reclaim (maintain) their social privilege?" (138). My analysis pushes this question further, positioning the Raths' vague emotional dis-ease within a relationally constructed ethnoracial hierarchy.
17. In their description of the "ever-expanding boundaries of whiteness," Jonathan W. Warren and France Winddance Twine write that "a not-so-new racial group has been transformed. Just as the White category was redefined in the 19th century to include the Celt, it has in the past century expanded to include ancestry from *anywhere* on the European continent" (206, emphasis in original).
18. Schultz, 8–9.
19. Frye Jacobson, 68.
20. Lipsitz, 1.
21. Doane defines a "dominant group" in ways that clarify the nature of the relatively unspoken dominant group into which Tom and Betsy were born:

> I define a dominant ethnic group as the ethnic group in a society that exercises power to create and maintain a pattern of economic,

political, and institutional advantage, which in turn results in the unequal (disproportionately beneficial to the dominant group) distribution of resources. With respect to intergroup relations, a key element of dominance is the disproportionate ability to shape the sociocultural understandings of society, especially those involving group identity and intergroup interactions. Historically, the origins of dominance lie in processes such as conquest, colonialism, and labor migration—situations where intergroup contact, resource competition, and power differentials combine to produce a system of ethnic stratification.... Thus, dominance is grounded in the existence of unequal power employed to derive material benefit. (376)

22. As Ira Katznelson notes, although the 1944 Servicemen's Readjustment Act, popularly known as the GI Bill, did not contain overtly discriminatory stipulations, its enactment largely excluded black participation. One major problem was the decision to leave particular methods for implementation to state and local authorities:

> Shortly after he was hired by the Veterans Administration as a Special Assistant for Negro Affairs, Joseph Albright quietly noted to General Bradley that equal treatment under the act was likely to be a myth. Though the law contained no racial distinctions, the assignment of power to the states ensured discriminatory treatment for blacks. "The difficulties of the Negro veteran," he insisted, "are *not* the same as those of any other minority group of ex-servicemen, for the simple reason that all other minorities are considered as being white, and but with few isolated instances are treated as such." (128, emphasis in original)

23. Wilson, *All the Best People*, 365–66.
24. Ibid., 370.
25. Ibid., 372.
26. Ibid., 373.
27. In Wilson's memoir *What Shall We Wear to This Party?*, in which he primarily describes participating rather uneventfully in the Second World War, writing several novels, and meeting several women, he also refers at times to his wealthy, deep-rooted family history, including its situated position among northeastern elites. Wilson does so in ways that demonstrate much about the emotional and psychic remnants of an Anglo-Saxon heritage. He never refers to himself as a WASP in this memoir, let alone an Anglo-Saxon, and repeatedly mentions instead the burden of a "puritan" heritage, which he sometimes labels Protestant and

which he states drove him to work hard and to feel inhibited sexually. At one point, Wilson reveals his ambivalent membership in this tribe, by conflating the perception of a religious lineage with that of an English one, when he recalls introducing his mother to a fiancée, Betty, who happened to have an Irish father. Apparently mindful of his mother's Anglo-Saxon pride, Wilson remembers adding "hastily" that "'Her people are all Protestants.'" Much to his surprise, Wilson's mother claims that they too have Irish ancestors: "Never had I heard her speak of Irish ancestors. English, German, Danish and French, yes, but the Irish ancestors she seemed to be inventing on the spot." When he later asks for clarification, his mother says, with a "twinkle" in her "sternly puritanical" eye, "Well, they stayed in Ireland for a few generations on their way from England to America" (380). Wilson's mother, of course, had meant to welcome Betty into the family, but she did so by creating an ancestral connection that was both inclusive and, in a relational, status-conscious way, exclusionary. In this memory from his own life, Wilson condenses several culturally induced habits among those who still embraced this loosely, often fantasized hidden ethnicity, a fading affiliation that was embraced less and less affirmatively by those who came to be known, and increasingly so by others instead of themselves, as WASPs. In particular, this moment reveals both a reflexively nostalgic conflation of puritanism with English-ness and the status assertion that typically came with it. Finally, it's worth noting that by this point in United States history, another fabricated lineage that had once been proudly and openly claimed among such people, that of whiteness, goes entirely unspoken.

28. Morrison, x.
29. As Gary Gerstle writes in his study of twentieth-century "racial and civic nationalism," World War II as participated in by the United States could in several ways be fairly labeled a "race war," not only for the hyper-racialization of the Japanese and the ways in which their wartime conduct was described in ways that harkened back to Native American savagery but also "in the degree to which race remained the organizing principle of the U.S. military":

> Throughout the war, all branches of the military remained largely segregated. Black and white GIs trained, served, and socialized separately from each other. Proportionately far fewer black servicemen than whites ... were allowed to engage in combat. When they did, they almost always fought in all-black units commanded by white officers. The military segregated its blood supply to make sure that a white servicemen would never receive an infusion of black blood. (203)

30. Puwar, 141–42. In terms of race, as Morrison writes in her description of "metonymic displacement," this version of the Africanist presence includes descriptions of "physical traits [that] become metonyms that displace rather than signify the Africanist character" (68). Regarding stereotypical conceptions of black emotionality, as Derek Hook writes in his discussion of theoretical work by South African social psychologist Chabani Manganyi,

> one of the most persistent and categorical of the available symbolic equations in Western culture ... is that which equates whiteness with mind, and blackness with the bodily... These polarized sets of value not only replay the rudimentary dynamics of racism (its logics, that is, of superiority and inferiority), they also represent routes of identification: the upper pole (whiteness) provides a means of narcissistic self-valorization, affording its subjects the position of symbolic idealization; the lower pole (blackness) represents that which is devalued, deserving of denial and repression. (143–44).

31. As Gerstle notes, "the threat of communism prompted American leaders to depict the American nation as strong, unified, and steadfast in its devotion to timeless ideals ... This realization was an important factor impelling the U.S. Justice Department, first under Truman and then Eisenhower, to file amicus curiae briefs in support of the NAACP lawsuits challenging the legality of school segregation. In these briefs, the government repeatedly stressed the embarrassment that race discrimination was causing America abroad and the damage it was doing to national security" (241, 250).

32. Although Tom continually refers to Japanese soldiers as "Japs," a similar feel-good depiction of his wartime racial tolerance arises when Tom remembers empathetically imagining himself in the shoes of his enemy: "Suddenly the Japs had not seemed so much like caricatures of little yellow men grinning and holding bayonets anymore ..." (*M*, 90). An irony here, of course, is the nevertheless caricatured quality of Wilson's racial and ethnic characters.

33. As Wilson himself writes in an introduction to a 1983 edition of the novel (published also in a later edition as an afterword), "Underneath the bland exterior which the business world demanded of him, Tom Rath was of course a very angry man. When I named him 'Rath' I thought I might be criticized for making this too obvious in a rather corny way, but Tom's manners in the book were so good that very few readers picked that up. Men in gray flannel suits hide their emotions all too well, but younger readers are seeing through the disguise" ("Afterword," n.p.).

34. Dean, 171.
35. Ibid., 172.
36. Ibid., 90.
37. On Kennedy's trumped-up wartime heroism, see Dean, 37–62. Also at potential play here is the era's anxieties about the supposed threat to a stabilizing postwar social order of homosexuality, particularly the casting of effeminacy in terms of sexuality, as evoked by Tom's disparaging conception of his internal voice as "high, effeminate, [and] prissy." Although consideration of this factor is beyond the scope of this chapter, such anxieties about masculinity—in terms of both aristocratic and homosexual effeminacy—likely also informed Wilson's portrayal of the head of the Universal Broadcasting Company, Ralph Hopkins, who remembers being diagnosed by a psychoanalyst as suffering from "a guilt complex [that] was probably based on a fear of homosexuality..." and whom Wilson occasionally portrays in terms that echo such common mainstream stereotypes (*M*, 156). For a relevant explanation of the movement of associations of effeminacy from aristocracy to homosexuality, see Hennen, 32–58. For discussion of historical examples of aristocrat English men attempting to bolster their besieged classed and gendered identities through ostentatious pursuit of reckless adventure in the western American territories, see Rico.
38. My reading here thus counters those of other interpreters of this major theme of the novel, that of authenticity, which Tom is often said to regain by the novel's end, especially by leaving the corporate world. As Abigail Cheever writes in one such interpretation, "In *The Man in the Gray Flannel Suit*, the decision not to be buried in one's professional life is a choice in favor of balance, domestic harmony, and most important, 'honesty' or authenticity, rather than cynicism or phoniness" (192).
39. In an argument that Wilson uses various forms of clothing to symbolize different levels of economic stratification that the novel ultimately fails to register as iniquitous, Birte Christ writes that in this moment, "Tom is ashamed and knows that he is morally wrong in desiring to disassociate himself from a poorer member of society who even used to be a friend during the war..." While acknowledging that "Tom's uneasiness about their difference in wealth that is so clearly marked by their different 'uniforms' mingles here with his uneasiness about his affair during the war and Caesar's knowledge of it," Christ overlooks the further aura of authenticity evoked in the collective white imagination by the repeated highlighting of Caesar's ethnicity (36).
40. There is a crucial difference between Wilson and those Beat writers who romanticized racial and ethnic otherness: while they sought escape from what amounted to white middle-class conformity by "project[ing]

themselves imaginatively into the kind of primitiveness that was marginalized in respectable white society and repressed within white men themselves" (Forth, 210), Wilson's romanticizing springs from an unacknowledged well of nostalgically missed Anglo-Saxonism, a hidden ethnicity revealed as a missed site of social dominance by narrative usage of Africanist and ethnicist presences. On the self-reflexive usage during the 1950s of romanticized ethnoracial others by Kerouac, Mailer, and others, see Brayton, Holton, Nicholls, and Traber, 85–87.

41. As numerous scholars have noted, white Anglo-Saxon romanticizing of subjugated others has a long history. See, for instance, Todd Vogel on nineteenth-century sentimental treatments of Native Americans (4–62).

42. As Judge Bernstein ponders small-town life and its suitability for more informed judicial dispensation, he evokes the past in a way that further constructs the novel's depiction of a feudally hierarchical setting in nostalgic terms: "It was, of course, difficult to resurrect the past, but not impossible. In a small town, the past clung to the present more permanently than in a big city. People's footprints lasted longer before they were stamped out" (M, 189).

43. That Wilson was more interested in using the character of Judge Bernstein in the service of a plot centered on the ostensibly open-minded Raths than in depicting a Jewish American in anything approaching equally complex terms is also suggested by a description of the judge's life as implausibly comfortable: "Saul Bernstein had prospered in South Bay... He had grown reasonably rich, and respected, and might have been happy except for one thing: he detested justice almost as much as he detested violence or cruelty of any other kind" (M, 133). Bernstein is depicted elsewhere as fully aware of his exclusion not only from the country club but also from elite South Bay social circles generally; such a person was, of course, unlikely to feel socially content and "respected" in the face of such degrading subordination and isolation.

44. Brodkin, 30.

45. Regarding the limitations of access to returning veterans' benefits for black service personnel, see Katznelson, 209, Note 19.

46. Ngai, 94.

47. Ibid., 95.

48. Yet another minor character who functions in these ways is the Raths' housekeeper, Mrs. Manter, whose animatedness primarily takes the form of continuous, unself-conscious shouting. Wilson gains further comic effect with this character by rendering her dialogue accordingly. When Tom expresses his interest in hiring her because Betsy is sick, Wilson next writes, "'DON'T TELL ME!' she thundered. 'I HAD EIGHT KIDS MYSELF, AND ONCE WHEN THEY WAS ALL DOWN WITH

MEASLES, I BROKE MY LEG!'" (*M*, 34). As with other minor characters of this sort, Wilson next goes on to emphasize, apparently in the service of humor, Mrs. Manter's corporeal being, by having her describe tying her broken leg to a chair and dragging it around as she continued her motherly duties. Wilson never mentions Mrs. Manter's ethnicity, limiting description of her background to the fact that she's a "farm woman." Nevertheless, the animatedness that Ngai describes has narrative utility for expressing stereotypical associations in terms of other social hierarchies, and in the case of Mrs. Manter, the stereotypes seem to coalesce into the categories of "working class" and "rural."

49. Gonsalves, 9.
50. Ibid.
51. Ibid., 10.
52. The last glimpse of Tony happens in Judge Bernstein's court, where the Raths plead their case for a zoning variance before a skeptical crowd of fellow South Bay residents, who fear that an influx of less wealthy people into a new housing development will result in a "slum." Once again, Wilson delineates Tom's quiet, seemingly sensible reserve by juxtaposing it with Tony's excessive, lively animatedness:

> Immediately a dozen people were on their feet asking Bernstein for permission to be heard. [Tony] began an impassioned plea for increased business opportunities. For more than an hour the argument raged back and forth, the voices becoming louder and more strident... [Tom's] head started to ache, and he longed for the cool air outside. (*M*, 245)

53. Robinson, 29.
54. Doane, 380.
55. Puwar, 1.
56. Babb, 43.

BIBLIOGRAPHY

Babb, Valerie. *Whiteness Visible: The Meaning of Whiteness in American Literature*. New York and London: New York University Press, 1998.

Barrett, James, and David R. Roediger. "Inbetween Peoples: Race, Nationality and the 'New Immigrant' Working Class." *Journal of American Ethnic History* 16, No. 3 (1997): 3–44.

Baum, Bruce. *The Rise and Fall of the Caucasian Race: A Political History of Racial Identity*. New York and London: New York University Press, 2006.

Brayton, S. "'Black-lash': Revisiting the 'White Negro' Through Skateboarding." *Sociology of Sport Journal* 22, No. 3 (2005): 356–72.

Brodkin, Karen. *How Jews Became White Folks: And What That Says About Race in America*. New Brunswick, NJ: Rutgers University Press, 1998.

Cheever, Abigail. *Real Phonies: Cultures of Authenticity in Post-World War II America*. Athens: University of Georgia Press, 2010.

Christ, Birte. "More Trouble with Diversity: Re-dressing Poverty, Masking Class in Middlebrow Success." *Amerikastudien/American Studies* 55, No. 1 (2010): 19–44.

Dean, Robert D. *Imperial Brotherhood: Gender and the Making of Cold War Foreign Policy*. Amherst, MA: University of Massachusetts Press, 2001.

Doane, Ashley W., Jr. "Dominant Group Ethnic Identity in the United States: The Role of 'Hidden' Ethnicity in Intergroup Relations." *The Sociological Quarterly* 38, No. 3 (1997): 375–97.

Forth, Christopher E. *Masculinity in the Modern West; Gender, Civilization and the Body*. London; Palgrave Macmillan, 2008.

Frye Jacobson, Matthew. *Whiteness of a Different Color: European Immigrants and the Alchemy of Race*. Cambridge, MA: Harvard University Press, 2015.

Gerstle, Gary. *American Crucible: Race and Nation in the Twentieth Century*. Princeton: Princeton University Press, 2001.

Gonsalves, Joshua David. *Bio-Politicizing Cary Grant: Pressing Race, Class and Ethnicity into Service in 'Amerika'*. Alresford, UK: Zero Books, 2015.

Hennen, Peter. *Faeries, Bears and Leathermen: Men in Community Queering the Masculine*. Chicago: University of Chicago Press, 2008.

Hoberek, Andrew. *Twilight of the Middle Class: Post-World War II Work American Fiction and White-Collar Work*. Princeton: Princeton University Press, 2005.

Holton, Robert. "Kerouac Among the Fellahin: On the Road to the Postmodern." *Modern Fiction Studies* 41, No. 2 (1995): 265–83.

Hook, Derek. "The 'Real' of Racializing Embodiment." *Journal of Community & Applied Social Psychology* 18, No. 2 (2008): 140–52.

Horsman, Reginald. *Race and Manifest Destiny: Origins of American Racial Anglo-Saxonism*. Cambridge, MA: Harvard University Press, 1981.

Hutner, Gordon. *What America Read: Taste, Class, and the Novel, 1920–1960*. Chapel Hill: University of North Carolina Press, 2009.

Jurca, Catherine. *White Diaspora: The Suburb and the Twentieth Century Novel*. Princeton: Princeton University Press, 2001.

Katznelson, Ira. *When Affirmative Action Was White: An Untold History of Racial Inequality in Twentieth-Century America*. New York: W. W. Norton, 2006.

Kaufman, Eric P. "The Decline of the WASP in the United States and Canada." In *Rethinking Ethnicity: Majority Groups and Dominant Minorities*, edited by Eric P. Kaufman. London: Routledge, 2004a: 61–83.

————. *The Rise and Fall of Anglo-America*. Cambridge, MA: Harvard University Press, 2004b.

Lipsitz, George. *The Possessive Investment in Whiteness: How White People Profit from Identity Politics*. Philadelphia: Temple University Press, 1998.

Long, Christian. "Mapping Suburban Fiction." *Journal of Language, Literature and Culture* 60, No. 3 (2013): 193–213.

Lowenthal, David. *The Past Is a Foreign Country*. Cambridge, UK: Cambridge University Press, 1985.

Martschukat, Jürgen. "Men in Gray Flannel Suits: Troubling Masculinities in 1950s America." *Gender Forum* 32 (2011): 8–27. http://genderforum. org/wp-content/uploads/2017/02/HistoricalMasculinities_Complete.pdf. Accessed 10.13.2017.

Matt, Susan J. *Homesickness: An American History*. New York: Oxford University Press, 2011.

Mills, Charles. "Global White Ignorance." In *Routledge International Handbook of Ignorance Studies*, edited by Matthias Gross and Linsey McGoey. Routledge, 2015: 217–27.

Morrison, Toni. *Playing in the Dark: Whiteness and the Literary Imagination*. 1992. New York: Vintage Press, 1993.

Ngai, Sianne. *Ugly Feelings*. Cambridge, MA: Harvard University Press, 2007.

Nicholls, Brendan. "The Melting Pot That Boiled Over: Racial Fetishism and the Lingua Franca of Jack Kerouac's Fiction." *MFS Modern Fiction Studies* 49, No. 3 (2003): 524–49.

Puwar, Nirmal. *Space Invaders: Race, Gender and Bodies Out of Place*. Oxford: Berg, 2004.

Rico, Monica. *Nature's Noblemen: Transatlantic Masculinities and the Nineteenth-Century American West*. New Haven: Yale University Press, 2013.

Robinson, Sally. *Marked Men: White Masculinity in Crisis*. New York: Columbia University Press, 2000.

Roediger, David R. *Working Toward Whiteness: How America's Immigrants Became White: The Strange Journey from Ellis Island to the Suburbs*. New York: Basic Books, 2006.

Schultz, Kevin M. "The Waspish Hetero-Patriarchy: Locating Power in Recent American History." *Historically Speaking* 11, No. 5 (2010): 8–11.

Traber, Daniel S. *Whiteness, Otherness, and the Individualism Paradox from Huck to Punk*. New York: Palgrave Macmillan, 2007.

Vincent, Jonathan. "'America e Italia': U.S. World War II Novels and the Occupation of Italy." *Fictions* 13 (2014): 17–30.

Vogel, Todd. *ReWriting White: Race, Class, and Culture in Nineteenth-Century America*. Brunswick, NJ: Rutgers University Press, 2004.

Warren, Jonathan W., and France Winddance Twine. "Americans, the New Minority?: Non-Blacks and the Ever-Expanding Boundaries of Whiteness." *Journal of Black Studies* 28, No. 2 (1997): 200–18.

Wilson, Sloan. *All the Best People*. New York: G.P. Putnam's Sons, 1970.
————. *What Shall We Wear to This Party? The Man in the Gray Flannel Suit Twenty Years Before & After*. New York: Arbor House, 1976.
————. "Afterword." *The Man in the Gray Flannel Suit*. 1983. Cambridge, MA: Da Capo, 2002, n.p.
————. *The Man in the Gray Flannel Suit*. 1955. Cambridge, MA: Da Capo, 2002.

CHAPTER 3

Moralizing White Male Nostalgia: Richard Wright's *Savage Holiday*

After Richard Wright moved to Paris in 1946, his work of the 1950s was often dismissed as out of touch with that which he had famously exposed in his early writing, the travails of black American citizens in a social order that remained to varying local degrees white supremacist. By 1954, his depiction in *Savage Holiday* of a murderous middle-class white male protagonist who kills a mother and her young son garnered him not only no laudatory reviews in the United States press; like most of the crime-laden potboilers it ostensibly resembles, the book was not reviewed there at all. Since this novel by a black author contained a white protagonist, it likely seemed unconcerned with the racial themes that had become Wright's well-known métier. Indeed, when Wright addressed the novel in interviews with French journalists, he himself seemed uncertain about its primary concerns. At times, Wright described *Savage Holiday* as an examination of "universal" subject matter, especially the existentialist "problem of freedom," as well as "completely non-racial, dealing with crime per se."[1] At other times, Wright described the novel's themes as "mostly moral" but also driven by his interest in "the historical roots and the emotional problems of Western whites which make them aggressive around colored peoples.... I was looking for explanations of the psychological reactions of whites."[2] I will argue here that these latter two themes, morality and white aggression, wound up conjoined—that *Savage Holiday* amounts to a satiric portrait of domineering white men who resort reflexively, and sometimes violently, to restorative nostalgia when confronted with the hypocrisy of their collective's long-standing claims to moral superiority.

© The Author(s) 2018
T. Engles, *White Male Nostalgia in Contemporary North American Literature*, https://doi.org/10.1007/978-3-319-90460-3_3

As scholars have begun to explain, *Savage Holiday* has long been over-looked for its critique of collective white male pathologies. In an era in which mainstream Cold War culture in the United States was exacerbating the national fetish of individualism by starkly contrasting itself with Soviet collectivism, Wright's novel scrutinizes domineering white masculinity by situating a representative psyche within that which shaped it—the collectively formed frameworks of categorically induced habits, fears, and modes of self-deception. His construction of protagonist Erskine Fowler as a man who feels his status threatened by a changing social order also examines a common white male response in such circumstances: the attempt to restore a sense of power, and to assuage pain caused by that loss, by resorting to nostalgic reveries of imagined conditions in which people like themselves enjoyed a seemingly unquestioned eminence.

Throughout the several stages of philosophical, psychological, and sociological inquiry that Wright pursued during his career, he repeatedly identified white supremacist aggression as a primary authorial target. By the 1950s, Wright had adopted a broader global outlook, which led him to recognize white supremacist ideology as not only a historically grounded system of oppression but also one that had already moved significantly toward what became America's widespread denial in the late twentieth century of white supremacy's history and its ongoing abuses. One manifestation of this latter shift was that a middle-class man like Erskine Fowler, *Savage Holiday*'s forcibly retired and pathologically anxious protagonist, had little daily awareness of being taken by one and all as "white," and only slightly less of being taken as "male" and of being treated accordingly. Nevertheless, the categorically induced effects for any white American man were many, and in depicting for the first time in his fiction the interior machinations and ultimately murderous impulses of a white male protagonist, Wright could only provide plausible characterization by portraying such effects. That Wright instead sought to focus on non-racial, non-gendered, or seemingly universal matters was a common claim among *Savage Holiday*'s few early critics. Although later scholars sometimes repeat this contention, primarily to focus on traditionally psychoanalytic or seemingly autobiographical elements in the novel, more have come to recognize in *Savage Holiday* an incisive dissection of a representative white male psyche from a critically cognizant black authorial perspective.[3] I will argue that with the satiric extremes exhibited by its protagonist, *Savage Holiday* also foresees new elements of middle-class white masculinity as it took shape in subsequent decades, particularly the psychic embeddedness of its members in their own misrecognized history, their longing for past conditions of supposedly unchallenged eminence, and their consequent moral hypocrisy and blindness.

During a radio interview with Raymond Barthes, Wright was clearly speaking of his protagonist as a representative white American man when he stated that because Erskine is no longer working and is living in a culture that encourages men "to consider work as a kind of religion, your *raison d'etre*," his sudden unemployment renders him afraid of "assuming the responsibilities entailed by his new kind of life, a holiday, i.e., a life deprived of the props and supports of a daily task to perform."[4] As *Savage Holiday* suggests, that which is propped up and supported by work, and by the intertwined religious injunction that a primary goal of a man like Erskine should be the pursuit of the material results provided by hard labor and proper membership in a family, is one's assigned role in life as an upright Christian, white American man. As in earlier times (and later), an operative self-justification for American white men of the postwar era was the claim that whereas they deserved what they had because they had (supposedly) worked for it, others had less because they worked less—indeed, racial and ethnic others were often accused of being inherently incapable of working hard enough and of managing resources improperly if and when they did have control of them. While white men have sincerely believed such self-justifying deceptions, many also sense at times the contradiction between their stated principles regarding hard work and the fact that they have much of what they do because they and their ancestors have extorted it from others. From Wright's perspective, as he told an interviewer in 1956, "the most important problem white people have to face [is] their moral dilemma. This is why I have chosen this white New Yorker as a protagonist."[5]

The moral conundrum that Wright locates at the heart of white masculinity is the donning of a mask of morality while knowing at some level of a collective immorality. Between the world and themselves, white American men have always inserted a mask of self-absolving rectitude, suppressing knowledge of how their dominant collective position in relation to others is the ongoing result of historical inequity, as wrought by the lies of whiteness and masculinity and buttressed by religious belief. As Jennifer Harvey writes in her analysis of the morally fraught state of historically cognizant white allies within the context of social justice work, to be white, and to be in any degree realistically self-aware of one-self *as* white, "is to exist socially in a state of profound and fundamental moral crisis that goes to the heart of our selfhood."[6] Emphasizing what amounts to moral self-righteousness and such American manifestations of it as the Protestant work ethic, along with the nostalgic connotations that such notions carry, helps to assuage guilt provoked by awareness of raced and gendered social inequity. Such an emphasis also quells misgivings about the confining self in which domineering white men tend to encase themselves, by projecting conceptions of what amounts to their own supposedly negative characteristics out onto denigrated others, a reflex that furthers the concealing and containment of such characteristics in themselves.

Because Erskine suddenly lacks the setting and scheduled tasks of daily work to help him function in these identity-forming ways—as Wright put it when describing his novel, Erskine "had been capable [while working] of forgetting, we can even say repressing, his feeling of guilt through his acquisition of material wealth"—he stands figuratively naked, free of the iron cage of labor that had helped to restrain his unsanctioned emotions and desires, including not only his classically oedipal mix of desire, frustration, and anger but also those characteristics that a respectable, civilized man supposedly did not have or, if he recognized that he did, was always careful to contain.[7] Historically, an insistence on the inherent superiority and moral righteousness of white men had not only justified the theft from and slaughter of other peoples and the subjugation of white women; it also fostered the perception of more vivid life in others, as the white male subject perceives in them and misses in himself that which he has been led to repress. In Erskine's time, as subjugated others pushed for equality, domineering white men often reasserted control by castigating resistance in moral terms, squelching the humanity of others as well as their own. Ultimately, such a denial of life aligns white masculinity in this more conceptual mode with mortality—with imposed, premature death.

WHITE MALE HISTORIES

On *Savage Holiday*'s opening page, Wright establishes a distinctly patriarchal white national context. Erskine is the central focus of what would seem to be a satisfying, career-capping event, a lavish retirement party thrown for him by Longevity Life, the insurance company that he helped to build while rising up its ranks. Wright tweaks with this company's alliterative name both the budding prominence of corporate branding and, at a deeper thematic level, a certain white-male American obsession with immortality, an obsession that evinces deeper, guilt-ridden denials and fears about death. Off-kilter elements in this ceremonial gathering quickly become apparent, including Erskine's remarkably young "retirement" at the age of forty-three (readers soon learn that Erskine has been forced out to make way for the company president's son), and more generally an overblown patriotic tinge to the entire affair, as if a man of much greater importance and stature were being feted. The event, over which hangs an enormous red, white, and blue banner, is held in a grand hotel's "Jefferson Banquet Room"; the narrator describes Erskine as "Lincoln-like"; and as part of the retirement ritual, the company's president hands him a commemorative medallion, a coin-like object which, in a more absurdly presidential vein, bears Erskine's embossed profile.[8] Such hyperbole establishes not only this novel's satiric mode but also its analytic target—a vaunted form of idealized American masculinity buttressed by a nostalgically cast backdrop of American history.

In the novel's 1950s United States setting, a man who could plausibly feel at home within the center of such a scene could only be a conventionally successful white man. Indeed, Wright emphasizes that Erskine has felt entirely at "home" at Longevity Life, working with people who amount to surrogate family members. Given that Erskine joined Longevity Life at the age of thirteen, his sense that his coworkers are also his family may not seem implausible, but the company's paternalistic structure treats its employees this way as well, and the president twice refers to the assembled workers as "brothers and sisters of the Longevity Life Family," a phrase that Erskine also uses in his own mechanically jocular farewell speech (S, 13, 16). As the novel progresses, Wright's theme-establishing sendup of patriotic white American paternalism settles into an allegorical dissection of hypocritical, abusive white masculine morality as it becomes evident that this seemingly mature, successful man cannot embrace his newfound freedom, nor establish life-affirming connections with others, in part because membership in a surrogate family that had cast him as an underling has not prepared him for mature, full-fledged adulthood. Read in this way, *Savage Holiday* suggests that the expectation of white masculine hyper-independence from others, the lengthy history of which is ironically bound to ontologically confirming abuse of others, has resulted in a collective white male psyche that is stunted in its failure to realize, nurture, and cherish inevitably necessary connections to others. As a result, an inculcated set of predispositions and desires that arise when confronted with *actual* freedom in this sense—that is, sudden severance from identity-confirming connections to others—would render an ostensibly successful middle-class white man like Erskine Fowler bereft, and thus anxious to scurry back into a seemingly "independent" sense of himself, a reasserted white male identity that Wright exposes as illusory by again suggesting its fundamental dependency on projected conceptions of others.

After fleeing from the ceremony, Erskine reflects that he has plenty of money to retire, but he also frets about his sudden status as unemployed, vaguely realizing that it makes him feel not only unsure about what to do with himself but also vulnerable: "His hated freedom was simply suspending him in a void of anxious ignorance that was riveting his consciousness with self-protective nostalgia upon the familiar atmosphere of the Longevity Life Insurance Company" (*S*, 31). Erskine's sense of a need for protection springs from the attendant feeling that without "a prison-cage of toil," consisting of an energy-draining and time-consuming career, something tamped down inside himself by his former labor, and by the armor of the identity that his labor had helped to construct, threatens to burst forth (*S*, 33). Accordingly, frustrated by a "haunting sense of not quite being his own master," Erskine touches "the tips of his four pencils in his inner coat pocket to free himself of these filmy cobwebs dusting at his mind" (*S*, 32). Wright eventually reveals that Erskine unconsciously associates these pencils with his own mother; in this moment, then, the concept of "family," and another loss thereof, has come to mind for Erskine. Later, as he tries to sort through his mixed feelings about Mabel Blake, the neighboring woman whom he hastily pursues after causing her child's death, Erskine remembers an old "uneasiness in the presence of women," as well as the accompanying sense that "he was being claimed by that which he thought he'd surmounted long ago with God's help and his incessant toil" (*S*, 121). As Erskine registers the emotions and desires provoked by the thought of Mabel—disturbing feelings that arise within the body that he thought he had mastered and thus distanced himself from—he flinches, oddly "feeling his feelings realizing the idea of being with her" (*S*, 121). While the narrator alludes in such moments to the familial childhood trauma eventually revealed as the oedipal mess that ostensibly results in Erskine's murder of a surrogate mother figure, Wright also calls attention by intermingling it with Erskine's new anxiety about unemployment to a severe psychic split in the ordinary white male American identity. This collective schism—between a desire for freedom and leisure and a felt responsibility to squelch such desires with purposeful, preferably exhausting labor—was formed historically, within a broader white supremacist context that proclaimed a supposedly inherent propensity toward productive labor as a distinguishing difference between white men and their perceived others.

At one point, Erskine rejects the talk he's been hearing about "'complexes' and the 'unconscious'; and a man called Freud," whose name, he thinks, "always reminds him of *fraud!*" (*S*, 61, emphasis in original). Nevertheless, Erskine's more personal longing for an idealized past with his mother does plausibly reflect standard psychoanalytic interpretations of the lingering, nostalgic effects of family-of-origin trauma. As Zachary Boren explains in his analysis of common psychoanalytic understandings of nostalgia, the feeling "manifests unconsciously," and "yearning for that original oneness with the mother, is the base principle of almost all manifestations of nostalgia.... This nostalgia is inherent to the human condition. We are all designed to experience it, and find ways to compensate for it."[9] Although *Savage Holiday* long struck most readers as a bluntly simplistic dramatization of some basic psychoanalytic concepts, its exposure of causes and consequences of Erskine's lack of psychic self-awareness subtly functions at much broader levels, registering how nostalgia is shaped, and even prompted by, any person's particular positioning within a sociohistorical context. While the mainstream postwar culture of *Savage Holiday*'s era trumpeted a rejuvenated American social scene peopled with idealized model citizens, it was underpinned at a collective psychic level by white supremacist, masculine, and Christian ideologies, which predate even the nation itself. Just as Wright had thrown himself into communism, only to reject it, *Savage Holiday* suggests that he may have also shifted from an initial adherence to individualized psychoanalytic principles to those that functioned at collective levels.[10] In effect, Erskine's vexed state and its consequences suggest that the standard Freudian limitation of psychic phenomena to an individual's immediate familial circumstances is indeed a fraud.

Delineating key features of a larger sociohistorical context, in which a person like this protagonist would have been influenced by notions of proper masculine, white, and Christian behavior, renders Erskine's destructive thoughts and actions more plausible and significant than

would attributing his deep-seated, murderous disdain for Mabel merely
to unresolved trauma initiated by fraught interaction with his own
mother. As Shannon Sullivan writes regarding interpretive limitations in
the traditional Freudian conception of the psyche,

> Clearly a person's environment is crucial to the formation of his or her
> unconscious. The other is the core of who I am. And the other encom-
> passes more than the mother and the father, the adult components of the
> Oedipal triangle that are so crucial to Freud's account of the develop-
> ment of the infant psyche. This is why Freud's familialism is inadequate
> as a challenge to standard individualism... While it might be a contingent
> fact that much of [the] adult world comes to the infant through the mes-
> sages of its parents or other primary caregivers, what is being transmitted
> is not just a familial meaning, but also a complex tangle of local and global
> significations.[11]

While Wright ostensibly frames his depiction of Erskine's murderous
violence in terms of classically oedipal anxieties, he also indicates the
shaping influence on his protagonist's feelings of hegemonic ideologies. Of particular apparent interest to Wright are those that masquer-
ade as morality, especially as a function of masculinity, white supremacy,
and Christianity. Indeed, Erskine's murderous actions not only register
how his era's masculine imperative calls for control of a womanhood
perceived as irrational and impure; they also echo how, for the founders of what became the United States, the conception of indigenous and
African people as the unrestrained, "savage" embodiments of the lethal
propensities that were actually central to settler colonialism itself was a
foundational mode of collective projection that bolstered the victor's
claims to moral justification and superiority. Thus, what some part of
Erskine feels nostalgic for in his new, enforced freedom from a previously
stable white male identity as an insurance executive is not just devoted
attention from his mother but also a nationally grounded network of
meaning and rules that tells him how the world should work, who he is
as a morally superior being within it, and thus how he should regard and
treat others.

When Wright was asked during a 1957 interview with a French peri-
odical for his assessment of current racial conditions in the United States,
he began by pointing backwards: "It is impossible to understand the
racial question in the United States without first putting that question in

its proper historical setting." Wright went on to explain that the enslavement of Africans initiated a "moral" problem, "for the introduction of slavery in America violated the ethical convictions of the men who did it. Economic motives overruled these ethical doubts when the cultivation of cotton became the dominant economic activity of the South."[12] Slavery, and the profits it provided, violated white male American ethical convictions by overriding compassion and a sense of justice for other human beings. In *Savage Holiday*, Wright further demonstrates the continuance, deep within his own era's white American men, of such early compromises with their professed morality, including their claims of moral superiority over those whom they had long subordinated. As Wright knew all too well and often sought to depict in his work, racial whiteness is a fiction emphasized and instrumentalized in the service of power. Like masculinity, white supremacy has always called for relational assertion in order to maintain ontological stability, in large part by controlling the lives of others on the basis of their supposedly inherent inferiority, which is in turn cited as justification for white male assistance and oversight; in order to morally justify expropriation from others, dominant men have narcissistically sought reflection of themselves in subordinated others. A primary motivation for the continual need for such self-assurance, and for nostalgic conceptions of United States history, has been the ongoing contrast between domineering white men's professed moral values and their own contrary actions. In these terms, Wright's satirical target in *Savage Holiday* can be read as a broad nationalized consciousness that draws on reality-obscuring, morally assuaging nostalgia in order to imagine its white male citizenry as entitled beneficiaries of dominance and prosperity.

That Erskine's identity and anxieties are framed by a national history comprised of mythological notions of the proper relation of a person like himself to others is suggested by one of his satirically suggestive dreams. Prior to Erskine's finding himself naked in his apartment building's corridor while trying to retrieve his Sunday newspaper, a neighboring boy's beating of a toy drum awakens him from a fraught dreamscape, that of a forest through which he'd been wandering anxiously. In a novel so heavily larded with Freudian tropes, this closely described set of images calls for interpretation. However, we deny the novel its social insight if we stop at straightforward, individualized Freudian analysis. In his dream, Erskine knows that the forest belongs to him and further that he will harvest its lumber for profit. As he proceeds, assessing the potential value of this resource, he encounters a man chopping furiously into the V of a tree. Frightened by this man's actions and his "brutish and criminal-looking" face, Erskine tries to hide behind another tree, only to have the chopped one come crashing down on him as he awakens (*S*, 37). Traditional analysis of this dream in light of other biographical information about Erskine would likely find a latent castration anxiety; the tree's V would represent his mother, and by extension all women, and the chopping man would figure as a composite of the many men whom Erskine remembers visiting his mother at night. Furthermore, the sense of these trees as his property, and the threat of losing that property at the hands of this man, would seem to represent more prosaically his lost job, and a symbolic castration would also suggest the lost sense of potency formerly provided by his successful career.

However, the dream has broader implications if we follow Wright's stated suggestions of reading *Savage Holiday* in light of a more collective white American masculinity, particularly of its "moral dilemma." Part of that dilemma involves the collective white male sense of ownership—how can white men who profess egalitarian principles in proud appreciation and defense of the country that earlier white men supposedly built ignore the horrific costs to others in the thieving establishment and maintenance of that country? In these terms, the contested vaginal tree evokes another woman in Erskine's life, Mabel, and the possessive desire that Erskine has felt for her, well before Tony's death; with his family-bound identity as a member of the Longevity Life collective no longer intact, marrying Mabel comes to strike Erskine as a way to reassert a traditionally masculine (and thus woman-possessing) identity. Possessiveness is racialized in the dream as well, as Erskine wanders among the trees with a sense that any profit from harvesting them will also be his: Erskine's consciousness registers no awareness of a prior presence of indigenous people, from whom such lands and resources were relentlessly stolen, yet Wright inserts a reminder for readers of this presence by having Tony awaken Erskine with the stereotypical beating of a drum while shouting, "The Indians are coming!" (*S*, 38). Those who took the land and resources that became the United States justified their theft in large part by conceiving of themselves as civilized, God-fearing opposites, that is, as white Christian men like Erskine. Since the primal, seemingly forested past of American beginnings, awareness of the insistently possessive bent of its Christian white supremacy has faded as part of a general psychic retreat from the country's foundational realities. Regarding the nation's beginnings in possessive colonial conquest, historian Roxanne Dunbar-Ortiz writes,

> part of the Christian colonizers' outlook was a belief in white supremacy. As an 1878 Protestant hymn suggests—"Are your garments spotless? / Are they white as snow? Are they washed in the blood of the lamb?"— whiteness as an ideology involves much more than skin color... . White supremacy can be traced to the colonial ventures of the Christian Crusades in Muslim-controlled territories and to the Protestant colonization of Ireland. As dress rehearsals for the colonization of the Americas, these projects form the two strands that merge in the geopolitical and sociocultural makeup of US society.[13]

Instead of acknowledging these realities, when white American men in general have harkened back to their nation's past, they've usually done so nostalgically, bolstering their exceptionalist presumptions of paragon status by emphasizing such self-congratulatory and supposedly foundational virtues as freedom, independence, and democracy. A general collective amnesia embedded in Wright's representative white male psyche about indigenous people, and about what one's own people did to them and to others, effectively renders the original landscape empty, and thus pristine or pure, as the "nature" of the North American landscape is still widely represented.[14] Nevertheless, as George Lipsitz puts it, "race is produced by space," as is gender; accordingly, "wilderness" has been conceived not just as a conquest-justifying, guilt-relieving emptiness but also as a staging ground for seemingly unencumbered white male action.[15]

Aside from portraying Erskine in the grip of a vexed anger toward women because of his mother's apparent sexual behavior, Wright depicts him as nostalgic for a stable sense of ownership and control because, in his state of forced retirement, the setting and role that provided his sense of mastery, including control of himself, have been taken from him. And because an accurate memory of the past would include acknowledgement of the slaughter of Native Americans and the theft of their lands by people like himself, unconscious erasure of such morality-challenging realities in a dream of possessed wilderness, which registers more nostalgic versions of a historic national context, functions for Erskine in a compensatory mode, not only by registering the quotidian source of his new fears and anxieties (that is, his forced retirement, which amounts to banishment into uncharted territory) but also by providing assurance that a man like him is justified in perceiving that his very identity and status are under threat. By labeling his novel's first section "Anxiety," Wright points to immediate and personal sources of anxiety for Erskine, but his depiction of a representatively white American man, and thus the sort who is likely, in Wright's words, to be "aggressive around colored peoples," also reflects the underlying, historically rooted sources of his era's common white male anxieties.[16]

In this way, *Savage Holiday* suggests via Erskine's dream of a possessed landscape how the very conception of "nature" or "wilderness" as depopulated was intrinsically binarized in racial terms—the concept's "purity" implies an absence of that which would sully it, namely "savage" people, who were conceived of (when conceived of at all) in relationally contrary terms. In traditional Protestant, Anglo-American terms, a proper white man's duty, the material results of which were widely considered the very sign of his suitability for Heaven, was the hard work of cultivating one's own sector of previously unsullied (by people) "nature." In Wright's time, collective white historical memory had become almost necessarily nostalgic, given the unacknowledged abuses at the hands of white masculinity, but also because white masculinity in the mid-twentieth century had become an individualizing force; to a degree that became stronger in subsequent decades as overt declarations of white supremacy faded, white men had generally moved toward not seeing themselves *as such,* and thus they dis-identified that much more with historical and ongoing collective racial abuse. In terms of racial identity, Veronica T. Watson helpfully labels this phenomenon "the nonrelational epistemology of Whiteness," that is, "the belief that Whiteness, unlike any other subject position, is forged and formed independently as the ultimate act of unencumbered self-fashioning.... Thus, Whiteness fails to acknowledge or recognize the ways in which conceptions of the White self are bound up with and juxtaposed to constructions of Blackness, Otherness, and foreignness."[17] There is, of course, a parallel to be made to an intertwined, relational phenomenon in terms of gender; conceptions of the male self are bound up with and juxtaposed to constructions of womanhood and femininity. In these terms, Erskine's dream reflects as well the historical continuity of white masculinity's conceptual erasure of its own actions and of other people and thus of its own morality-challenging relations to such abuses—the twentieth-century movement of whiteness toward a hegemonic nonrelational epistemology and ontology is but a continuation of this process. In addition, the novel exposes the general white American Christian-based morality as not just one more underpinning in the dominant mindset that Erskine represents, but also as an ideology that white masculinity instrumentalizes as a justifying framework for morality-challenging abuses of others.

PURIFIED WHITE MALE BODIES

In terms of the sociohistorical context that *Savage Holiday* repeatedly registers, an inevitable conflict had arisen between egalitarian social values and the exploitative behavior of the white male collective. One result of this conflict was an extremely tight, self-justifying "mastery" of emotions within many white men. As Wright's narrator notes at one point, "Never in Erskine's life had his emotions been a problem to him; indeed, he had lived with the assumption that he had no emotions. From puberty onwards, he had firmly clamped his emotions under the steel lid of work and had fastened and tightened that lid with the inviolate bolts of religious devotion" (*S*, 80). In such a confined state, the white male psyche can find itself perceiving and longing for that which it has suppressed in itself, as when Erskine thinks in directly relational terms about Minnie, "his colored maid": "Erskine was somewhat calmed by Minnie's naturalness.... [He] didn't believe that servants were quite human, but he felt that having them around brought one some standing; one could always depend on them for simple, human reactions" (*S*, 140–41). As Erskine uses Minnie's subservient status to assert a class-based superiority, he simultaneously projects onto her, while also missing in himself, seemingly unbound, natural reactions and emotions.[18] Here and elsewhere in the novel, Wright depicts how the rational side of a psyche thusly split can sense an alienated detachment from and even denial of one's own emotions and sometimes, perhaps bizarrely, watch another part of oneself feel them. As numerous historians have explained, white American men had long considered it a moral duty to "master" their desires and emotions in order to labor instead of "indulge" or "play," and they had long considered others inherently less capable of doing so and, furthermore, in need of white male "mastery" to spur them into productive labor.[19]

Again, in a novel in which Wright meant to portray a white moral dilemma and that which led white men to be aggressive toward their racial others, the repeated trope of "mastery" has clear historical resonance. Wright's ultimate suggestion in this regard is that the collective white male insistence on control of others operates concurrently with an insistence on mastery of themselves. That which is within themselves and seemingly in need of mastery—not only desires and emotions but also sloth, appetites, bodily matter and secretions, and so on—becomes a despised and rejected part of oneself, as well as something projected outward onto others as supposedly inherent and unmastered qualities that *they* possess. As a result, the white male formation of an identity so fundamentally grounded in control of oneself for the sake of productive labor can plausibly leave a suddenly unemployed man feeling "trapped in freedom," unsure of how to act because action had previously been premised in a self-contained, other-oriented identity that no longer exists (*S*, 33). At the same time, as *Savage Holiday* also suggests, the occasional attraction to the despised, abjectified qualities projected onto others amounts to a nostalgic longing and even mourning for that which the white male collective has repressed and denied in itself.

In the remainder of *Savage Holiday*'s opening "Anxiety" section, Erskine's highly neurotic response to winding up naked in a corridor after locking himself out of his apartment, and to then accidentally killing Mabel's son Tony, provokes a desperate scramble to get back into his apartment. Although a fugitive killer's desperation is a typical potboiler plot device, Erskine's anxiety arises as much from fear of being connected to Tony's death as from simply being seen naked: "He was still nude; he had to hide… regardless of what happened to Tony, he had to seek shelter for his nakedness" (*S*, 55). Indeed, this fear of a censorious communal gaze propels him at such a rate that his sheer alacrity, as much as his "naked and wild-eyed" appearance, is apparently what scares Tony into his deathward fall (*S*, 58). Erskine's palpitating, sweaty response to the possibility of moralizing communal censure arises primarily because the image he presents so directly counters that of his recent self—the successful, wealthy, Christian and properly contained insurance executive. Wright devotes a great deal of description in these moments to his protagonist's "hirsute body that gleamed wetly in the sunlight" and to Erskine's disgusted apprehension of it (*S*, 54). Several narrative elements—Erskine's recent forced retirement, his extreme awareness of his own exposed and unfamiliar (even to himself) body and its excretions, and his great fear that other upstanding white people will see him in this state—combine in Wright's hyperbolic emphasis on Erskine's corporeal form to underline the dyad between the blunt facts of a human body and a disdainful and common white male psychic distance from it. Again, the allegorical framework that Wright suggests in his exterior commentary on *Savage Holiday* implies that what amounts to Erskine's feverish effort to regain a clean, properly contained white male identity in which he can safely perform calls for elaboration of the suppressed historical context that would account for it.

After the choice of a white American male protagonist for this novel's satiric analysis of hypocritical racialized and gendered morality, Wright's further choice of the potboiler genre, grounded as it is in narrative realism, confined the novel's characterization to plausible feelings and actions. Erskine's desperate alarm over his own exposed body is indeed plausible, but only because it also reflects an actual collective, historically grounded sense of disgust with corporeal physicality, an estrangement that can be so thorough that an individual's own identity can occlude effectively incorporated awareness of an actual, living body. This ontological detachment largely arises in the United States context from how Christian-oriented white male ideology has long conceived of others, both women and non-white people, in excessively corporeal terms, underestimating in them the rational or "mind" side of a severe mind/body split and overemphasizing it in themselves. As a representative "fouler," Erskine Fowler is not just repelled by the suddenly undeniable fact of his own physicality; he has been trained to detach in a sense his very identity from it to the point that he believes the exposure of his body to the eyes of others would present to them a version of himself that differs fundamentally from the version he assumes they had come to know. By dramatizing a frantic anxiety about these matters that prevents Erskine from simply knocking on a neighbor's door to ask for help, Wright emphasizes that his era's white male sense of self is grounded in a pathological distancing not only from who and what one actually is, beginning with one's very own body, but also from what one is therefore capable of doing, as well as from what one is morally responsible *for* doing. After Erskine manages to get back into his apartment and pull himself together, he eventually decides that he could not be fairly accused of responsibility for Tony's death, because as a respectable, morally upstanding person, he simply could not be the sort of monster who would kill a child. Someone whose identity is in some way or ways the opposite of Erskine's own (supposed) identity must be to blame instead.

In a narratively philosophical mode, Wright thereby prompts consideration of the ways in which in the United States, hegemonic conceptions of hierarchically arranged identities had become both a key component and a result of white masculine morality. Through centuries of interaction with and abuse of their perceived others, white American men in general became convinced at a deeply psychic level that they were the group most inherently prone toward civilized behavior, and thus that acts of savagery and impulsive behavior driven by unbridled emotions were actions that other people were more likely to commit, because they were constitutionally less capable of restraining themselves from doing so.[20] As a result, historical atrocities committed by the white supremacist collective, some in the very name of "white Anglo-Saxon" supremacy, are not collectively remembered as brutal savagery but rather, when remembered at all, as natural and inevitable results of an organically expanding nation. Men who led the expansion, as represented in this novel by the directly referenced Jefferson and Lincoln, have been hailed nostalgically by white collective memory as glorious leaders of morally righteous settlement and healthy and vigorous expansion, and not as the often brutal leaders they were: a relentlessly barbaric collectivity that systematically exploited and often murdered its subjugated racialized and gendered others. Indeed, collectively repressed genocides played a crucial part in building the collective white male American identity.[21]

As Wright moves from the farcical retirement ceremony that ejects Erskine from the familial, identity-confirming sense of structure that work had provided and as Erskine's role in Tony's death apparently goes undiscovered by the police and his neighbors, a more directly domestic structure, his apartment, comes to represent the shell of a protective self that Erskine feels is missing. Desperately "naked," having lost the armor that was his identity as a successful, respectable man, the anxiety inside him boiling over like the coffee pot inside his apartment, Erskine seeks restoration of a sense of family, which would provide him with a relationally constitutive, reassuringly dominant, and morally sanctioned role. Crucially, he does so less because he misses a sense of communal belonging than because he wants to rivet himself back into the protective armor of a proper white masculine identity; the "self-protective nostalgia" he feels for the company's "familiar atmosphere" is an urge to rebuild and protect a particular, proper white masculine self (S, 31). This identity needs conceptions of grouped others in which to insert itself as a functioning member, "work" and one's bosses and coworkers being one group and "family" and one's spouse and children being another. Having suffered poor relations with women all his adult life (thanks, we later learn he feels, to his negligent mother), Erskine fumbles to construct a new family, this time as a man with a wife and future children instead of as a man-child with "brothers and sisters." He conceives of such a relation to Mabel as a chance to reassert not just himself but also a sanctioned and controlling white masculine self: "he'd be the boss; he'd dominate her completely..." (*S*, 134). Here, Wright emphasizes the ontologically constitutive overlap for his era's well-behaved white American men between the ostensibly separate spheres of work and family by having Erskine conceive of his masculine spousal dominance with the word "boss." An even broader psychic intertwining, which consists of raced, gendered, and Christian-oriented ideologies, is further reflected in his conviction that given how wild and even savage Mabel appears to him, his proper role is to civilize her, a role formed as well by his conception that his task in doing so is a missionary one (*S*, 87). In these ways, Erskine's psychic framework for conceiving of himself and others represents a common white male longing in moments of identity-challenging instability for historically resonant modes of more firmly enforced dominance, and thus for a more securely established and supposedly independent white masculine identity. Yet, ironically, as Wright in effect points out, white male identity is not dependent only on conceptions of other people; it depends also on peopled places, on a sense of oneself as situated within such places. These functionally symbolic physical spaces contain networks of bosses and coworkers as well as an immediate family but also, in broader terms, a nation, which moral, Christian-oriented people like oneself supposedly built and most suitably inhabit and lead as full-fledged, properly pure and contained citizens.

Accordingly, another ideologically laden place in which Erskine can assure himself that he is a self-restrained, decent person, and not the sort who could ever let his own hysterical fears lead to a child's death, is his Baptist church. Having made it back into his apartment but still shuddering with the feeling that while naked he "looked anything but pious or Christian," Erskine takes a shower and then dons his formal Sunday attire (*S*, 40–41). Nevertheless, in a psychic sense, he remains naked, unsure of how to conceptualize himself as an agent in the disaster that has just happened. Stiffly clad in identity-defining clothing, Erskine feels a revival of his sense of morality, and it prompts him to wonder just why he hid his part in Tony's death: "The honorable, Christian thing to do was to tell the police; he had money; he could hire a lawyer" (*S*, 81). In another ironic twist that continues filling in Wright's portrait of self-serving and self-constituting white masculine morality grounded in nostalgia,

Erskine's visit to church instead steers him directly away from doing the "honorable, Christian thing."

Functioning in church under the self-defining gaze of his fellow parishioners steers Erskine in this sense by reminding him of who he "is"—a respectable, pure, and honorable Christian, and therefore not the sort of person who could have been at fault in Tony's death. Indeed, he becomes convinced that someone else must have been at fault, given who and what she supposedly is: "Yes; that accident was God's own way of bringing a lost woman to her senses... hadn't she wallowed shamelessly in the fleshpots of nightclubs?... God was giving him a mandate to face Mrs. Blake and have it out with her!" (S, 87). Thus, by going as usual to church, Erskine veers toward another protective family of sorts, his fellow parishioners, an audience before whom he has long presented himself as a successful and admirable man, even if, once again, the construction of that seemingly independent, adult role has depended on a confirming collective gaze. As with the version of himself that became a successful man by in effect becoming a son of the Longevity Life family, this person has been a certain *kind* of man, one distinguished as such by a community's recognition and acceptance of him as one of their kind— and thus also as a potential white masculine savior of a woman he conceives of as a fallen harlot.

Erskine's reconstitution in this scene of a familiar self demonstrates that fully apprehending the "moral question" Wright poses for white Americans in *Savage Holiday* calls for consideration of several axes of social value, overlapping communities formed by both inclusion and exclusion. In the United States, patriarchal and white supremacist modes of categorical division have been formed concurrently with Christian modes, producing a specific concatenation of identity-based notions involving transcendence and purity.[22] When Wright positions Erskine standing naked outside his apartment door, imagining neighbors who would be shocked and disgusted by the sight of him, he describes Erskine's quickly mounting anxiety and subsequent actions as a direct result of his "sheer passion for modesty" (S, 44). This description, with its conjunction of opposing intensities, points to a conflicted passionate modesty at the heart of domineering white masculine morality—the obsessive desire to stamp out and expel the immodest, the indecent, and the "filthy" as qualities opposed to righteous purity. This relationally constructed ontological purity had long been represented in terms of Christian morality, but also by racial whiteness and masculinity. As Wright noted in a radio interview, Erskine's last name "suggests that his problem is mostly moral, or it has been defined in terms of social morality. Fowler brings to mind the notion of being 'foul,' of defiling, of not behaving according to social rules."[23] The "social rules" that Wright's representative protagonist calls on to pull his self together, and then to impose himself on Mabel, entail a nostalgic longing for a purity that never was, an ultimately child-like innocence to which the white male psyche commonly longs to return in moments of status-threatening duress.

While Wright underscores in this episode the more gendered uses made by white masculinity of family-oriented American Christianity—or, as Margaret Atwood puts it in a recent *New York Times* piece, "the 17th-century Puritan roots that have always lain beneath the modern-day America we thought we knew"—he goes further to emphasize concurrent, historically resonant raced and gendered elements as well.[24] As Erskine approaches the building, the narrator describes it as "a huge white sandstone church topped by a white cross," the organist has "snow-white hair," and the Sunday school secretary is named Mrs. White. Wright doesn't have to spell out that on this, "one of the most segregated hours" in Christian America, the parishioners are all racially white as well. Yet the repeated adjective functions as more than a sardonic reminder of racial segregation and counterpoised homogeneity (*S*, 83–84).[25] As part of Wright's depiction of the intertwined categorical influences on the identities of American men like Erskine Fowler, this whiteness motif in a Christian context also highlights the function of "purity" in binarized constructions of a dominant collectivity and its subordinated others. Here, Wright anticipates more recent analyses of binarized ideologies, including those that instrumentalize counterpoised notions of the pure and the defiled. In Dana Berthold's analysis of the current overconsumption in the United States of purified and purifying commodities, such as bottled water, antibacterial soap, and household cleaners, she delineates a sociohistorical "genealogy" of purity, an ultimately self- and other-defining set of associations that people in the United States still evoke in their excessive fears of contamination. As Berthold explains, this genealogy stretches back to early Christian conceptions of "dirty" others in need of purifying salvation, both those who were considered physically dirty in corporeal and phenotypic terms and those considered morally impure in terms of their excessively worldly actions. In a sense that has helped to bolster religious, racial, and masculine forms of dominance, "Whiteness, as it has come down to us, is conceived in part as a sort of physical hygiene—the lack of a mark of pollution. The lack of a mark physically has symbolized the lack of a mark morally, and this, in turn, has helped to bolster a dominant identity."[26]

As Erskine recomposes himself in church soon after his "passionate modesty" about his exposed corporeal form has caused Tony's death, he reasserts a morally purified sense of himself. He does so by rejoining a Christian collective, a particularly dominant-American one forged relatively long ago in the morally assuaging casting of others as impure: decimated indigeneity as savage and heathen and both blackness and femininity as wantonly, dangerously sexual. As Rebecca Anne Goetz explains in her study of the influences of an evolving Christian doctrine on colonial American racial formations, "Over the course of the seventeenth century, English people in the New World redefined Christianity and came to view Africans and Indians as hereditary heathens.... By the beginning of the eighteenth century, the idea that Christianity was a religion almost exclusively for white people was a conceit commonly held among Virginia's planter class."[27] Having repositioned himself within this ideological fold, Erskine finds his church calming, and then strengthening, as he reasserts his membership within a collectivity that has long conceived of its elevated (white male) members as relatively pure to the extent that they have supposedly lacked or kept at bay those elements of humanity with which they have ironically "fouled" others, by projection onto them. That the self-righteousness of this collectivity is grounded in historical amnesia is suggested by Wright's description of that which initially calms Erskine in church, "The nostalgia of singing voices..." (*S*, 84). The particular forms that Erskine's reconstitution of himself take render it insightfully representative of common white male feelings of Wright's time, a broader, collective nostalgia for what amounts to sharply divided and hierarchical group formations that had long served to bolster white male dominance.

Thus, as Erskine settles in among and then speaks to fellow members of "GOD'S ETERNAL FAMILY" (*S*, 85), the reassuring recognition of a version of himself reflected in their reactions enables him to slip back into enactment of the supposedly upright and morally pure man that he had taken himself to be before the unmoored independence of retirement and the terrifying thought of himself as a murderer. While the reassertion of his ties to a Christian community supplies Erskine with a conceptual framework that leads him back to a sense that he is a proper man, it also reminds him that such a figure is constituted by proper, rule-adhering action. Others, merely because of who they are and the qualities they thus supposedly embody, become proper objects of that action. A "sense of mission" seizes Erskine, and indeed, missionary-like, he comes to see Mabel not only as a woman who refuses to properly confine her sexual desires, and as the woman who thereby caused Tony's death because God took him away as a form of punishment, but also as a person in need of saving by a good Christian man like himself.

When he leaves church and sits on a park bench to sort through his thoughts and feelings, Erskine recalls talking to Tony about life at home with Mabel, which reminds him of his own childhood with a similarly single mother, one who also subjected him to "watching strange men tramping in and out of the house ..." (*S*, 105). As his anger about unresolved trauma from his own childhood surges toward the surface, Erskine displaces feelings about his own mother onto Mabel. Underlining how Christian morality provides a framework for this sexist displacement are Erskine's three newly resolved convictions: that his duty now is to "redeem" Tony's death, that it had not been his fault, and that "Mrs. Blake is the guilty one..." (*S*, 105). The ironic immorality of these conclusions, reached as they are by the reassertion of an identity buttressed by pious Christian morality, could hardly be more starkly presented. Having riveted himself into proper Sunday attire, Erskine has used his time in church to further don an ideological coat of armor, which in turn enables the reassertion of a superordinate white male self. As he shifts homicidal guilt from himself to Mabel, Erskine casts himself not only as judge but also as executioner, an ominous hint of the repressed awareness of death and thus of the ultimately deathward teleology that Wright goes on to illuminate at the very core of the vexed collective white male psyche.

The White Male Death Drive

When Wright told an interviewer about his efforts to examine in *Savage Holiday* that which makes white people "aggressive toward colored peoples," he spoke in a relatively muted manner about a topic that he'd long been exposing relentlessly.[28] Wright's earlier work repeatedly details his enforced awareness as a black American that since white male aggression toward perceived racial others so often resulted in the latter's demise, death was a far more haunting and imminent presence in black American life and consciousness than it typically was for white Americans.

At one point in his 1945 memoir *Black Boy*, Wright inserted a parenthetical aside that describes the consumerist obsessions of so many white Americans, as well as the frustration that many black Americans felt over having their egalitarian claims subordinated to those obsessions. Wright also assesses what amounts to the overarching, white male-dominated social order:

> Our too-young and too-new America, lusty because it is lonely, aggressive because it is afraid, insists upon seeing the world in terms of good and bad, the holy and the evil, the high and the low, the white and the black; our America is frightened of fact, of history, of processes, of necessity. It hugs the easy way of damning those whom it cannot understand, of excluding those who look different, and it salves its conscience with a self-draped cloak of righteousness.[29]

In *Savage Holiday*, Wright effectively allegorizes with a fictional case study how a broad American fear of history had provoked his era's common white male donning of "the cloak of righteousness." The novel goes further by suggesting that to be "frightened" of history is also to be aware at some level that history lives in the present, in the sense not only that historical abuses and murder of non-white others have yet to be accounted for, but also that they continue—an awareness of both of these circumstances counters the self-righteous morality buttressing the nation's claims to global exceptionalism.

As Wright also dramatized in much of his other work, death is a much more prominent, known presence in the lives of most black Americans. At *Savage Holiday*'s more strictly Freudian level, the novel contains the standard primal scene at its narrative center—aside from Erskine's killing of Tony, having witnessed their mothers having sex is their primary connection. Although this scene has been taken as central to a particularly middle-class white consciousness that is grounded in the biological family, shocking the child into a new sense of identity marked by separation, threat, and exclusion, a similar though explicitly racialized primal scene for black children would be that of white supremacy's inflicted awareness of one's racial status as black. Indeed, three years before the appearance of *Savage Holiday*, Frantz Fanon had published his foundational analysis of colonized subjectivity, *Black Skin, White Masks*, in which he described his own childhood apperception of the "white gaze" in just such traumatizing, identity-distorting terms.[30] Fanon's chapter on the ontologically warping power of the white gaze opens with words he remembers from childhood, words flung at him by children empowered by their white skin to be more than mere children: "'Dirty nigger!' or simply 'Look! A negro!'"[31] The shock of such moments, as often portrayed as well in black American cultural production, has tended to include a sudden sense of separation and exclusion, even from oneself, a sensation that Fanon also described: "Disoriented, incapable of confronting the Other, the white man, who had no scruples about imprisoning me, I transported myself on that particular day far, very far, from my self, and gave myself up as an object."[32] In addition to this relationally cognizant sense of enforced alienation and (non)subjectivity, such moments can include a new, very early apprehension of one's own mortal vulnerability. Confusion about parental sexual activity could, of course, be a significant moment in the development of black children, including the fear that Tony expresses about his mother's sexual activities with men—a fear that the adults are fighting and thus fear of the mother's death. Yet the black child's awakening to the collective "white" perception of oneself as "black" often entailed the sudden awareness and fear of *one's own* death.

Wright portrayed such a foundationally identity-forming scene as early as 1935, when his poem "Between the World and Me" appeared in *Partisan Review*. While walking through a peaceful woodland setting not unlike the opening of Erskine's forested dream, the poem's speaker stumbles upon the gruesome remains of a lynching. The speaker quickly notices not only the body's charred bones amidst tar, feathers, and ash but also the discarded evidentiary remains of the perpetrators. Given the context, these remains betray them as white and as both executioners and celebrants: "butt-ends of cigars and cigarettes, peanut shells, a / drained gin-flask, and a whore's lipstick." Gathering what has happened in this place and the likely race and gender of the person to whom it happened, the speaker's mind goes "frozen within cold pity / for the life that was gone." Immediately, racialized and gendered identification collapses the separation between the lynched person and the speaker, who imagines his own body "cooled by a / baptism of gasoline. / And in a blaze of red I leaped to the sky as pain rose like water, boiling my limbs / Panting, begging I clutched childlike, clutched to the hot / sides of death." In stark contrast to the life-affirming and identity-swelling direction in which Erskine's woodland dream moves, personal identity in this nightmare becomes consciously bound with death, as the speaker imagines himself reduced to "dry bones ... my face a stony skull staring in / yellow surprise at the sun...."[33]

An unspoken awareness imposed on the poem's speaking persona is the same as that expressed by Fanon, that "not only must the black man be black, he must be black in relation to the white man."[34] In addition, both authors dramatize this relation as a deadly one—as fundamentally grounded for the black subject in his or her reduction to an object, and thus in the pervading possibility of death at the hands of unpredictable, potentially murderous white people. While in many ways racial whiteness provides the sensation of safety and security for its occupants, white supremacy often imposes the opposite on its racial others. While Wright made intellectual forays into many realms of inquiry, he remained determined to expose how, thanks to Jim Crow laws and mores in the American South and to a persistent fear of blackness elsewhere in the nation, black Americans remained ontologically bound to death. Indeed, this is likely why, as Abdul R. JanMohamed writes, awareness of death itself "furnish[es] the underlying teleological structure" of Wright's work.[35]

Although JanMohamed does much in his chapter on *Savage Holiday* to elucidate its psychoanalytic portrayal of longings that appear fundamentally matricidal, including Wright's own, he disregards consideration of Erskine's internal machinations in terms that Wright himself suggested: as a representative depiction of white masculinity that is not merely aggressive but also collectively death-dealing and, as a result, death-denying. Arguing that "this novel has nothing to do with Jim Crow society or slavery," JanMohamed instead echoes earlier critics who saw the novel as unconcerned with racism, by reading its "displacement of race" via a white protagonist as illustrative of Wright's effort to sort through his own fixation with "matricidal desire, which Wright can contemplate adequately only if it is sufficiently 'distanced,' via racial difference, from implicating his personal life."[36] However, if we compare the intense existential experience of the persona in Wright's early poem not only to that experienced by Erskine in his forested dream but also to Erskine's broader identity crisis, an undeniable thematic focus on white masculinity arises, especially in terms of personal security versus mortal vulnerability. Whereas black Americans often learn early on of the vulnerability imposed upon them by their racial status, white Americans gather, usually more unconsciously, that whiteness is a protective, existentially reassuring status. In this sense, white Americans, as opposed to ordinary black Americans, have been encouraged to extreme degrees to repress the facts of death—not only the deaths wrought by the hands, as it were, of their own collective, but also their own.

In these terms and in terms that apply as well to domineering masculinity, theological historian Christopher Driscoll aptly describes whiteness as *"the racialized expression of a fundamental inability to accept limitation and uncertainty."*[37] In *Savage Holiday*, Wright allegorically suggests that although nearly all humans know that they and others must die, a certain avoidance of death awareness lurks within the dominant collective American consciousness. One historical reason is that the establishment of Christian white men as paragons of moral superiority provoked repression of the countervailing historical realities of large-scale abuse, theft, and murder. Indeed, what James W. Perkinson points out in terms of race is more specifically true of domineering white masculinity: "'White' skin is essentially a latent denial of death."[38] Absurdly enough, this deferral of death can go so far as a refusal of sorts to acknowledge, and adequately prepare for, the fact that one is eventually going to die. I will argue that in Erskine's desperation to reassert and enact a morally upright white masculinity, his murder of Mabel constitutes Wright's exposé of the imposing lengths to which those who adhere to white masculinity's dictates can go to regain their sense of an indomitable identity.

Erskine's forms of death denial are in part inspired and structured by a collective psychic need to suture the gaping contrast between a rigidly maintained moral righteousness and the fact of people like oneself as exploiters and murderers of others who have been cast as non-white. One extreme yet illustrative way for white American men to do so has been to anoint their people as the ones who continue existing in an "afterlife" and to deem those whom one abuses and extorts subhumans, and thus as lacking the souls that would enable such de facto immortality. Of course, not all early Christians conceived of racial others as irredeemable and many instead sought their religious conversion, yet the moralizing quest for immortality often provoked such ironic forms of immorality. As the young United States took shape and a Christian emphasis on an eternal afterlife endured, the deserving were increasingly cast in liturgical and more widespread representations as white, along with a phenotypically whitened God, his son, and angels.[39] Attendant to and indeed constitutive of a horizon-free conception of ontological continuity in America's full-fledged "white" citizens was that of an earth-bound, closer-to-nature quality in non-white others, a quality often extended into a supposed inability to transcend mortality. Broader conceptions of non-white peoples as animal-like helped to foster such conceptions, which were symptomatic of attempts not only to denigrate racialized subordinates but also to assert white superiority, in this case via a certain denial of white death.

For decades after the end of the Civil War, American intellectuals continued to debate in such terms the ontological status of people of African descent. In 1867, Nashville-based clergyman and publisher Buckner H. Payne, writing under the pseudonym Ariel, entered the fray in a way that was common at the time, by issuing a pamphlet on the "ethnological origin of the negro." Payne's tortured racial logic illustrates this morally assuaging, white American conception of an existential boundedness to death among non-white races. Payne wrote in a Southern context, but like many white Americans of his day, he conceived of the black race as an entirely different species and as preexisting Adam and Eve. His argument that "the negro... like all other beasts or animals, has no soul" resonated with readers nationwide, resulting in a second printing, likely because it reflected common conceptions of an afterlife cast in exclusively white terms.[40] In 1902, Adamic Publishing House, based in St. Louis, published a book written in a similar vein, Charles Carroll's *The Tempter of Eve*. In addition to furthering the claim of black soul-lessness, Carroll argued that Eve's satanic tempter was not a snake but rather Eve's black maidservant. According to theological historian Colin Kidd, such believers partook in a lengthy national debate on racial difference and helped to foster "a consistent interpretation of blacks as an inferior, pre-Adamic race whose members did not have immortal souls."[41] Such conceptions were common and enduring and their remnants persisted in Wright's time, and still do in ours.

In these and other dehumanizing conceptions of non-white peoples, an attendant, countervailing sense had become embedded within white American self-consciousness of one's own being as not only superior but also (if one lived morally enough) limitless, boundless in terms of linear temporality. Although a white person obviously knew that he or she would one day physically die, the concept of a whitened afterlife that was counterposed to black soul-lessness provided a reassuring sense of continuity, making it that much easier to displace, and even disassociate oneself from, the end of one's own corporeal form. As strained as the logic may now seem in such common ways of casting people of African descent into a lower realm of being, the hint of desperation in such arguments reflects the lengths to which white Americans have been willing to go in order to paper over the undeniable contrast between their professed egalitarian moral principles and not only the horrors of slavery and its aftermath, but also the similarly dehumanizing treatment of indigenous peoples. In equally conceptual terms, not only were the nation's morally righteous white citizens cast with an implicit aura of immortality, so was the nation itself, as an ever-expanding, quasi-organism, reflecting a sense of endless expansiveness that has also lingered, long after the apparent establishment of fixed geographical borders.

Wright initially registers in *Savage Holiday* the psychosocial context of his own era's manifestations of white American quasi-invulnerability in the name of Erskine's former employer, Longevity Life. Aside from the intertwined, identity-structuring frameworks of religious and racial ideologies, a reason that a person like Erskine may well have felt unprepared for the freedom of retirement from paid labor is that, in a sense, middle-class, white male working life has also discouraged cognizance of his own inevitable death. Longevity Life had been a place where Erskine felt at home because he could dream along with his collectivity a fantasy of quasi-immortality, a suspended present tense enhanced by the 1950s consumerism that pictured people like him as the rightful, entitled residents of the horizon-free American Dream. Thrust into a new freedom and feeling vulnerable, Erskine quickly reverts to the habitual psychic framework that prompted middle-class white male proclivities and prerogatives. In this sense, having shed an idealized yet immature white masculinity, Erskine is unprepared to step into the role he so hastily tries to assume, that of husband/father. Thus, his unresolved oedipal trauma is, beneath its repressed anger, a naïve restorative nostalgia for conditions before his mother supposedly had sex with so many men, a time in which he imagines he had a connection to her that went unchallenged. Without the protective, death-deferring armor of a "successful" masculine identity, and with the psychic comfort of the "home" that was Longevity Life and his coworkers undeniably lost forever, Erskine's sudden awareness of his own human vulnerability prompts a longing for an infantile psychic state, one in which death was not quite denied—it was, to him, entirely unknown.

In these terms, Wright constructs a historically resonant critique of white masculinity's ironically immoral refusal of accountability for death brought about by its own self-serving ideology. He lays the groundwork for Erskine's representative refusal by initially depicting him causing Tony's death with his "passionate modesty," his fear of being seen as what his projected identity pretends he is not, just another flesh-bound human. As with its other modes of life suppression, twentieth-century hegemonic white masculinity remained grounded in suppression of the identity- and morality-challenging awareness of death. As societal norms changed and white men felt their dominance come increasingly under fire, white male consciousness often hearkened backwards in ways that amounted to wistful longings for a time when its own collective power, and its future, seemed unchallenged and, in a sense, infinite. Approved middle-class white masculinity entailed enactment of a steady, supreme confidence, a projection of *in*vulnerability that had long asserted itself by ruling in seemingly unquestioned ways over others. Its ironically relational sense of freedom, asserted most potently by the ability to impose death on others, also seemed in a sense a freedom from one's own mortality, or at least from needing to remain as aware as others had to be about imminent possibilities of one's own. This near-belief in one's own immortality also resembles actual adolescent self awareness: the sense teenagers often have that their own mortality, though undeniable, is nevertheless so far off as to be nearly unimaginable. This common attitude in white American male adults ultimately amounts to a childish deferral of death rather than a present awareness of and preparation for its inevitability. What *Savage Holiday* suggests is that this denial is prompted in part by the guiltily repressed awareness of the massive death inflicted on others by white Christian-oriented masculinity. Accordingly, as noted earlier, church is the place where Erskine suppresses his initial, ethical sense that he should go to the police and admit his role in Tony's death and where he forms instead a twisted conviction that Tony's death was not at all his fault but rather Mabel's. Christian emphasis on the afterlife, including the proffered possibility of his own soul's immortal transcendence, is part of the ideological framework that helps him repress the recent, horrific reminder of earthbound mortality, both Tony's and, should he be put on trial, his own.

Wright thus illustrates in Erskine's internal machinations and resultant actions how the individual white male psyche can respond when its status feels threatened, by reasserting various underpinnings of a social order run and regulated by people like themselves and by insisting that others assume the subservient roles that they once supposedly accepted without question. As the novel approaches its dramatic climax, Erskine presents himself to the grieving mother Mabel as a source of masculine (and thus automatically able) support. His vexed feelings for Mabel ostensibly consist of desire for a sexually attractive woman and anger with a supposedly negligent mother who reminds him of his own. However, as Mabel resists Erskine's advances, his moralizing, censorious judgment of her rises fully to the fore, propelling him into entirely self-centered destruction. Unlike most of Wright's female characters, Mabel displays complex agency, including persistent defense of her independence and privacy, and a staunch resistance to Erskine's efforts to confine her, so quickly, to the role of chaste, subservient housewife and child-bearer. Though initially intrigued in her shocked state by Erskine's clumsy offer of marriage, Mabel soon sees through his guise, ultimately calling him out as the killer of her child. Wright also refrains from depicting Erskine's sudden love interest as a formulaic crime-narrative femme fatale, who would manipulate Erskine into committing crimes and murder on her wicked behalf.[42]

Shattered by the death of her son, a loss which is compounded by her status as a recent widow, yet also clearly in possession of a firmly agential sense of herself, Mabel repels Erskine's confining advances. "Listen," she tells Erskine when he asks how many men she's been sleeping with, "I sleep with whom I damn please. I'm a woman; I'm free" (*S*, 213). As much or more than his unconscious perception of her as a proxy mother, what drives the fury that leads Erskine to kill Mabel in another starkly "white" space, his kitchen (with its "white refrigerator, the white gas stove, the gleaming sink, the white-topped table"), is her refusal to submit, which would mean taking him as the man he has long pretended to be (*S*, 214). Wright thusly allegorizes his era's challenges to traditionally dominant, aggressive white men, challenges represented as well by Mabel's vacillation at most points between indifference and mocking refusal of Erskine's efforts to control her. The more Mabel resists his efforts, the more she reflects back to Erskine his own failure to assert relationally a controlling, narcissistic, and fundamentally abusive version of himself. As before, Erskine reacts to his newfound freedom and the fearful, diminishing feelings it evokes by in effect attempting to reinsert between the world and himself an entire history of white male conceptions of others deemed lesser, and by trying to drape it like clothing over Mabel's conceptually naked (and thus, eventually, literally naked) self. Although Erskine is desperate to restore a sense of family and a home—a *nostos*—his restorative nostalgia is actually a longing for the seemingly unquestioned status that dominant figures like himself once had. All of Erskine's sudden trials widen fissures in his white masculine façade, prompting his desperate efforts to reseal them. A point thereby conveyed is that, as in any social order, white America's hegemonic moral code is not a universal or God-given set of values but instead a dominant group's constructed set of self-justifications for the willful and grossly hypocritical enactment of its members' baser instincts and desires.

In 1945, a reporter for the *Des Moines Register* paraphrased similar insights offered by Wright during a book tour: "Wright said slavery came to America when Europe was coming out of the feudal world; that America's conscience was troubled and to soothe it, the myth of Negro inferiority was invented. He said this concept was deeply implanted in the white's mind; that white children at the age of six believed it and to challenge it is to hit directly at the white's primal ideas on morality."[43] Although the precise accuracy of this reporter's summary is indeterminable, Wright does display in *Savage Holiday* not only the imprint on an adult psyche of childhood phenomena but also, in a broader mode, the effects at the individual level of a collective adherence both to the legacy of white Christian-oriented patriarchal morality and to the ironic immorality of nostalgic collective fantasies, particularly in the minds and feelings of white American men, that obscure from conscious awareness their costs to others. The highest costs to others include large-scale expropriation and suffering, and at times communal levels of death, a historical fact of such ethically challenging magnitude that it accounts for much of the collective white tendency toward nostalgic remembrance as a form of denial. Ultimately, this denial serves as a form of power, enabling further extraction from others, including, as always, self-aggrandizing reflection of oneself in relation to them.

Earlier in the novel, Erskine exhibits how the white male psyche also denies life by pouring itself into zombifying work, but also by denying parts of itself, especially its emotional and corporeal components, as it projects perception of those features onto others. An emphasis on containment is a feature of the collective white masculine psyche that *Savage Holiday* dramatizes effectively and presciently. Judging oneself and others by such metrics as the "Protestant work ethic" became a way of denying life as well as a way of *justifying* the denial of life. In Freudian terms, repressed life forces left unfulfilled by deadening labor tend to return, often in grotesque ways, another problem dramatized by Erskine's murder of Mabel. In his freed state of retirement, Erskine has lost his role/uniform of successful American man, and just as he scrambles back into his apartment, he scrambles back into his identity, a received role in which a successful man needs relationally defined and self-defining personages to perform within a family. Having also riveted himself into a

Christian missionary role, Erskine attempts to channel his energies into enacting what amounts to his era's version—to the extent that men were still conceived of as stabilizing forces bringing irrational women safely under control—of the husband role. He simultaneously imposes on Mabel the fiancée role and becomes enraged when she behaves in ways deemed inappropriate to her assigned part.

As Erskine attempts to form an absurdly and satirically hasty bond with Mabel, what he perceives as her earthly sensuality both attracts and repels him. He feels repelled because his white Christian sense of morality tells him that she isn't acting the way a proper woman should (and, at a more personal oedipal level, because what he construes as "whore"-like behavior reminds him of his dead mother) and attracted because her sensuality evokes that which he, in a state that is both deadened and deadening, has suppressed in himself and in his conception of properly acting women (*S*, 133). In this sense, domineering white American masculinity encourages a self-inflating conception of women as an abjectified other in the same way that it does racial others. In sum, while Wright ostensibly portrays Erskine's murderous rage toward Mabel as oedipal and thus as a release of repressed rage toward his mother, Erskine's feelings about women more generally are an imposition of masculinity-defining "proper" womanhood onto both of these women (and ultimately to all women), who, of course, have reasons for their actions that Erskine fails to see since he sees them instead through the distorting lens of white male nostalgia. Wright thus critiques an automaticity built into white masculinity, a set of induced, unacknowledged drives that encourage men to act out robotically a teleology that is ultimately death-oriented.

The automatized state grotesquely depicted in Erskine's stabbing of Mabel, which Erskine commits in part because she refuses to submit to his single-minded, self-defining possessiveness, highlights an ultimately life-denying orientation toward oneself in relation to others, as white men inflict a suppression and denial of life onto them while also nostalgically longing for those lost qualities that the collective white male psyche represses and projects onto others. Having suggestively covered up and repressed his own sexualized, panic-inducing corporeal form in stiffly formal attire, Erskine finds glimpses of Mabel's body tantalizingly distracting. A twisted result of this hegemonically oriented sexual repression—which can flare into action when confronted with the demands of abjectified others and a concomitant challenge of one's elevated status—is a longing for prior subjective states that never actually existed.

White American masculinity's automaticity itself has a lengthy collective history and its robotic, "riveted" quality has long bolstered a broader, exceptionalist sense of both American morality and immortality. Yet, given the demands for egalitarian recognition from white men's others, the cracks in white masculinity's armor were becoming more evident gaps by the mid-twentieth century.

If morality can generally be defined as a set of socially sanctioned rules for right and good versus wrong and bad behavior, *Savage Holiday* emphasizes that Erskine's moral codes derive from his tripartite positionality as a Christian-oriented white man. Furthermore, the novel depicts his actions as allegorically representative in that they revolve around two constant interrelated themes—received, operative versions of history and the reality of death, particularly of white masculinity's denial and consequent fear of it. As the novel closes, Erskine turns himself in at a police station, finally finding actual iron bars that both replace his "prison-cage of toil" and suggest the iron cage in which domineering white masculinity has encased him (*S*, 33). Reflecting the broader international concerns of Wright's later career, the novel assesses postwar possibilities for a new form of Cold War American identity and power by ominously predicting how domineering white, Christian-oriented American men will adjust to—or rather, fail to adjust to—the increasingly vocal and assertive presence of their collectivity's subjugated others. As much a satiric warning as a horrific forecast, *Savage Holiday* suggests that unless the wielders of white male power begin to acknowledge the obstinate psychic underpinnings denied by nostalgic longings for times and conditions in which their status and power supposedly went uncontested, white American masculine hegemony will continue inflicting its self-sustaining moral codes on others, assuring the destruction not only of many more of those others, but ultimately of the social order built so heavily in its image and favor.

Notes

1. Charbonnier, 236. The quote regarding crime is from Fabre, who excerpts a letter that Wright wrote in 1952 while working on the novel to his agent, Paul Reynolds (376).
2. Barthes, 167.
3. Recent scholarship that fully or partially examines *Savage Holiday* in terms of racial whiteness include Charles, Demirtürk, Dubek, and Li.

Early scholars who read *Savage Holiday* in terms of non-racial or seemingly universal themes (or both) include Gounard and Gounard, Fabre, Margolies, Reilly, and Vassilowitch. Other recent scholars have focused on the novel's non-racial, traditionally psychoanalytic, or seemingly autobiographical elements: Kiuchi traces autobiographical parallels in the novel; as in Tate's earlier analysis, JanMohamed draws parallels between Erskine's Oedipal Complex and Wright's own supposed matricidal urges; Smith connects Erskine's actions with those of Kwame Nkrumah; Cassuto examines the novel in terms of masculinity, drawing little distinction between white, black, or other raced masculinities; and Kuhl draws parallels to the ideas of Fredric Wertham to argue that *Savage Holiday* shows "that individual and social forces are at work simultaneously" in our treatment of others (although Kuhl places little emphasis on either whiteness or masculinity as social forces) (667).

4. Barthes, 168.
5. Ibid., 167.
6. Harvey, 35.
7. Barthes, 168.
8. Wright, *Savage Holiday*, 11, 13. Hereafter cited as *S*.
9. Boren, n.p.
10. In these terms, my interpretation of the novel resonates with that of Laura Dubek, who writes, "Recognizing the political nature of the drama of psychosis that lies at the heart of *Savage Holiday* necessitates returning the novel to its historical and social context, a move that underscores Wright's life-long commitment to critiquing American culture" (599).
11. Sullivan, *Revealing*, 70–71. It also bears noting that Freud himself devoted little attention to racial influences on human psychology and, indeed, in a way that ironically resembles white masculine presumptions of (dis)embodiment, largely presented himself as a fount of ideologically unencumbered rationality and scientific objectivity. On both Freud and his concepts in terms of race and ethnicity, see López and Nast.
12. *La Nef*, 174.
13. Dunbar-Ortiz, 36.
14. Similarly, in his analysis of the utility of the "myth of a primeval New Zealand" for promoters of tourism, Alfio Leotta writes, "the representation of a pure nature implicitly suggested that the country was a good terrain for the colonial enterprise. Purity is equated with emptiness and, in turn, emptiness justifies the settler enterprise" (196).
15. Lipsitz, 4. As Lipsitz adds, and as I explain more fully in Chapter 4 in regard to Shields's depiction of a representative white American male identity in *Happenstance*, "The lived experience of race takes place in actual spaces ...", spaces in which histories are imagined and promulgated

to the material, psychological, and emotional benefit of the dominant and thus to the detriment, and often the conceptual erasure, of the subordinate: "The racial meaning of place makes American whiteness one of the most systematically subsidized identities in the world" (Lipsitz, 5).

16. Barthes, 167.
17. Watson, 131. At one point, as Erskine enters Central Park after spending time in church, Wright registers the relational yet unmarked quality that whiteness was increasingly attaining in white consciousness: "Children skipped and ran. A little girl blew bubble gum. A black boy sat on a bench reading a comic magazine" (*S*, 90). Wright depicts not only the status of white children in the white mind as *just children* but also how that status exists in relation to the overtly racialized status of other children, in this case, that of the boy on the bench markedly perceived as "black."
18. For an extended analysis of Erskine's use of Minnie "to further the charade of his manufactured and ultimately derivative identity," see Li, 80–82.
19. See, for example, Takaki, *Iron Cages*, 3–42. Such is the projection onto raced and gendered others of the bodily, a corporeality which white men have long been encouraged to abjectify, suppress, and ultimately fear in themselves, that James Baldwin was led to write in 1961, "It is still true, alas, that to be an American Negro male is also to be a kind of walking phallic symbol: which means that one pays, in one's own personality, for the sexual insecurity of others" (*Price of the Ticket*, 290).
20. Localized and class-inflected exceptions to this general tendency exist, of course, in such conceptions of white irredeemability as late-nineteenth and early-twentieth-century beliefs in eugenics. Nevertheless, such beliefs still tended to hold that such supposedly irreformable and sometimes provisionally white people were inherently superior to members of other races.
21. In his analysis of genocidal efforts during the 1990s in Rwanda, Philip Gourevitch puts this point more succinctly: "Genocide, after all, is an exercise in community building.... Killing Tutsis was a political tradition in postcolonial Rwanda; it brought people together" (95–96).
22. In his discussion of the intertwining of ideologies into "whiteness as Christianity," James W. Perkinson writes,

> Modern Western Christian association of goodness and purity with whiteness, evil and sin with darkness, impurity with mixtures and off-colors, divinity with transparency, Christology with European physiognomy, and soteriology with a progressive 'enlightenment'

gained its historical intransigence in [a] reciprocal process.... The theological meanings invested in epidermal appearances served the function of theodicy, legitimizing the exploitation of both (indigenous) native and (imported) slave labor for European and later imperial enterprises. (157)

23. Barthes, 167.
24. Atwood, "Margaret Atwood on What 'The Handmaid's Tale' Means in the Age of Trump," n.p.
25. This observation about racially segregated churches is, of course, from Martin Luther King, Jr., who in 1960 said on the television show *Meet the Press*, "I think it is one of the tragedies of our nation, one of the shameful tragedies, that eleven o'clock on Sunday morning is one of the most segregated hours, if not the most segregated hours, in Christian America" (King).
26. Berthold, 2. For a more detailed elaboration of the historical development within the United States of common conceptions of racially non-white impurity, see Zimring, 27–106.
27. Goetz, 169. For elaboration of even earlier roots for denigrating Christian white American conceptions of darker otherness as a sign of immorality, see Thomas DiPiero, who writes, "Europeans' association of moral and intellectual wretchedness with dark complexion seems to have become fixed in the popular imagination during the Middle Ages" (66).
28. Barthes, 167.
29. Wright, *Black Boy*, 272.
30. Fanon, 90.
31. Ibid., 89.
32. Ibid., 92.
33. Wright, "Between," 18–19. For extended analysis of this poem as illustrative of Wright's "radical capacity for 'intransitive identification'... a capacity to overcome intersubjective boundaries and understand the predicament and the capabilities of the death-bound subject," see JanMohamed, 28–31.
34. Fanon, 90.
35. JanMohamed, 2.
36. Ibid., 211, 215.
37. Driscoll, 261, italics in original.
38. Perkinson, 199. As Perkinson also writes,

Perhaps one of the most difficult and cogent things that must be said about white identity in the modern world is that it is fundamentally a structure of denial. It is elusive to talk about... precisely in its function of hiding history and domination under a presumed normalcy and a naturalized superiority. What has been hidden in particular is the degree to which white identity and white wherewithal [are] relational phenomena, gathered from a history of exploiting and oppressing peoples of color that remains largely opaque—ungrasped and unfelt—by white people. (175–76)

39. On the gradual whitening of representations of Jesus and other Christian figures during European contact with non-white others, see Gayraud Wilmore, who describes "The Aryanization of Christ" (228), and Edward J Blum and Paul Harvey's *The Color of Christ*.

40. As quoted in Jared Gardner, 210, note 65. Payne's pamphlet first appeared in 1840. For more on Payne's pamphlet within the context of other mid-nineteenth-century efforts to justify white supremacy on the relational basis of perceived inherent inferiority in people of African descent, see Colin Kidd's *The Forging of Races*, 121–67.

41. Kidd, 150. The full title of Carroll's book is *The Tempter of Eve: or, The Criminality of Man's Social, Political, and Religious Equality with the Negro, and the Amalgamation to Which These Crimes Inevitably Lead. Discussed in the Light of the Scriptures, the Sciences, Profane History, Tradition, and the Testimony of the Monuments*. Its St. Louis-based publisher, Adamic Publishing Company, also published Carroll's 1900 effort, *"The Negro: A Beast" or "In the Image of God."*

42. Reflective of her era's newly assertive white femininity, Mabel is not at all malleable. Few critics have examined this *Savage Holiday* character, perhaps because Mabel ostensibly appears to be another of his poorly drawn, even misogynistic, female characters. In an early biography of Wright, Margaret Walker sets the tone for most of the later, brief considerations of Mabel that have appeared, failing to distinguish Wright's apparent estimation of her from Erskine's: "Wright's negative treatment of women is perhaps most extreme in *Savage Holiday*. He regards [Mabel] as 'degraded,' and like all the women in his fiction she is whore, cunt, and bitch—the fallen woman.... Never does he see her in the light of a grief-stricken mother. She is never a real human being. She is stupid, hysterical, emotional, silly, evil, and low-class" (247). Tara T. Green also offers a narrow reading of Mabel as, in Erskine's eyes, a reminder of the Biblical Eve. In his afterword to the 1994 reissue of *Savage Holiday*, Gerald Early describes Mabel as "one of Wright's most intriguing female creations," but he does not elaborate (229).

43. *Des Moines Register*, 85–86.

BIBLIOGRAPHY

Atwood, Margaret. "Margaret Atwood on What 'The Handmaid's Tale' Means in the Age of Trump." *New York Times*, March 10, 2017, n.p. https://www.nytimes.com/2017/03/10/books/review/margaret-atwood-handmaids-tale-age-of-trump.html. Accessed 10.14.2017.

Baldwin, James. *The Price of the Ticket*. New York: St. Martin's Press, 1985.

Barthes, Raymond. "Interview." In *Conversations with Richard Wright*, edited by Keneth Kinnamon & Michel Fabre. Jackson: University Press of Mississippi, 1993: 166–68.

Berthold, Dana. "Tidy Whiteness: A Genealogy of Race, Purity, and Hygiene." *Ethics and the Environment* 15, No. 1 (2010): 1–26.

Blum, Edward J., and Paul Harvey. *The Color of Christ: The Son of God and the Saga of Race in America*. Chapel Hill: University of North Carolina Press, 2012.

Boren, Zachary. "The Nature of Nostalgia." *Contemporary Psychotherapy* 5, No. 1 (Spring, 2013): n.p. http://www.contemporarypsychotherapy.org/volume-5-no-1-spring-2013/the-nature-of-nostalgia/. Accessed 5.22.2018.

Cassuto, Leonard. "A Father's Law, 1950s Masculinity, and Richard Wright's Agony over Integration." In *Richard Wright: New Readings in the 21st Century*, edited by Alice Mikal Craven & William E. Dow. New York: Palgrave Macmillan, 2011: 39–54.

Charbonnier, Georges. "A Negro Novel About White People." In *Conversations with Richard Wright*, edited by Keneth Kinnamon & Michel Fabre. Jackson: University Press of Mississippi, 1993: 235–38.

Charles, John C. *Abandoning the Black Hero: Sympathy and Privacy in the Postwar African American White-Life Novel*. New Brunswick, NJ: Rutgers University Press, 2013.

Demirtürk, E. Lâle. "Mapping the Terrain of Whiteness: Richard Wright's *Savage Holiday*." *MELUS* 24, No. 1 (1999): 129–40.

Des Moines Register. "Asserts Negro's Fight for Equality Benefit to Nation." In *Conversations with Richard Wright*, edited by Keneth Kinnamon & Michel Fabre. Jackson: University Press of Mississippi, 1993: 85–86.

DiPiero, Thomas. *White Men Aren't*. Durham and London: Duke University Press, 2002.

Driscoll, Christopher M. *White Lies: Race and Uncertainty in the Twilight of American Religion*. New York: Routledge, 2016.

Dubek, Laura. "'Til Death Do Us Part: White Male Rage in Richard Wright's *Savage Holiday*." *Mississippi Quarterly: The Journal of Southern Cultures* 61, No. 4 (2008): 593–613.

Dunbar-Ortiz, Roxanne. *An Indigenous Peoples' History of the United States*. Boston, MA: Beacon Press, 2015.

Early, Gerald. "Afterword." *Savage Holiday*. 1954. Jackson: University Press of Mississippi, 1994: 223–35.

Fabre, Michel. *The Unfinished Quest of Richard Wright*. Urbana and Chicago: University of Illinois Press, 1993.

Fanon, Frantz. *White Skin, Black Masks*. 1952. New York: Grove Press, 2008.

Gardner, Jared. *Master Plots: Race and the Founding of an American Literature, 1787–1845*. Baltimore: Johns Hopkins University Press, 2000.

Goetz, Rebecca Anne. *The Baptism of Early Virginia: How Christianity Created Race*. Baltimore: Johns Hopkins University Press, 2012.

Gounard, J. F., and Beverley Roberts Gounard. "Richard Wright's *Savage Holiday*: Use or Abuse of Psychoanalysis?" *College Language Association Journal* 22 (1979): 344–49.

Gourevitch, Philip. *We Wish to Inform You That Tomorrow We Will Be Killed with Our Families: Stories from Rwanda*. New York: Picador, 1999.

Green, Tara. "The Virgin Mary, Eve, and Mary Magdalene in Richard Wright's Novels." *CLA Journal* 46, No. 2 (2002): 168–93.

Harvey, Jennifer. *Whiteness and Morality: Pursuing Racial Justice Through Reparations and Sovereignty*. New York: Palgrave Macmillan, 2007.

JanMohamed, Abdul R. *The Death-Bound-Subject: Richard Wright's Archaeology of Death*. Durham: Duke University Press, 2005.

Kidd, Colin. *The Forging of Races: Race and Scripture in the Protestant Atlantic World, 1600–2000*. Cambridge: Cambridge University Press, 2006.

King, Martin Luther, Jr. Interview transcript, "Meet the Press" April 17, 1960. The Martin Luther King, Jr. Research and Education Institute, Stanford University. https://kinginstitute.stanford.edu/king-papers/documents/interview-meet-press. Accessed 10.14.2017.

Kinnamon, Kenneth, and Michel Fabre. *Conversations with Richard Wright*. Jackson: University Press of Mississippi, 1993.

Kiuchi, Toru. "Psychoanalysis as Self-Reflection in Richard Wright's *Savage Holiday*." In *Richard Wright: Writing America at Home and from Abroad*, edited by Virginia Whatley. Jackson: University Press of Mississippi, 2016: 118–38.

Kuhl, Stephan. "Guilty Children: Richard Wright's *Savage Holiday* and Fredric Wertham's *Dark Legend*." *Amerikastudien/American Studies* 55, No. 4 (2010): 667–84.

La Nef. "Are the United States One Nation, One Law, One People?" In *Conversations with Richard Wright*, edited by Keneth Kinnamon & Michel Fabre. Jackson: University Press of Mississippi, 1993: 173–79.

Leotta, Alfio. *Touring the Screen: Tourism and New Zealand Film Geographies*. Bristol and Chicago: Intellect/University of Chicago Press, 2011.

Li, Stephanie. *Playing in the White: Black Writers, White Subjects*. Oxford: Oxford University Press, 2015.

Lipsitz, George. *How Racism Takes Place*. Philadelphia: Temple University Press, 2011.

López, Alfred J. "The Gaze of the White Wolf: Psychoanalysis, Whiteness, and Colonial Trauma." In *Postcolonial Whiteness: A Critical Reader on Race and Empire*, edited by Alfred J. López. Albany, NY: State University of New York Press, 2005: 155–82.

Margolies, Edward. *The Art of Richard Wright*. Carbondale: Southern Illinois University Press, 1969.

Nast, Heidi J. "Mapping the 'Unconscious': Racism and the Oedipal Family." *Annals of the Association of American Geographers* 90, No. 2 (2000): 215–55.

Perkinson, James W. *White Theology: Outing Supremacy in Modernity*. New York: Palgrave Macmillan, 2004.

Reilly, John M. "Richard Wright's Curious Thriller, *Savage Holiday*." *College Language Association Journal* 21 (1977): 218–23.

Smith, Virginia Whatley. "Lying, Deception, Truth-Telling, and Self-Negation: Ironies and Failures of Nation-Building in Wright's African Parody *Savage Holiday*." In *Richard Wright: Writing America at Home and from Abroad*, edited by Virginia Whatley Smith. Jackson: University Press of Mississippi, 2016: 98–117.

Sullivan, Shannon. *Revealing Whiteness: The Unconscious Habits of Racial Privilege*. Bloomington and Indianapolis: Indiana University Press, 2006.

Takaki, Ronald. *Iron Cages: Race and Culture in 19th-Century America*. Oxford: Oxford University Press, 2000.

Tate, Claudia. *Psychoanalysis and Black Novels: Desire and the Protocols of Race*. Oxford: Oxford University Press, 1998.

Vassilowitch, John, Jr. "'Erskine Fowler': A Key Freudian Pun in *Savage Holiday*." *English Language Notes* 18, No. 3 (1981): 206–8.

Walker, Margaret. *Richard Wright: Daemonic Genius*. 1988. New York: Amistad Press, 1993.

Watson, Veronica T. *The Souls of White Folk: African American Writers Theorize Whiteness*. Jackson: University Press of Mississippi, 2015.

Wilmore, Gayraud. "Black Theology: Its Significance for Christian Mission Today." *International Review of Mission* 63 (1974): 211–31.

Wright, Richard. "Between the World and Me." *Partisan Review* 2, No. 8 (1935): 18–19.

———. *Black Boy*. 1945. New York: HarperCollins, 1998.

———. *Savage Holiday*. 1954. Jackson: University Press of Mississippi, 1994.

Zimring, Carl A. *Clean and White: A History of Environmental Racism in the United States*. New York and London: New York University Press, 2015.

CHAPTER 4

Spatialized White Male Nostalgia: Carol Shields's *Happenstance*

Although Carol Shields lived the majority of her life in Canada and is widely identified as a Canadian author, she was born and raised in suburban Chicago. As she said in a 1998 interview, she considered "the WASP culture I was born into," which straddles these two North American nations, her primary "piece of territory" as a literary author.[1] Although the settings of Shields's novels span numerous eras and geographical locations, her work has sometimes been characterized as insular domestic fiction that expresses only mild, second-wave feminist discontent with patriarchal dominance. In a recent study of Shields's fictional women writers, Brenda Beckman-Long offers a more subtle assessment, perceiving instead "a body of work that represents a significant and sustained political project."[2] As Beckman-Long writes, Shields reacted in responsive, evolving ways to both the second- and early third-wave feminist movements by producing "highly theoretical novels [that] are deceptively simple. … She questioned dominant discourses, such as masculine selfhood and Western individualism, implicating in them even white middle-class feminists who are, ironically, among the largest segment of her readers."[3] In the paired stories that comprise *Happenstance*, Shields dramatizes the restorative nostalgia commonly prompted in 1970s-era white American men by the psychological groundings of their ironically collective identity in a fantasized national past. The American past has often been conceived in spatial terms, particularly as an appropriate staging ground for assertive white male action. This is a form of spatialized self-staging that Shields symbolically appropriates in the novel for women

© The Author(s) 2018
T. Engles, *White Male Nostalgia in Contemporary North American Literature*, https://doi.org/10.1007/978-3-319-90460-3_4

while also countering masculine dominance with feminized figurations of reflective, communal nostalgia.

CONTEXTS FOR *HAPPENSTANCE*

The two novellas paired together as *Happenstance* depict an emblematic week in the late-1970s marriage of a middle-aged couple living in Chicago, Jack and Brenda Bowman. The Bowmans spend nearly all of both stories apart from each other, she at a quilting convention in another city and he mostly at their home. An implication of their temporary split is that although the Bowmans clearly enjoy each other and their marriage, social forces are nudging their lives in opposite directions, particularly in terms of gender roles. Brenda is a budding artist and entrepreneur gaining emotional independence from the sphere of home while Jack is moving away, if less enthusiastically, from the traditionally masculine sphere of family-supporting labor by dabbling in caretaking domestic life. In this chapter, I will follow the lead of various publishers by reading these novellas together, interpreting the two halves of *Happenstance* as a meditation on the effects on middle-class American women and men of wider societal movements toward (primarily white) women's liberation. At another level, with her depiction of Jack as a frustrated academic historian, Shields provides an incisive portrait of the era's common middle-class white male emotions, anxieties, and tendencies. She anchors these companion stories in ultimately nostalgic constructions of history, both a solipsistic, restorative form that springs from a geographically resonant sense of besieged white male power and a counterpoised reflective form that arises in light of the newly empowered social status of white women like Brenda.

A novella told from Jack's perspective was originally published in 1980 as *Happenstance*, and Brenda's version of the same week in their lives appeared in 1982 as *A Fairly Conventional Woman*, a punning title suggested by an editor.[4] In the 1990s, they were printed together as *Happenstance*, with two sections entitled "The Husband's Story" and "The Wife's Story," and sometimes in an unusual format. As Wendy Roy explains,

> In many editions the volume has two front covers (in the 1993 Vintage edition, featuring a blue quilt for Jack's story and a pink flipside for Brenda's), with the narratives progressing so that the chronologically

simultaneous endings of each book converge toward the middle of the volume. There is no sense that one novel comes first and the other second, and in fact when my sister read the volume, she began with Brenda's story, not Jack's. This reading order, which contradicts the publication order of the novels, may be encouraged by the fact that the ISBN code and price, normally on the back cover of a book, can be found at the bottom of the cover that introduces "The Husband's Story." (Roy, 72)

In a 2013 edition published by Open Road Integrated Media, to which I will refer in order to eliminate confusion about page numbers, a subtitle was added (*Two Novels in One About a Marriage in Transition*), and "The Wife's Story" appears first despite having been published second. When read together, the stories and their protagonists comment on and interlock with each other, producing intertextual commentary that often privileges Brenda's insight on Jack while rendering ironic Jack's occasionally condescending presumptions about Brenda.

Reflecting changes in the era's working status for white middle-class women, Shields has Brenda spend most of the novel away in a city commonly referred to as the birthplace of American freedom, Philadelphia. Repeatedly on the move in this symbolic setting, Brenda gains confidence as a professionally successful artist, temporarily liberated, as it were, from the home and family that have come to define her. In the husband's half of the story, Jack tries to nurture intimate connections with his children, his parents, and a male friend while occasionally working on a book in his professional guise as a historian. Throughout Brenda's account, she feels for the most part exhilarated while away from home, if also uncertain about just how far to take her burgeoning artistic identity. Although Jack is the more privileged and unencumbered of the two, the feeling he exhibits most often is anxiety, a feeling that in turn inspires restorative nostalgia in him in both domestic and professional terms. Jack's anxiety is brought about not only by his potential emasculation in the domestic sphere but also by the apparent professional competition of a new book on his own research topic, written by a woman and former lover, as well as by challenges to his patronizing conceptions of women, including Brenda.

As a critique of unwittingly empowered status in terms of race and gender, Jack's story reflects an observation that Shields once offered in an interview: "I do not believe that men wake up every morning and think: How can I oppress women today? They are as caught up as we are in our assigned roles—but they have power and we don't."[5] Indeed, a thematic concern of *Happenstance* is the exposure and analysis of such hegemonic power in terms of masculinity and, to a more subsumed degree, of race as well. As Coral Ann Howells writes more broadly, Shields's fiction often "transforms large public concerns about identity into personal terms," thereby suggesting "that identity is both unstable and relational..."[6] In regard to racial whiteness, and in terms that apply to masculinity as well, Howells adds, Shields "deconstructs whiteness as a category through her scrutiny of the process of identity formation based on family background and inheritance, class, education and profession, age..."[7]

Although Jack spends most of his half of *Happenstance* at home, his thoughts and feelings are largely about his professional role. As a white male academic historian struggling to write a book about what he continually terms "Indian trading practices," Jack offers ruminations that reveal his commitments to a conventional American—that is, white patriarchal—conception of American history and of his role as a historian. Shields ultimately figures the arc of Jack's internal drama as less that of movement toward a better, fuller sense of self and more a question of whether Jack will continue on the path he seems to have found toward reconsidered, less dominant relations with others. A less dominant version of himself would acknowledge, incorporate, and practice more fully the kind of personal, nourishing connections with others that traditionally have been cast as a feminine concern, and thus omitted as well from the mode of reconstruction that white patriarchy posits as seemingly objective "history." Throughout his story, Jack's thoughts, feelings, and behavior often reflect a nostalgic longing for times when white men supposedly functioned as independent individuals who relied little on the assistance of others. Shields expresses hope for change by depicting Jack as open at times to new conceptions of others and of himself in relation to them, and by depicting him also as occasionally self-aware of, and at times even skeptical about, his adherence to what amount to the foundations of domineering white masculinity. Although both Jack and Brenda are by and large conventional middle-class white Americans committed to the mores of their era, the "transition" that their marriage undergoes moves toward a positive shift in gendered power relations, in part because of Brenda's newfound confidence in embracing and acting upon a communal conception of the past and also because of Jack's apparent willingness to move from his own white supremacist, phallocentric framework toward greater acceptance of a merging of the domestic and professional spheres.

For white American men, the restorative nostalgic impulse often arises as a conception of earlier, seemingly open space, and that which Jack seeks to restore within such space is ultimately a sense of unencumbered mobility. Shields repeatedly depicts Jack evincing what geographers Owen J. Dwyer and John Paul Jones III identify as a "white socio-spatial epistemology," a largely unwitting conception of geographical space that correlates with largely "masculinist and colonial spatiality."[8] As Dwyer and Jones add, "places are far from neutral or empty containers. Rather, they can be charged with white [and masculine] supremacy, and are co-constitutive in [their] production."[9] The white male imagination commonly objectifies women and ethnoracial others within such imagined space, figuring them instrumentally in terms both of exploitability and, ironically enough, of contradistinction to their supposedly independent selves. Shields contrasts the fantasized independence of this idealized white-male figure performing in seemingly open territory with, in Svetlana Boym's terms, Brenda's reflective conceptions of the past, a communal perspective that recognizes and embraces interdependency. This recognition is missing perhaps most representatively in Jack's isolated research focus on indigenous peoples, a topic in which he actually has little personal stake and genuine interest. *Happenstance* effectively critiques a common mode of white American masculinity by suggesting that a professional historian like Jack could regain his professional passion if he were to see himself as a direct descendent and inheritor of those who subjugated and decimated Native Americans. What partly hinders Jack from such a healing understanding of abusive interaction is his common white male conception of aggressive action in imagined geographical space, space that he casts nostalgically, and alternately, as both empty and selectively populated. On the other hand, Brenda gradually gains confidence in a communal, reflectively nostalgic conception of the past that the novel portrays positively, in part by having her stride confidently through the effectively appropriated space of a Philadelphia. As Beckman-Long writes, quoting Shields, "Her novels intentionally contain 'the lives of women whose stories [have] more to do with the texture of ordinary life and the spirit of community than with personal battles, goals, and prizes' of a masculine-dominated literary tradition."[10] By counterposing Brenda's more personally collective memories and her sense of history in general with Jack's more abstract and appropriative conception, Shields reveals how the latter is grounded in a subsumed reactionary nationalism, with certain feelings and perceptions arising in response to identity-challenging efforts towards egalitarianism. As Shields demonstrates with her characterization of Jack, a common white male response to such challenges is to seek restoration of white masculine prerogatives. Of particular interest to Shields in this novel are sociohistorically resonant conceptions of open yet selectively populated geographical space and the relative freedom that white men have to move within such spaces with relatively unencumbered and self-serving agency.

An Unwittingly White Male Historian

At one point, Jack pauses to assess his current circumstances, including the question of whether he is "happy": "Happy? Happiness? Happiness is relative, Jack was ready to say (with an agreeable shrug); within the framework of relativity, he is a happy, or at least fortunate, man. Pure happenstance has made him into a man without serious impairment or unspeakable losses."[11] In ways that render the novel's title ironic in Jack's case (and less so in Brenda's), "pure happenstance" is not all that has led to this middle-class white man's happiness. Having been raised, as Brenda also was, in decidedly working-class circumstances, Jack now considers himself very fortunate to have reached a state of ease and material success that would likely be the envy of men who work in "gangs tearing up the streets" or otherwise perform physical labor all day, as his father did while working as a postal clerk (*H*, 278). Jack reflects that he owns his own home (instead of registering that he and Brenda occupy it together), "which was now valued at an astronomical eighty thousand dollars," and also that he holds what amounts to a sinecure at "the Great Lakes Research Institute, the Chicago branch" (*H*, 278). What he does not consciously acknowledge is that these are comforts that a non-white, non-male person would have found far more difficult to attain. While pondering his happiness, Jack goes on to take stock of his other bits of apparent luck (including loving parents, nuclear family members, and "one good friend, Bernie Koltz"), omitting again the further enabling benefits of being white and male. Although Jack does not attribute his advantages solely to his own hard work, he nevertheless fails to situate himself in sociohistorical terms. This failure is no small oversight, particularly for a man who prides himself on having found a suitable profession because he supposedly possesses an innate "sense of history" and who openly derides his wife for lacking one (*H*, 169). In these terms, both his happiness and his identity as a historian—particularly as one who writes about "Indian trading practices" in isolation from European contact with and abuse of indigenous peoples—are rendered suspect. As Sara Ahmed points out, "So much happiness is premised on, and promised by, the concealment of suffering, the freedom to look away from what compromises one's happiness."[12] The happiness felt by a man like Jack, as well as his attribution of it to "pure happenstance," would be threatened by a genuine accounting of the hierarchical connections between people like oneself and others. As with other white American men, Jack's inherited legacy includes a non-relational social epistemology that omits such connections in historical memory, replacing them with romanticized, literally self-serving fantasy.

Shields nevertheless allows for the reformability of unwittingly privileged men, in this case by depicting a protagonist who realizes at times that he is performing a set of scripted roles and that the power and prerogatives of those roles are coming under fire in a "new era" (*H*, 504). Jack's roles are usually segregated between the stage sets of work and home, but both take place within ideologically resonant geographical contexts. When Jack reflects on the masculine names of streets in his neighborhood—including North Franklin, Emerson, Horace Mann, Oliver Wendell Holmes, and James Madison—he sees in them "a kind of radiant idealism" (*H*, 287). When two more names arise—those of roadways that he uses for commuting, Shakespeare Boulevard and the Eisenhower Expressway—he thinks of his working day as being "sandwiched between the poetic and the pragmatic, as he had five or six times observed at parties..." (*H*, 287). Shields's portrait of Jack becomes more pointedly representative when he goes on to recall that "he loathed himself" for making this remark, a feeling that expresses awareness of the artificiality of the role he's playing as a contented middle-class denizen of these streets. However, Jack's discontent arises from an awareness of only one categorical sector of his identity, his class-based positionality as a person of working-class origins who has moved into middle-class comfort. What Jack fails to register is the exclusionary, power-entrenching white masculinity of the roll call announced by his neighborhood's street names, a homogeneity that from other perspectives would convey racism and sexism rather than "radiant idealism."

Perceiving such a list as comforting or inspiring arises from a sociohistorically positioned perspective that empowers itself in terms of race and gender at the same time that it enshrines that which it selects to perceive as disembodied, objective fact. Those born and raised into oblivion about how they are ensconced in this perspective fail to see not only its raced and gendered specificity but also its self-constituting historical underpinnings. As Trinh T. Minh-ha writes of the more explicit and similarly self-centering colonialist worldview,

> One can date it back to the immemorial days when a group of mighty men attributed to itself a central, dominating position vis-à-vis other groups; overvalued its particularities and achievements; adopted a projective attitude towards those it classified among the out-groups; and wrapped itself in its own thinking, interpreting the out-group through the in-group mode of reasoning while claiming to speak the minds of both the in-group and the out-group.[13]

In these terms, Jack can more readily critique the mores of his current middle-class in-group because he has been raised into the perspective of the working-class out-group. Yet, given his membership in both gendered and raced in-groups, Jack does not see his neighborhood's hagiographic street signs as markers of a nostalgic mindset regarding American history, a mindset that sees "a kind of radiant idealism" in a list of men rendered renowned by a particular self-constituting ideological tradition. As a white American male historian of indigeneity, he also registers no ambivalence about his appointed task of "speak[ing] the minds" of a decimated, largely banished out-group.[14] Such a list of renowned men can radiate ideally only when perceived in a way that isolates them from the abuse of racialized and gendered others who helped to construct their ideological eminence. As with other protagonists under consideration in this study, Jack has his own particular ways of perceiving the push for equality as oppression of people like himself. He pays closer attention to certain details in his residential neighborhood because he is home this week in a domestic role while his wife is away in a professional one. Jack is ostensibly okay with his wife's increased assertion of professional autonomy, yet this unwelcome role switch inspires his attention to the reassuring street names, an unconscious emotional attachment to a national past that registers in a specifically self-bolstering white male way.

That Jack also sees his professional life in fraught, anxious terms inflected by race and gender is suggested more fully in Shields's depiction of his feelings about his stalled book project, feelings that continually intrude on his domestic life, inflecting his interactions with various family members. Jack's authorial malaise takes the ostensible form of a simple "loss of faith" in this research, but Shields gradually connects his negativity about the book to other emotions, all of which arise from new expectations of Jack as both worker and family man and, all of which also circle back to historical realities that are papered over by the nostalgic vision of past relations between white men and their others that Jack unconsciously seeks to restore. Early in his story, Jack's desire for a more stable ontological grounding inspires a somewhat wistful effort to recover the past in more personal terms when he visits his parents. As Jack prepares to leave his own home for the visit, the "whiteness" of a new snowfall pleases him because such a "neat covering" simplifies and levels the neighborhood's details to "mere surface" (*H*, 372–73). The snow also has for Jack a "secret absolving power," although he has no concrete idea of why he or people in his neighborhood should seek absolution. Again, though, Shields depicts Jack in this scene not as a man entirely enveloped by white masculine ideology but rather as one who is thoughtfully self-reflective at times, registering in personal terms some of the people and settings that challenge his preconceptions, even as he functions within the habitual mode of his inculcated, empowered perspective.

As he sits with his parents and struggles for something to chat about, Jack asks his mother whether she remembers Harriet Post, a former lover of his and author of the imminent, apparently competing book. Jack fears that Harriet's book will pre-empt his own, and he seeks to assuage the anxiety wrought by this challenge to his masculine professional identity by sharing the bad news with his parents. However, his mother doesn't remember Harriet, and his attempts to broach the topic go nowhere, so he resumes the usual containment of his feelings. In this scene, Shields depicts, across three generations, another common, historically inflected white male tendency, the broader phenomenon of bodily containment. As I explained more fully in the previous chapter, the history of white American masculine identity formation includes a general, subordination-justifying conception of others as more bodily, as less able to control (and thus more controlled by) their own bodily and emotional functions; the obverse is encouragement of excessive personal control by white men. Accordingly, Jack's containment of his anxieties while with his parents about both his stalled writing project and the recent threat of another competing book is encapsulated in the title of a self-help book that Jack's father has been reading: "*You Are Your Own Keeper*" (*H*, 380). Jack's father, who fills his time in retirement with many such self-disciplining volumes, reports that the book's primary suggested method toward self-improvement is to write down a hoped-for change in behavior and then "hide it away" (*H*, 380). Jack disapproves of self-help books, ironically dismissing them as "a new American form of masochism, the new perversion of the old American dream" (*H*, 382). Although this professional historian places such readings, which often recommend ways of disciplining oneself and one's body and emotions, within a sociohistorical continuum, he neglects recognition of his own psychological and emotional enactment of particularly white male modes of containment, which again reflects the common failure of those like Jack to recognize their membership in the in-group of white men. Jack's fealty to the impractical and destructive dream of ideally contained white male embodiment is echoed not only by his father but also by his son Rob, who has taken up his own form of corporeal discipline (*H*, 378). As if in training for an adult life partly defined as white and male by personal containment, Rob has begun fasting, his reported reason being merely "to see if I can do it" (*H*, 487).

The trope of fasting soon arises again, as Jack and his father stroll through the suggestively named Columbus Park. This space is redolent for Jack with childhood memories, as he recalls childhood adventures with his current friend Bernie in this "microcosmic wilderness.... A chunk of wilderness at the city's edge, a wilderness the size of a handkerchief" (*H*, 388). Jack is conscious of the constructed nature of this "wilderness" but far less so of the conceptual framework through which he views and remembers it. While walking, he and his father meet a group of "hunger strikers" protesting the incarceration of dissident Russian scientists, whom Jack perceives, along with the members of other "post-Vietnam, post-Watergate demonstrations," as futile and bedraggled (*H*, 387). Having evinced vaguely liberal political inclinations, Jack feels he has little at stake personally in the issue, so he sees no reason to join in. Shields then depicts Jack's memory of finding himself in the midst of a violent protest during the 1960s and of receding at the time with the help of a "cool voice in his head" into a conception of public protests as a mere "phenomenon of the times," rather than as justified responses to inequity. In such moments, Jack reflects a conventional white American male ideological perspective, an assumed stance of detached, objective observation and a stance that he conceives of himself as having developed in a supposedly disembodied, non-situated way. Dwyer and Jones identify such a paradoxically non-positioned positionality in terms of ocularcentrism, as a "visionary point" occupied by "the omniscient white (male) subject, secure in his position as a surveyor of the social terrain."[15] Earlier, Shields symbolically represents the detached, incorporeal quality of such a perspective when Jack thinks of the "blinding" lighting at the institute in which he works, "a universalized whiteness that seemed to have no source" (*H*, 280). In their hegemonic forms, both whiteness and masculinity function this way, as a non-relational epistemology that discourages those who embody it from perceiving their own perspective *as* a particular, group-bound, and socially influenced perspective.

Shields devotes a lengthy scene to the artificial urban wilderness of Columbus Park, and Jack's casual disregard for the significance of its name is a clue to historical connections of other sorts that he fails to make consciously, even as historical events and contentious group-bound interactions such as those suggested by the park's name heavily influence his geospatial perspective. This scene emblematizes how, although he is a professional historian, Jack's sense of the past proves more instrumentalizing than historically accurate and, in response to threats to his white-male privilege, ultimately restorative within a lurking national context. As Svetlana Boym writes, "restorative nostalgia puts the emphasis on *nostos* [that is, on "home"] and proposes to rebuild the lost home and patch up the memory gaps."[16] Ultimately, Boym also notes, "This kind of nostalgia characterizes national and nationalist revivals all over the world, which engage in the anti-modern myth-making of history by means of a return to national symbols and myths."[17] At one point, Jack's perception reflects the influence of this sociohistorical context when he briefly notices the "rankness" of a clearly constructed stream's urine-like water but then focuses instead on how the air in his favorite part of the park has "a scrubbed, Wisconsin-like scent of pine pitch and earth-rot. Jack never came here without the phrase 'sylvan glade' popping into his head" (*H*, 389).[18] Despite Jack's awareness of the park's artificiality, this plot of constructed nature also evokes nostalgic memories of playing there as a child, when he and Bernie had "called it simply 'the woods'" (*H*, 389). The national "myth" that adds emotional resonance to Jack's fond memories of this place is that of certain sectors in American geography that have been set aside as "nature" or "wilderness." These places then serve as proving grounds for properly ambitious white men to act out their unfettered ideal selves.

As Jason E. Pierce points out in *Making the White Man's West: Whiteness and the Creation of the American West*, a geographically situated sense of identity has always informed masculine European (and then European American) experience in what has become the United States, including an ontological connection to parts that had yet to be conquered. Pierce notes that "From the moment the Pilgrims landed at Plymouth Rock, the frontier, just out there to the west, seemed redolent with possibility."[19] He goes on to explain that as the colonies turned into an expanding nation, land to the west became "the west," as well as an idealized backdrop for a specifically white American mode of masculinity: "if one possessed strength, intellect, fearlessness, and individualism (all soon considered 'American' traits), then one could be successful in this New World [, which] fostered characteristics that forged Englishmen into Americans."[20] Jack evinces the influence of a national inheritance of nostalgically conceived wilderness when he recalls that, as boys, he and Bernie had snuck past a No Trespassing sign to enter what seemed, to their budding white male selves, like a sanctuary: "Jack felt about the woods not so much a sense of possession, but a feeling of refuge, of safe enclosure—hardly anyone else was there…" (H, 389). They performed media-influenced white-male roles by building dams and playing war games, in which "recognition, gratitude, and fierce manly modesty all had a part" (H, 390). The fact that the park had been closed had seemed like just that, a fact, "and required no explanation—it was like the dark forbidden forests encountered in certain old folk tales, phenomena unassailable at the level of logic" (H, 391). Jack asks his father why the park had been closed and learns it was due to fears of spreading polio and furthermore that it had been closed for "only" a month or two. Significantly, Jack feels astonished that it wasn't longer, because the park had seemed such a private world, and the forbidden space's "aura of prohibition" had increased his sense not only of excitement but also of the place as in a sense belonging to him and Bernie. Jack also generally remembers feeling a sense of freedom, a feeling provided to two thrill-seeking white boys by the park's enclosed yet open sense of nature. As an adult, Jack consciously recognizes the park's natural-ness as an artificial construct amidst a large, densely populated, and racialized city, facts which Shields carefully brings to mind by having Jack and his father encounter there "three small boys, skinny, black… dangling fishing lines" into a stream that Jack's father describes as a "sewer" (H, 393). Nevertheless, the length Shields devotes to this scene and the strength of Jack's feelings while revisiting it suggest how a flagging white American masculine sense of self can be bolstered by nostalgic conceptions of seemingly untrammeled territory.

Jack's fond conception of this park is a particularly white male one, forged in an abusive history that his current social order discourages him from registering. Jack recalls conceiving of the place as an enabling setting for war games and other adventures with another white boy, identity-forming play that would not have felt right, and might not have happened at all, with black boys participating, given the segregation of the actual military services during World War II and that of the televised and cinematic versions that boys like Jack and Bernie would have likely imitated. "The woods" felt separate and empty, yet possessed as well, for two boys who were in effect practicing their identities on a stage set figured as "woods" by conceiving of it as empty "nature" and thus as an appropriate setting for the enactment of an ultimately possessive white masculinity. Jack's astonishment as an adult that the park had been closed so briefly reflects how large the time in which he and Bernie had played there has come to loom in his imagination, but also in his self-fashioning. Reflecting on this failure of memory, Jack decides that "History was no more in the end than what we wanted it to be" (*H*, 393). Yet a final irony remains in his disregard for the name of the park. While Christopher Columbus had yet to signify during the 1970s in any significantly popular sense as notorious for his treatment of indigenous people, Jack fails to conceive of "the woods" not only as a space formerly occupied, quite literally, by such people as those whom he studies professionally, but also as a place where "civilized" men who resembled himself interacted with and fashioned themselves in superior contradistinction to such people. In sum, these illusions arise from his sociohistorically inculcated tendency to conceive of this space nostalgically and from current challenges to his white masculine status.

Again, memories of less troubled times in this park feel restorative for him at this point because he is feeling emasculated by a professional threat, that of Harriet Post's apparently imminent and competing book, and by his suddenly increased domestic responsibilities. Jack's omission of any actual, vanquished indigenous presence from this personally resonant and suggestively named space is, of course, particularly striking in light of his current research subject, "Indian trading practices." However, although Jack does tell his father about the other impending book on the same topic, he does not correct his father's assumption that its author is a man; the implication is that the author's status as a woman would deflate even further his father's proud conception of him as an admirable son (*H*, 397). Shields casts this reflex on Jack's part in gendered terms, and, as I will explain, Jack's approach to the topic of his book points to his imbrication as well in a possessive, geographically oriented white supremacist mindset. That Jack does not seriously consider contacting Harriet Post to ask about her book until nearly the end of his story and that he ends up talking to her husband instead function to erase this other historian, a silencing of a women's voice and presence within an intellectual, professional realm—that of scholarly "history"—that Jack regards, perhaps unconsciously, as competitive masculine territory.[21]

Jack's masculine sense of individual entitlement also appears when readers learn that his earlier area of historical research had been "the explorer LaSalle and his voyages of discovery" (*H*, 61). Having written a graduate thesis on the French "explorer" René-Robert Cavelier, Sieur de La Salle, Jack dropped this research topic because "There was no point in going on with LaSalle; LaSalle had been done down to the last hangnail; it was time for Jack to move into a new and potentially rewarding area" (*H*, 433).[22] Jack then switched to "Indian trading practices," despite his lack of expertise, because the director of Jack's institute had told him that the topic was "open, available…. No real work had been done in the area… it was virgin territory" (*H*, 432). In such moments, Shields wryly casts Jack in the same mode as that in which "explorers" like La Salle actually operated. That is, she depicts him as, in Shannon Sullivan's terms, an ontologically expansive white man, one who feels both a right and an identity-bound duty to enter and "explore" territories that seem empty because the presence within them of other people has been deemed unworthy of respectful acknowledgement.[23] Just as the self-serving and often abusive quality of La Salle's incursions into indigenous territory belies the nostalgic conception of him as an explorer, so is Jack's ostensibly inquiring journey into American Indian history self-serving and ultimately abusive as well in its inattention to European and indigenous interaction. Despite his ignorance, Jack decides to write about "Indian trading practices" in order to make his own mark, to stake out his own territory in a supposedly empty field. His earlier motivation for writing about La Salle had been much the same. As Brenda recalls, he "admitted that he had chosen the topic because a professor had suggested it. Not much work had been done on LaSalle's last journey; it was open territory, so to speak" (*H*, 149). In sum, as Shields underlines with "so to speak," the conceptions of historical figures and events, and of the land on which they took place as "open," are just that, socially constructed conceptions that justify unfettered white male mobility and conquest.

In *The Myth of Emptiness and the New American Literature of Place*, Wendy Harding points out that such geospatial conceptions within the United States context have a distinctly self-serving yet ontologically relational lineage: "In the American and more generally in the colonial context, what was beyond the settlements was seen as 'empty.'... The land became ipso facto available, even urgently calling for human presence."[24] As a result, Harding adds, "land designated as empty became inscribable; it demanded to be materially claimed and conceptually informed."[25] In *Happenstance*, Shields draws a parallel between the conception of land occupied by indigenous peoples as empty "open territory"—as held by a Frenchman and other Europeans who claimed vast swaths of it for empire and no doubt for their own renown as well—and Jack's similarly appropriative conception of open, conquerable intellectual territory. His haphazard notion of research areas as especially appealing merely because they seem conceptually empty, and thus as well open territory for his own relationally defined male action and conquest, renders Jack an unwittingly white male historian in his approach to geographical space, other peoples, and historical fact.

As Jack pauses at one point to ponder his own "historical sense," Shields's portrait of this historian's specifically situated and habitually enacted perspective approaches parody when Jack attributes what he perceives as Brenda's supposed lack of any "sense of history" to her having "never had a father" (by which he means her never having known who her biological father was) (*H*, 429). However, as Brenda's own interior drama demonstrates, she does evince and gain confidence in her own strong sense of history a "reflective" form in Boym's terms that both acknowledges and embraces nostalgia while serving as well as a countering and more explicitly gendered perspective to Jack's unwittingly masculine one. Jack's patronizing conception of himself as suited to the profession of historian because of his "historical sense" takes the form of a claim that, nearly anywhere he goes, he visualizes layers of time in which people and even geological formations preceded the present moment in that space. Although Jack claims an ever-alert sense of history in broad terms of geographical space and geological time, his sense of these vectors is inextricably and ironically connected to himself as a white American man because, as I will explain, he conceives of historical pasts and settings primarily in order to imagine himself acting in relation to them. As Shields repeatedly demonstrates via Jack's conceptions and usages of history, idealized white American masculinity has been forged in direct relation to conceptions not only of other people but also of a romanticized original national landscape, which is generally conceived of as devoid of other people, except when they serve instrumentally as recipients of agential white male action. Shields's conjoining of Jack's conception of historical time with geographical space marks its crucial distinction from Brenda's sense of history as communal—as consisting of "a chain of stories" that are "as tentacled as the most exotic vegetation, reaching back impossibly far" (*H*, 170–71), a valorizing of human connections and memories that, while also nostalgic, can nourish understanding and appreciation of the importance of others in one's current life.

COMMUNALLY COGNIZANT REFLECTIVE NOSTALGIA

In the half of *Happenstance* that depicts Brenda Bowman's attendance at a quilting convention in Philadelphia, Shields again provides a deeply internalized account within a geographically resonant setting, including descriptions of Brenda's excitement regarding her artistic talent and her growing entrepreneurial opportunities, as well as her contemplative reflections on her marriage and various people back home. Brenda also grapples with the possibilities and implications brought about by another man's attention and the absence of her assigned hotel roommate, a woman who is apparently having a sexual liaison of her own. Brenda feels contentedly married to Jack, so extramarital possibilities remain secondary to her professional interests and to her thoughts about them as they relate to her own transitional state. Reflecting the era's increasing opportunities for middle-class white women, Brenda embraces her budding professional self with increasing confidence. The title of *Happenstance* evokes in Brenda's case as well not just randomness but also the concept of happiness, as her sense of her domestic life remains consistently positive. However, Brenda's new confidence and geographical distance also allow a sharper appraisal of Jack, including what readers come to see as the ironic condescension of his declaration that she lacks "a sense of history." As with her other female protagonists, particularly in the Pulitzer Prize–winning *The Stone Diaries* (1993), Shields depicts in Brenda a purposeful, more positive version of memory. Although Brenda's sense of history, like Jack's, is ultimately nostalgic, her opposing sense is both more reflective and more realistic, to the extent that it continuously incorporates currently living people in a conception of the past that is both relationally aware and consciously connected to the present.

Shields's later novel *The Stone Diaries* merits extended consideration here since it presents more elaborately this form of restorative memory—an awareness of reconstruction of the past as necessarily subjective and selective as well as relational. *The Stone Diaries* ostensibly relates the life story of Daisy Goodwill, a woman born in Manitoba, and an emigrant to the United States and resident of several places there, the last being a retirement home in Florida. Daisy is often the first-person narrator, but rather than tell her story in a straightforwardly linear fashion, Shields provides the perspectives of over a dozen other characters in a widely hailed postmodern mode that exposes the flawed nature of both memory and reportorial narrative, while also asserting the restorative value of empathetic imagination.[26] As an elder Daisy attempts to figure out just who she is, she discerns the performed versions of herself expected by various people she has known. As Daisy does so, the novel's temporally ranging and often chaotic structure renders personal memory and collective history themselves thematic subjects, especially as they intertwine, as well as how people tend to use them. As in *Happenstance*, Shields emphasizes the contingency of any attempt to capture the past upon the limited perspective of the beholder/constructor, particularly with Daisy's habit of trying to account for her life by continually reflecting not only on her own past but also on her connections to others and how those connections inextricably form the story of herself. As a child rendered bedbound for weeks by measles, Daisy "understood that if she was going to hold on to her life at all, she would have to rescue it by a primary act of imagination, supplementing, modifying, summoning up the necessary connections, conjuring the pastoral or heroic or whatever... getting the details wrong occasionally, exaggerating or lying outright, inventing letters or conversations of impossible gentility, or casting conjecture in a pretty light."[27] Appearing early in the novel, this description of Daisy's mental methods is both a warning of sorts about the difficulty readers will sometimes have in distinguishing between apparent "truth" and fancy in Daisy's accounting of herself as well as a more general reminder about how inevitably flawed and at times even fictional most acts of memory and historical construction are. However, the novel goes on to suggest that, although memory is often flawed, it can, if performed in certain reflective ways, be useful for better perceiving human relations in the present and for working more realistically toward better futures.

By way of underscoring her pervasive thematic point that the past shapes and lives in the present, Shields meticulously depicts men and women in both novels who construct and use conceptions of the past in differently gendered terms. The contrast between masculine and feminine modes of memory and historical construction in both *The Stone Diaries* and *Happenstance* depicts the former as injuriously solipsistic, self-serving, and domineering and the latter as preferable in ways that amount to the opposite. Early in Daisy's story, as she imagines her birth, which caused her mother's death, she expresses a metanarrative lack of confidence in her own memorial method: "Everyone in the tiny, crowded, hot, and evil-smelling kitchen... has been invited to participate in a moment of history. History indeed! As though this paltry slice of time deserves such a name. Accident, not history, has called us together, and what an assembly we make" (*SD*, 28). However, even while reconstructing the scene of her very own beginning, Daisy is already recalling the past in terms of the others around her who continually influence and form her identity, as well as asserting the value of doing so. Throughout her accounting of her own life, interwoven with the perspectives on it of many others, Daisy acknowledges that she "has a little trouble with getting things straight; with the truth, that is... she imposes the voice of the future on the events of the past, causing all manner of wavy distortion" (*SD*, 109). Nevertheless, by the end of the novel, Daisy's confidence in her own self-accounting method has solidified, as expressed by a series of questions that read as rhetorical since her method itself has answered them: "And the question arises: what is the story of a life? A chronicle of fact or a skillfully wrought impression? The bringing together of what she fears? Or the adding up of what has been off-handedly revealed, those tiny allotted increments of knowledge?" (*SD*, 252). As suggested by the next two sentences, an accurate story of a life is the story not of individualized efforts nor of inherent personality, but rather of the necessary, shaping connections one has with the witnessing presences of others: "She needs a quiet place in which to think about this immensity. And she needs someone—anyone—to listen" (*SD*, 252). In Elizabeth Reimer's study of biographical narrative in Shields's fiction, she identifies a repeated thematic point that, in most cases, "people's lives, especially women's, become diminished or lost in representations of them" (*SD*, 254). What the characterizations of both Daisy and Brenda affirm instead is "an appetite for connection to the whole mysterious rhizome of history, a shared history that draws in others" (*SD*, 255). As opposed

to Jack Bowman's distanced, non-collaborative, and personally instrumentalizing approach to the past, affirmative connection to and understanding of known others, however subjectively conceived, emerges as
paramount.

Shields depicts both Brenda and Daisy as women who reflect on their
own pasts and presents while actively resisting masculine historical methods. While thinking about a younger version of herself, Daisy recalls that
"Men, it seemed to me in those days, were uniquely honored by the stories that erupted in their lives, whereas women were more likely smoth-
ered by theirs. Why?... Why should men be allowed to strut under the
privilege of their life adventures, wearing them like a breastful of medals,
while women went all gray and silent beneath the weight of theirs?" (*SD*,
88). The narrative's implication is that men have been accorded recognition of their efforts, and women generally not, because women's stories
have gone largely ignored by men, the creators of the dominant, society-
forming discourse. In a summary of a critical consensus regarding *The
Stone Diaries*, Coral Ann Howells writes that "the disrupted narrative
with its flow of undifferentiated voices represents Daisy as a decentered
subject whose identity is invented for her by others—both within the
text and by the readers as well."[28] Although this common interpretation often constitutes criticism of the novel's characterization, as if the
absence of Daisy at many points in her own story suggests a lack of effective characterization and feminine agency, this absence conveys a profound point: "through the opinions of others in the social and cultural
discourses surrounding us, our identity is constructed as intelligible and
therefore representable."[29] Another answer for Shields then to Daisy's
question, as Jack Bowman's blinkered and self-serving conceptions
of memory as "history" especially demonstrate, is that men have been
"allowed to strut under the privilege of their life adventures" because
their patriarchal social order valorizes and falsely represents in an individualizing manner masculine identities, action, and achievement, while
omitting or otherwise failing to account for not only the life stories and
contributions of women but also for the contributions of all—men and
women—to what is actually and always communal interaction, including
the constitution of individual identities (*SD*, 88).

This emphasis on the greater value of a communal conception of the past, however admittedly nostalgic, often arises as well in
Brenda Bowman's story. After temporarily losing her new jacket to
a missing hotel roommate, Brenda dons her quilting contest entry like

a cloak in preparation for a newspaper interview. She then strides down a Philadelphia street with a newly felt confidence in herself, effectively appropriating the urban space commonly known as the City of Brotherly Love for a feminist self-staging in terms of the city's other renowned associations, freedom and independence. However, instead of continuing to revel in her own growing success and renown, Brenda reflects with sympathetic curiosity on the old-fashioned coat worn year round by a former neighbor, who also walked with unusual (for a woman of the time and place) self-possession. The deceased Miss Anderson, branded a witch by local children, was known for spreading hollyhock seeds in the neighborhood:

> [T]his afternoon the thought of Miss Anderson and her vigorous, purposeful back-alley striding spoke to that part of Brenda that she kept unexamined. Shouldn't she have tried to get to know her a little better when she was alive? The black coat and the eccentric preoccupation with hollyhock propagation had seemed, then, to make her impenetrable and unknowable, and her age had made her seem, to a younger Brenda, not worth bothering about. But it might have been interesting, and perhaps even profitable, to discover what mysterious childhood shaping had determined that Miss Anderson would be old, relentless, and, in some strange way, content. Something historical had predetermined that straightforward gait. Something historical, too, had touched her mildly with madness. Everyone had a history, after all, everyone—even Miss Anderson... (*H*, 168)

Having pondered this woman in relation to history, Brenda reflects on Jack and on his condescending claim that she has no "sense of history": "What he meant, of course, was that she lacked his own vivid pictorial sense of a world in which he had never lived. It was true enough, she had to agree" (*H*, 169). Here, Shields emphasizes the hegemonic power of ideology to penetrate the psyche, and thus to degrade the self-conception, of the subjugated. An implication is that Brenda has not examined this part of herself that reflects sympathetically and contextually on others she has known because, as a woman, she has been discouraged from having confidence in her ability to think historically. However, emboldened by her recent artistic success and independence, Brenda decides that she does actually have a sense of history; it's just a different one: "Jack was a romantic, and condemned to the broad stroke; his historical happenings were purpled with a flood of anonymous blood.... What he didn't seem to grasp (as Brenda did) was that history was no more than a chain of stories, the stories that happen to everyone and that, in time, came to form the patterns of entire lives, her own included" (*H*, 170). In contrast to Jack's conception of their neighborhood, which focuses on inanimate objects and eminent, long-dead men memorialized in street names, Brenda focuses on an actual person whom she encountered there. Her memory of Miss Anderson includes not only that of a largely forgotten woman and her actions but also recognition that larger "historical" forces had surely influenced her, and thus her seed-spreading actions, and that she in turn influenced in lasting ways the people with whom she came in contact (as symbolized by the perennially growing hollyhocks). This conception of history as grounded in individuals, shaped by context, and admittedly yet necessarily consisting of partially imagined stories contrasts positively with Jack's distanced, supposedly objective, and ultimately appropriative approach. Brenda's approach also recognizes that the past lives in and informs any individual's present, comprising a "true and ongoing story that pressed as tightly as clothing against the skin" (*H*, 173).

Brenda also has a more living, relational connection to the past in another "sense." As a daughter of an immigrant mother, Brenda has retained her facility with the Polish language—a direct ancestral connection that Jack has lost amidst his family's ascent into more full-fledged American whiteness—and with the French that she learned in high school. She remembers having listened to and spoken the latter for both of them while traveling in France, where she had felt that Jack "was being cheated and unfairly humbled. The flatness of [his] English words broke her heart, and particularly since Jack seemed innocent of any loss" (*H*, 169). Jack's ignorance of something vivid and alive here that Brenda apprehends is, of course, ironic given his rather arrogant oblivion to the connections that she exercises to the living history conveyed by other languages. Brenda repeatedly displays, then, something that she instead credits Jack with, "a sense of personal connection with the past" (*H*, 170), which Jack supposedly has because he can readily imagine people and events conventionally deemed "historical" while she "couldn't even picture Simone de Beauvoir sitting in a particular café with her notebook open on a table..." (*H*, 170). Nostalgia is also figured positively for Brenda in terms of affirmative memories about actual people whom one cherishes, in part because she understands how essential other people are for building one's own story, and other stories, including embellished ones and even pure fantasy (*H*, 171–72). While Shields acknowledges that conventional "history" ultimately consists of stories as well, she depicts these more personal stories positively, and even as more accurate, in part because they emphasize the necessity of other people in the creation of the story of one's self. Thus, such stories counter the unmoored and domineering fantasy of white male hyper-individualization, as commonly conceived in terms of action against alternately blank or selectively populated geographical backdrops.

The past is remembered by Brenda as composed not only of stories with connections to currently living people but also, given their connection to the present, of stories that can have several endings. Shields emphasizes this rhizomatic and future-oriented form of remembrance when Brenda attends a conference session presented by the famed Mrs. Dorothea Thomas, the seventy-eight-year-old "Grandma Moses of quilters" and a maker of "story quilts" (*H*, 186–87). Mrs. Thomas (as Shields's narrator refers to her) begins with memories of making quilts as a girl, something that she did along with multiple generations of other girls and women. A contrasting reminder for readers of Jack as an excessively isolated, solipsistic historian appears in the remembered form of Mrs. Thomas's father, a quiet, friendless man: "I'd stop and think of my father out there in the barn, doing chores all by his lonesome—it got freezing out there..." (*H*, 187). Mrs. Thomas's renowned quilts consist of panels of images that visually retell stories of people she has known. As Brenda listens to Mrs. Thomas relate the personal stories depicted in various prize-winning quilts, she recalls several events from her own family's past. Her "sense of history" as connective and contextually cognizant arises again as she reflects that she and Jack have together built up a "private stock" of such stories, a "shared history" that helps to tell them who they are, as a couple and individually. After the presentation, Brenda talks with Mrs. Thomas, who says that she now regrets confining stories in her quilts to one ending: "The fact is, most stories have three or four endings, maybe even more," including what actually happened, what one wishes had happened, and what could have happened (*H*, 191). Brenda summarizes the latter as "The road not taken," a phrase she quickly attributes to Robert Frost. Mrs. Thomas seizes on the image as a perfect expression for what she's been trying to say, but she displays no interest in who actually said it, a further rejection of the singularly possessive approach to knowledge that often guides Jack's professional approach.

As Brenda's story closes, her brief platonic liaison with a geologist ends amiably, her quilt wins honorable mention, and her thoughts return more strongly homeward. Having consciously progressed artistically and professionally, she thinks more directly about Jack's work and his apparent relation to it. After acknowledging that she's never understood his profession and the apparently painful isolation that the act of writing "history" imposes on its practitioners, she demonstrates that she understands fully the source of Jack's lack of passion for his current research: "What she hasn't been able to say to Jack is that she finds the project bewildering in its purposelessness" (*H*, 218). Brenda also knows that Jack's heart is not in the project, and given the contrasting conception of historical reconstruction presented in her half of the novel, what the project lacks for Jack, at least as he conceives of it, is a personal and motivating connection to his topic. Indeed, a focus on La Salle, his earlier topic, could be conjoined with his current work, as the actual La Salle interacted extensively with American Indians. This is not to say that Shields suggests such a conjunction, but as an inheritor of the legacy bequeathed by such forerunners of American white male supremacy, a historian of the sort that Jack represents would have entirely personal connections to such a topic. As noted by John P. Bowes, a historian of European and First Nations contact, the very name of Jack's birthplace was founded in such interaction: "The name 'Chicago' dates back in history to René-Robert Cavelier, Sieur de La Salle's, use of '*checagou*' to describe a specific portage along Lake Michigan in a 1682 exploration report. His use of that term is most likely indebted to the Miami-Illinois name for the river, *šikaakwa siipiiwi*, which originated from the wild leeks that grew so abundantly on its banks."[30] Instead of working in such integrating terms, Jack's current research treats indigeneity in isolation from people like himself, in isolation, that is, from the founders and enactors of a collective white-male ideology that enables men like himself to occupy positions of relative comfort and ease amidst an ongoing, open-ended history. Alternatively, via the increasingly confident perspective of Brenda, Shields figures the past as something that could be used toward the future, a potential social order that is less limited and determinative, particularly for women.

DEHISTORICIZED LAND

As Jack's memories of childhood play in Columbus Park demonstrate, although the construction of hegemonic white masculinity has required binarized, countervailing conceptions of grouped and labeled others, such interactions have occurred in light of particular conceptions of physical space. The history of such conceptions lives in the present for white American men by evoking a national context, one in which idealized figures like themselves perform both as independent actors and as leaders, builders, and maintainers of a nation. As Katherine Hodgkin and Susannah Radstone write in a discussion of the connections of nationalism to history, "Nationalist memory describes a geography of belonging, an identity forged in a specified landscape, inseparable from it. To study memory in the context of the nation, then, is to engage very directly with the relations between individual and collective memory, between the subject and the state, between time and space..."[31] In these terms, Shields provides a moment of foreshadowing for what I will later read as this internal drama's climactic scene, when she depicts Jack's thoughts while commuting in his car. As he drives in his Dodge Aspen (the name of which is another evocation, this time in corporate terms, of nostalgically resonant natural spaces[32]), Jack deploys his supposedly special historical sense to imagine not just "layers and layers of time" but also himself, moving in relation to a backdrop consisting of intertwined conceptions of time and geographical space:

> Driving home from work, he was never entirely unconscious of the fact that he and the Aspen were skimming across the surface of a great alluvial basin; under the concrete of the expressway, just at the rim of consciousness, was the old glacial lake, Lack Chicago. For him, the lake was still there, would always be there, a sub-image that a thousand layers of concrete couldn't obliterate. He could, if he wanted to, keep going, driving straight through Elm Park, out into the country, past small country towns and the sad rural frosts of the Illinois farmland, following the path of the old glacier to its westernmost limit, populating the spaces as he went with overlapping generations. (H, 431–32)

Jack often conceives of historical time and geographical space in such ways, that is, primarily in order to conceive of himself in active relation to it. Significantly, especially for a historian of American Indians, this conception of "overlapping generations" imagines no particular indigenous presence. In what I will read as the climax of Jack's internal plot, he conceives of Chicago's snow-covered streets as even more of a blank space, yet also as a selectively populated one, primarily because he also sees the streets as a stage on which to enact a newly confident sense of himself.

In collective terms, such a relation to time and space serves to ease what amounts to a broader white masculine conscience because it includes conceptual erasure of exploitative white male interaction with raced and gendered others. In Jack's case, this erasure allows for the relief of morality-challenging guilt over the near literal and often intentional erasure of American Indians by European and white American men. In his recent memoir *Not from Here* (2015), Allan G. Johnson describes his own attempt to discern within himself habitual elements of the legacy of white American masculinity, particularly its repressed and denied relations to indigeneity. Johnson's highly self-conscious account was initially prompted by the death of his father, who, when asked by Johnson just where he would like his ashes spread, gave an answer that reflected a lack of felt attachment to any particular geographical location: "It makes no difference to me at all."[33] In response, and like many white American male literary characters, Johnson sets off on a westward journey, in search of an appropriate place for his father's ashes. However, Johnson's efforts become less a search for a paternal resting place than for an honest contextualization of his own identity-defining positionality, as situated in relation to America's history, its ideologically freighted geography, and the peoples who have occupied its land. As Johnson visits various places in the western United States connected to the backgrounds of his immigrant Norwegian ancestors, and having moved residentially from place to place throughout his own life, he feels like a "a man from nowhere."[34] A paradox that Johnson comes to realize is that, in terms of geographically based identity, being a white American man also makes him particularly prone to such a rootless identity precisely because people like him have been classified as "white" and "male" in "America."

As many critical whiteness studies scholars have noted, whiteness has defined itself less in terms of what it supposedly is than in unnamed contradistinction to what it is not, and the same conceptual disembodiedness is an element of conventional masculinity.[35] A similar subjective blankness is particularly encouraged for white American men in terms of the geographical component of their identities. Men like Johnson and Jack would likely not hesitate to identify as "Americans," but for United

States citizens gendered as men and raced as white, that geographically bound affiliation is as much or more about who they are in terms of a place, and again what they can or should do in it, as it is about the place itself. The non-relational epistemology of hegemonic white masculinity discourages the asking of questions that Johnson learns to ask when he begins thinking about himself more relationally: "Why does it matter who we are in relation to the land? And how am I to know?"[36] Confronting the morality-challenging specter of the land as the former residence of indigenous people, as Johnson eventually does, raises the issue of just where "Americans" are actually "from." Severed from "crude attachments to ethnicity and place to roam the earth and claim and settle land that is [already] home to someone else," white male American identity has been constituted more in terms of what one can or should do against the backdrop of a land mass conceived of as open, demographically empty territory.[37] What Jack demonstrates, and what Johnson comes to realize about himself as an ideologically imbricated white American man, is an inherited disposition toward effectively evacuating historical memory and geographical space of anything which does not serve the conception of oneself as an independent, free-ranging actor. Jack also demonstrates an inherited disregard for those people who have ironically helped to establish his own categorically induced sense of autonomy.

In part because "indigenous" peoples are precisely so because of their primary occupancy of a place, those who came later—"European Americans," as they have sometimes called themselves—are not fundamentally from that place. As Johnson writes, "I am not indigenous to anywhere, not what you would call 'aboriginal' or 'native,' qualities I grew up equating with primitive and savage, uncivilized and invariably 'dark.'"[38] Here, Johnson identifies a particularly white American male rootlessness, which arose in conjunction with a restless, entitled drive to roam, conquer, and appropriate, and, of course, dominant masculinity has been a co-constitutive influence. Part of Jack's general anxiety stems from the challenge wrought to his general conception of his wife Brenda by her week-long absence from her usual role as the one who stays home while he goes out and purposefully "works" (as if her domestic tasks, and her artistic ones, are not also forms of purposeful work). As I will explain, Shields also depicts Jack's interactions with an office worker, Moira Burke, as almost entirely objectifying—Jack's conceptions of her mainly involve what she does for him as a professional underling, as she points out. In sum, as Shields's characterization of Jack continually demonstrates, white American male identity has been idealized in an active, dominating, and wandering modality because white people have relinquished overt "ethnic" ties that would geographically tether their self-conceptions, while also erasing, expropriating, or romanticizing other peoples, and because men have also conceived of themselves as the non-defined definers, and de facto controllers, of women.

GEOGRAPHICAL SPACE AND WHITE MALE MOBILITY

Toward the end of his narrative, Jack awakens one morning with plans to submit a half-hearted book chapter to his supervisor, Gerald Middleton. He soon realizes that an enormous overnight snowfall will prevent the use of his car, so he takes a subway and arrives half an hour late. Only Moira is in the office; this is also her last work day, and since a scheduled retirement party will not happen, Jack takes her to Roberto's, the same restaurant where he and Bernie meet every Friday. Jack again complains in an emasculated way about his threatened book project, focusing again on the gender of his apparent competitor: "after all these years of hard work, he told Moira, he was going to be stomped upon by a woman in Rochester, New York, called Harriet Post" (*H*, 458). After several glasses of wine, Moira admits that she's long had sexual fantasies about Jack, fantasies that she knows he has never even suspected. When Moira then blurts out a request that Jack have sex with her that afternoon, he politely declines and summons her a taxi. Moira has complained earlier about being treated more like a piece of furniture than a professional colleague, a form of objectification amplified by both her gender and her positional subservience at the institute.[39] Moira's "outburst" leaves Jack feeling "giddy," "overwhelmed and dizzy," with a "shaky euphoria fill[ing] his head" (*H*, 464). After hustling her into a taxi, Jack feels elated by the boost to his masculine ego and not at all sympathetic or concerned over Moria's further revelations about her frustrated, stunted professional existence. He then decides for no particularly conscious reason to walk the ten miles back home through the snow. As he does so, Shields uses the whitened landscape symbolically, in both literary and sociohistorical terms.

Prior to embarking on his walk, Jack reflects, again in a decidedly subjective manner, on how the snow and the cloud-filled sky have changed Chicago's landscape: "All the sky was filling with whiteness. Amazing how the corrupt, old downtown sky could be so quickly transformed and widened" (*H*, 426). Given that Shields depicts her two protagonists as being "in transition" during an era of widened opportunities for women (and for men, if they could but see it that way), she seems intent here on portraying the snow-covered urban landscape as a purified, blank page of sorts, a setting for the new path in life that Jack might discover and learn to follow. However, her further descriptions of Jack's perception of this urban landscape, particularly in relation to his mobile, agential self, also suggest that there is much about his socialization as an ordinary white American man that will likely hinder his progress. In a study of common white male conceptions of urban space, Steven D. Farough reminds us that "white male racial identity is linked to unequal race, class, and gender power relations within a specific geographical context."[40] In terms of the physical mobility so integral to common conceptions of white male embodiment, Farough adds that "white men's movement across urban space is not only geographical, but discursive, structural, and psychological as well."[41] As Shields creates a plausibly realistic psychological portrayal of Jack during an era in which white men often felt besieged by the egalitarian claims of others, she depicts him perceiving the snow-covered Chicago landscape as he moves through it in ways that, instead of being open and receptive, reflect a continued search for bolstering signs of self-reflection amidst a landscape imbued with historical resonance by its being (for him) alternately empty and selectively populated.

The ironically and inevitably communal form that Jack's ostensibly self-sufficient identity takes arises when, as he considers taking a long walk home, which would be rendered extremely arduous by the snow, he also thinks of how others would see him in light of such a trek: with awe and even wonder. He would walk alone but also partly sustained by thoughts of how others will supposedly regard it as nearly heroic and at least noteworthy—as distinguishing, that is, *for him*: "'Is it true you walked all the way from… ?' 'Are you the guy who actually…?'" (*H*, 464–65, ellipses in original). Shields often portrays Jack as somewhat self-aware, in this case, of himself as an actor: "why was it that he could never do anything, never even think of doing something, without playing at doing it; there was something despicable in his small rehearsals and considered responses; was he the only one in the world who suffered these echoes?" (*H*, 465). Shields embeds that thought in parentheses to signal how subdued or insignificant it is for Jack, but the concerns it expresses are central to this narrative's internal plot. Jack is self-aware in terms of how others see him, but he is also unable to conceive of or find a version of himself that is not grounded in an *insecure* sense of how others see him. In broader terms, Shields depicts a masculine, late-1970s version of the vulnerability that Jason E. Pierce identifies as a historical legacy of the lengthy history of white American westward movement: "As Americans ventured into the West, they wore their beliefs in Manifest Destiny and their own racial superiority like armor, but like all armor it covered up their own uncertainty and vulnerability."[42] Instead of suggesting that Jack fails to construct a sense of self on his own, one free of socially instilled constraints, Shields demonstrates that because we are social beings, we cannot help but construct our identities relationally; in Jack's case, he often uses the perceptions of himself apparently held by others to shore up his own sense of self. To the extent that Shields constructs an alternative form of history, it valorizes instead of denigrates social connections and context, recognizing them as necessarily influential and indeed constitutive of anyone's perspective, including, of course, those of professional historians. Supposedly objective white men as well as the liberal, supposedly benign, Whitmanian white man that Jack next enacts during his walk fail to account for the social influences on themselves, influences that necessarily differ for them because of their positioning atop the white supremacist patriarchy.

In terms of the space itself into which Jack sets forth, he realizes in a common white male way that he'd never taken such a walk before because he's long conceived of the space between his office and home as full of "tough urban clutter" but also "a wide alien terrain [and] a dry basin." These are competing conceptions of both peopled and unpeopled land, both of which combine into a place "which could be safely traversed only within a closed vehicle" (*H*, 465). Shields deploys an enormous amount of irony in Jack's subsequent conceptions of the "seedy nexus of city blocks," which seem rife to him with the danger of "gangs on corners, knives, strange tongues and taunts, hucksters, pickpockets, drunks, pimps. Today, though, it was easier to believe that these dangers might be quelled. The snow was less a hindrance than a form of mitigation. It was whiteness that made the idea of walking home seem possible. Snow and purity: a symbolism effortlessly grasped... offering as it did a casual coat of simplicity atop Chicago's jumble-heap" (*H*, 465). This is indeed a symbolic whiteness, representative as it is of Jack's common white and fearful conception of peopled urban space, space he perceives as safely traversable on foot only if it can appear unpeopled for a day by those with whom one habitually avoids personal interaction. Jack explicitly thinks about the snow in terms of "purity" and "symbolism... offering as it did a casual coat of simplicity atop Chicago's jumble-heap," that same "heap" of vice and danger that he's just thought of from a white middle-class perspective (that is, fearfully). An aesthetic conception of snow helps to quell his apprehension, inspiring a sense of safety that feels "odd" to him primarily because he fails to recognize the racial whiteness of his geographically oriented fear:

> One snow-plugged city block would look like all the others; one traffic-less city street like the next; neighborhoods would meld together, one after the next, a blurring of postal districts, precincts, schools. It pleased Jack, made him feel oddly safe, to think of this new namelessness, and the way in which the snow had obliterated geographic boundaries, stretching even beyond the city limits to bind this rusty downtown sprawl to the stillness of forest preserves, small farms, villages, lakes. (*H*, 466)

This ultimately self-staging vision prompts in him a "quirky mushrooming of faith in his own feet and in the huge white light of the sky" (*H*, 466). Such thoughts and feelings reflect how his historical imagination is a decidedly white male imagination since it conceives of other people in terms of group membership, groups that in turn are defined by specifically conceptualized geographical location. To a limited self-aware extent, Jack also characterizes himself in terms of peopled space, as when the manner of speaking displayed by a woman in a flower shop (where he grandly stops to buy flowers for Moira, a gesture that again reads as more about him and his own actions than about how it will make Moira feel) tells him that he's getting close to "home," which is not just his house but also its named and characterized neighborhood. This conception of distinct, historically resonant urban spaces and the people in them functions as a representatively white American male one in being broad, nostalgically distanced, and instrumentalizing in terms of asserting oneself relationally. Conceiving of others in these ways has long helped to justify the acts of stealing from them and conquering them, a historical continuum of white male relations to the oppressed that Jack fails to acknowledge yet nevertheless reenacts in his professional approach to "Indian trading practices," an approach that is not only uninspired and feckless but also, by his own social order's moral code, unprincipled and ultimately immoral in its failure to account for the costs to American

Indians that have helped to produce Jack's unwitting social eminence. His conception of the "harsh, seedy" city between the institute and his home resembles that of the securely encapsulated commuters on trains or highways constructed to carry white middle-class suburbanites through such spaces. As for Tom Rath in *The Man in the Gray Flannel Suit*, the clean, orderly commute, properly conducted within an enclosed vehicle (be it automobile or train car), allows and indeed encourages a distanced perspective on the multiracial, multiethnic city and its residents, a perspective that can be both fearful and romanticizing.

The danger of Jack's exposed trek within urban space feels further exacerbated in racial terms for him by the lack of any "channel of softened parkway to scurry along," parkways being a particularly white form of nostalgic, pseudo-naturalistic cityscaping, as with the memory-laden park that Jack has visited with his father with mixed feelings of nostalgia and security (*H*, 465). Jack conceives of the whiteness of the snow-covered city as a border-obliterating force of sorts that renders the city conceptually blank, an open territory that is also selectively populated. As he imagines the snow-covered landscape "stretching even beyond the city limits to bind this rusty downtown sprawl to the stillness of forest preserves, small farms, villages, lakes," he finds comfort and even solidarity in images of places that contrast for him with urban ones in terms of not just their seemingly crime-free quietude but also their racially white homogeneity (*H*, 466). Feeling (as noted earlier) a "quirky mushrooming of faith in his own feet and in the huge white light of the sky," Jack decides to take, of all streets, Washington Boulevard, which "seemed to him the most civilized of the east-west streets, straight as an arrow, but with certain continental softenings here and there..." (*H*, 466). Within the context of highly segregated Chicago, Jack's conception of this street could hardly be more racially white or more resonant of a whitened, patriarchal national context; favored buildings have "facades [that] glowed in good weather like trustworthy faces," and "downtown Washington" Street has "something better-behaved about it, something cooler, more mannerly" (*H*, 466).

Jack again feels "fortified" by the thought that a woman, Moira, has told him she loves him, and in another masculine way, this trek and the bravery and fortitude that he feels it demonstrates also seem to raise his self-esteem. Although Jack feels fearful and separate from urban racial, ethnic, and classed otherness, there is again a Whitman-like cast to his appreciative thoughts of the gritty city that he's traversing and of its people. At first, he feels afraid of racially coded "hucksters, pickpockets, drunks [and] pimps" but these fears subside as he encounters some of the city's actual residents (*H*, 465). Nevertheless, an encounter with a black teenager in another store again reveals Jack's insistence on casting other people in his own terms, for his own purposes. After the teenager fixes a string that's been holding up his boot, he feels increasingly revitalized and optimistic about his trek, and he wants this young man to react in kind: "He smiled hard across the counter, trying to force this young boy to smile… why couldn't he smile?" (*H*, 472). Jack is frustrated by not being able to make him do so—instead of trying to understand why a black teenager might not want to do so, especially when encountering a privileged, potentially authoritative middle-class white man. Jack reaches across racial lines here in an insistently equalizing way, failing to register what may be a rejection as well as a signal that no such equalization is taking place. This mode of connecting with others, or trying to do so while not actually connecting with them, contrasts with the mode of connection that Brenda's story dramatizes (as does Daisy Goodwill's), a sense of human connection that does not make overly broad, and thus inevitably inaccurate, summations and claims about the past and its relations to the present, and instead conceives of the past in terms of *actual* connections, especially between individuals whom one knows.

When Jack arrives at home and his daughter Laurie expresses skepticism about both the point of such a reckless adventure and his having been out of touch for a long time during extreme weather, his former sense of purpose evaporates. When Laurie asks more directly why he walked instead of taking the usual train, he realizes the trek was actually "whimsical and foolhardy," and the only answer he can muster is vague and evasive: "Just because I'd never done it before" (*H*, 479). When Laurie begins to challenge this response, Rob—again demonstrating his status as a normalized white male in training—cuts her off with a masculine "clink of comradeship": "You don't have to have a reason for everything you do, stupid" (*H*, 479). To the contrary, Shields has demonstrated that Jack did have reasons, albeit largely subconscious ones, for conceiving of snow-draped Chicago as an appropriate stage for such a "foolhardy" performance.

In their analysis of a printed credit card advertisement, which shows two people sitting in a sport utility vehicle, Dwyer and Jones point out that the tagline ("MasterCard. Accepted wherever you end up.") is especially suited to the raced, classed, and gendered status of the occupants—two middle-class white men, whose status as such evokes "classic images of carefree adventure associated with the road trip, that particularly American coming of age ritual."[43] As Dwyer and Jones go on to ask more broadly and as Shields also asks with her depiction of Jack's road trip, "for whom is travel play, and for whom is travel better understood by making reference to its shared etymological roots with *travail*, to toil and labour, to suffer?"[44] People who are differently raced, classed, or gendered would surely regard such a trip differently in terms of its various dangers, including how they would likely be regarded by various onlookers. More to Shields's point, men like Jack are more likely to regard it whimsically or adventurously because they have inherited a certain geospatial epistemology, which encourages them to resort to fantasized memories of times and places in which white men felt freely confident about enacting a prerogative of purposeful, acquisitive mobility.

As Jack's story closes, the possibility that he will gradually transition toward more genuinely relational and appreciative interactions with others is suggested when he acquiesces to Bernie's request that a troubled neighbor, Larry Carpenter, join their Friday lunch sessions and when he goes out of his way to help Laurie with a school project. However, Bernie has also served as a countervailing foil for Jack in these terms by taking over domestic duties that Jack has neglected, including cooking dinner and cleaning the house. Jack picks up Brenda at the airport and will apparently resume happy relations with her, but Shields has suggested, particularly with hegemonically resonant figurations of geographical space and unfettered white male mobility, that like Frost's traveler, Jack, in his self-conception, is still at a crossroads.[45] In terms of his identity, Jack has been floundering, sinking into a morass of self-doubt because he has lost "faith" in his professional identity—all while his wife has been gaining confidence and success in her own—and because he thought another historian, a woman no less, was about to publish a book on "his" research area. Jack's sense of himself as a man has been flagging and it may now be on the rise in a more positive sense because he is more willing to appreciate and nourish connections with others. Yet, when he finally calls Harriet Post's home and learns that her research area is actually India, Jack plans to resume the book project that he'd been ready to give up, a project he'd embarked upon for ultimately selfish and even cynical reasons. Jack has domestic and social affiliations that could be not only sustaining personally but also influential for his historical practice. However, conceiving of the past as Jack apparently still does, in terms of homogenized groups of people within ethnoracially segmented land masses, has long provided morality-based justification for abuse, including the seizure of land being "wasted" by indigenous others. A strong and representative chance remains that any longing Jack has for *nostos*, or home, will instead continue to take the form of restorative, identity-bolstering dreams about seemingly open, potentially conquerable territory.

Notes

1. Shields, "An Interview with Carol Shields," Krolik Hollenberg, 350.
2. Beckman-Long, 10.
3. Ibid., 127.
4. "Lord, I hate that title!," Shields once said of *A Fairly Conventional Woman* (Shields, "A Little Like Flying," De Roo, 45). She also said of Brenda Bowman's story itself, "I think it's my best book..." ("An Interview with Carol Shields," Wachtel, 35).
5. Shields, "Interview: May 10, 2002," Weissman.
6. Howells, 80.
7. Howells, 81. In a 1989 interview, Shields directly addressed the racial whiteness of her own upbringing in Oak Park, Illinois: "It was an exceedingly WASP suburb of Chicago. For instance, there were 750 students in my high school graduating class, and we were all white, every single one.... What a place to grow up! Like living in a plastic bag, is how I think of it" (Shields, "Interview with Carol Shields," Wachtel, 5).
8. Dwyer and Jones, 210.
9. Ibid., 217.
10. Beckman-Long, 8.
11. Shields, *Happenstance: Two Novels in One about a Marriage in Transition*, 277. Hereafter cited as *H*.
12. Ahmed, 196.
13. Minh-ha, 1.
14. Ibid.
15. Dwyer and Jones, 212.
16. Boym, 41.
17. Ibid., 81.
18. Located immediately north of Chicago, the relatively forested state of Wisconsin has been a common summer vacation place for white middle-class residents of Illinois since the late 1800s. Their presence in Wisconsin is common enough that well-known statewide terms have emerged to describe them. In a study of Wisconsin resort areas published

shortly after *Happenstance* appeared, John Fraser Hart notes, "Local people refer to outsiders, and especially those from Chicago, as 'flatlanders...'" (Hart, 209). At the online crowd-sourced *Urban Dictionary*, an entry has, as of this writing, seven attempts to define "FIB." The current winning definition, with 1379 up-votes: "Fucking Illinois Bastards—just pronounced as fib by Wisconsinites referring to people from Illinois, how they drive and act. They drive really fast at home but slower than an old lady with a walker when they're vacationing in Wisconsin and don't know were [*sic*] they're going" (*Urban Dictionary*).

19. Pierce, 10.
20. Ibid., 10–11.
21. See Sarah Gamble for a discussion of Harriet Post as one of several absent writers in Shields's fiction and for an argument that Post represents, especially in being absent, "the contingency of endings, which impose an artificial sense of finality on an ever-proliferating pool of narratives" (Gamble, 49).
22. In *Happenstance*, Shields identifies the seventeenth-century Frenchman Rene-Robert Cavelier, Sieur de La Salle, commonly known as La Salle, with a variant spelling: LaSalle.
23. As Sullivan explains, "One of the predominant unconscious habits of white privilege is ontological expansiveness. As ontologically expansive, white people tend to act and think as if all spaces—whether geographical, psychical, linguistic, economic, spiritual, bodily, or otherwise—are or should be available for them to move in and out of as they wish" (Sullivan, 10).
24. Harding, 11.
25. Ibid.
26. As Lisa Johnson writes, "In *The Stone Diaries*, Shields employs common postmodern aesthetic strategies—the fragmented narrator, hybrid genre, and metafictional narrative, for example—but she joins them with a thematic insistence on the transformative female imagination, foraying into new parts of this aesthetic field, enacting an *embodied, woman-centered,* and *politicized* postmodernism" (Lisa Johnson, 203, emphasis in original).
27. Shields, *The Stone Diaries*, 57. Hereafter cited as *SD*.
28. Howells, 84.
29. Ibid.
30. Bowes, 152.
31. Hodgkin and Radstone, 169–70.
32. Associated in the wider American imagination primarily with winter skiing, Aspen, Colorado more broadly evokes, particularly for many white Americans, images of winter vacationing and adventure amidst open,

forested wilderness spaces. As an advertising executive for the Chrysler Corporation, R. H. "Ham" Schirmer, said of "Aspen" as the name chosen for the car model that Jack drives, "Aspen is a very pleasant name…" and when people hear it, they "think of the outdoors…" (Gainor, 5-F).
33. Allan G. Johnson, 1.
34. Ibid., 32.
35. As Grace Elizabeth Hale writes, "Central to the meaning of whiteness is a broad, collective American silence. The denial of white as a racial identity, the denial that whiteness has a history, allows the quiet, the blankness, to stand as the norm" (xi). Similarly, the heterosexual masculinity of people like Jack also functions to (un)mark them as the norm.
36. Allan G. Johnson, 102.
37. Ibid., 22.
38. Ibid.
39. In response to Moira's replacement, a young man, the institute's male scholars react to the change he represents, that of increasing numbers of men and women swapping gender roles. They do so by calling attention to his long hair, colorful clothes, supposed moodiness, and a strong manufactured scent—in other words, to features that emphasize his supposed effeminacy. Their judgmental, somewhat nervous discussion of him is focused on the same characteristics that would interest them were Moira's replacement a woman. In *Happenstance*, more than the Bowman's marriage is "in transition" and this response to change suggests that (white) American men in general had a ways to go in transitioning toward more egalitarian gendered mores.
40. Farough, 242.
41. Ibid.
42. Pierce, 20.
43. Dwyer and Jones, 216.
44. Ibid.
45. In a 1981 radio interview on Winnipeg Radio 2, Shields said of this protagonist's progress, "I think that in the book the hero, Jack Bowman—I suppose you had better call him an anti-hero—he does have something of a growth of self-awareness…. But it's not much. He opens a little bit but it's about an inch and [he] just has a glimpse I think into other people's inner lives as well as his own" (Transcript; Shields, "Interview with Carol Shields about *Happenstance*," Interviewer unknown, 2).

Bibliography

Ahmed, Sara. *The Promise of Happiness.* Durham, NC: Duke University Press, 2010.

Beckman-Long, Brenda. *Carol Shields and the Writer-Critic.* Toronto: University of Toronto Press, 2015.

Bowes, John P. *Land Too Good for Indians: Northern Indian Removal.* Norman: University of Oklahoma Press, 2016.

Dwyer, Owen J., and John Paul Jones III. "White Socio-spatial Epistemology." *Social & Cultural Geography* 1, No. 2 (2000): 209–22.

Farough, Steven D. "The Social Geographies of White Masculinities." *Critical Sociology* 30, No. 3 (2004): 241–64.

Gainor, Paul. "Surprise in Naming of Aspen." *The Detroit News,* December 18, 1975: 5-F.

Gamble, Sarah. "Filling the Creative Void: Narrative Dilemmas in *Small Ceremonies,* the *Happenstance* Novels, and *Swann.*" In *Carol Shields, Narrative Hunger, and the Possibilities of Fiction,* edited by Edward Eden and Dee Goertz. Toronto: University of Toronto Press, 2003: 39–60.

Hale, Grace Elizabeth. *Making Whiteness: The Culture of Segregation in the South, 1890–1940.* New York: Vintage, 1999.

Harding, Wendy. *The Myth of Emptiness and the New American Literature of Place.* Iowa City: University of Iowa Press, 2014.

Hart, John Fraser. "Resort Areas in Wisconsin." *Geographical Review* 74, No. 2 (1984): 192–217.

Hodgkin, Katharine, and Susannah Radstone. "Patterning the National Past." In *Contested Pasts: The Politics of Memory,* edited by Katharine Hodgkin and Susannah Radstone. London: Routledge, 2003: 169–74.

Howells, Coral Ann. *Contemporary Canadian Women's Fiction: Refiguring Identities.* New York: Palgrave Macmillan, 2003.

Johnson, Allan G. *Not from Here: A Memoir.* Philadelphia: Temple University Press, 2015.

Johnson, Lisa. "'She Enlarges on the Available Materials': A Postmodernism of Resistance in *The Stone Diaries.*" In *Carol Shields, Narrative Hunger, and the Possibilities of Fiction,* edited by Edward Eden and Dee Goertz. Toronto: University of Toronto Press, 2003: 201–29.

Pierce, Jason E. *Making the White Man's West: Whiteness and the Creation of the American West.* Boulder: University Press of Colorado, 2016.

Roy, Wendy. "Revisiting the Sequel: Carol Shields's Companion Novels." In *The Worlds of Carol Shields,* edited by David Staines. Ottawa: University of Ottawa Press, 2014: 63–80.

Shields, Carol. "Interview with Carol Shields About *Happenstance* (*The Husband's Story*), Winnipeg Radio 2, 1981, Transcription of Audio Tape." Interviewer unknown. Winnipeg Radio 2, 1981. http://www.carol-shields.com/happenstanceinterview.pdf. Transcript: 1–6. Accessed 6.19.2017.

———. "A Little Like Flying: An Interview with Carol Shields." Interview by Harvey De Roo. *West Coast Review* 23, No. 3 (1988): 38–56.

———. "Interview with Carol Shields." Interview by Eleanor Wachtel. *Room of One's Own* 13, Nos. 1–2 (1989): 5–45.

———. *The Stone Diaries.* 1993. New York: Penguin Group, 2008.

———. "An Interview with Carol Shields." Interview by Donna Krolik Hollenberg. *Contemporary Literature* 39, No. 3 (1998): 339–55.

———. "Interview: May 10, 2002." Interview by Kathy Weissman. *Bookreporter,* May 10, 2002. http://www.bookreporter.com/authors/carol-shields/news/interview-050902. Accessed 6.19.2017.

———. *Happenstance: Two Novels in One about a Marriage in Transition.* 1980, 1982. Open Road Integrated Media, 2010.

Sullivan, Shannon. *Revealing Whiteness: The Unconscious Habits of Racial Privilege.* Bloomington: Indiana University Press, 2006.

Trinh, T. Minh-ha. *Woman, Native, Other: Writing Postcoloniality and Feminism.* Bloomington: Indiana University Press, 1989.

Urban Dictionary. "FIB." https://www.urbandictionary.com/define.php?term=FIB. Accessed 10.23.2017.

CHAPTER 5

Denying White Male Nostalgia: Don DeLillo's *Underworld*

In 1999, Don DeLillo received the Jerusalem Prize, which is awarded biennially to "a writer whose work best expresses and promotes the idea of freedom of the individual in society."[1] DeLillo has long been hailed for his compelling depictions of pervasive threats to contemporary personal autonomy, yet few studies have considered the significance not only of his own ironically individualizing white masculinity but also of his Italian American origins in the Bronx. Particularly lacking is attention to the different perspective that such an outlook may well have granted to his efforts to gauge the pulse of quotidian life in the United States against the highlighted backdrop of late capitalism. When asked during a *Paris Review* interview whether growing up in an Italian American household influences his writings, DeLillo replied, "I think it translates to the novels only in the sense that it gave me a perspective from which to see the larger environment. It's no accident that my first novel was called *Americana*."[2] Born in 1936 to immigrant parents, DeLillo waited as a novelist until the third decade of his career to include in *Underworld* (1997) extensive depictions of Italian American characters and settings. This authorial elision of ethnic affiliation, which helped to produce DeLillo's reception as a white male author—and thus as an individualized and supposedly more objective one—likely accelerated his eventual ascendancy to the rank of high master of postmodern fiction.[3] Yet, unlike other (white male) postmodern masters, DeLillo has often demonstrated his concern with the ontological and emotional dependence of individuals on others, as when David Bell, the protagonist of his first

© The Author(s) 2018
T. Engles, *White Male Nostalgia in Contemporary North American Literature*, https://doi.org/10.1007/978-3-319-90460-3_5

novel, ponders the crowds around him while walking home from work: "it occurred to me that perhaps in this city the crowd was essential to the individual; without it, he had nothing against which to scrape his anger, no echo for grief, and not the slightest proof that there were others more lonely than he."[4] Indeed, in his numerous depictions of protagonists who follow the dictates of middle-class white masculinity, DeLillo has repeatedly exposed the late-twentieth-century American hyper-individualism most fully embodied by middle-class white men as a pathological sham, stripped as it was of the sociohistorical context that so thoroughly undergirded and shaped it.

In his later novels, DeLillo hones in more intensively on the irony that sociohistorical forces in the Cold War era contributed to specific constructions of white-male individualism, a conundrum that Daniel S. Traber succinctly terms the "individualism paradox."[5] As scholars in many disciplines have recently argued and as all of the novels considered in this study demonstrate, such constructs as race and masculinity are better understood in relational terms, thereby situating identities within the abusively hierarchical relations that inevitably form them. Perhaps because DeLillo is commonly grouped with other white male literary postmodernists, whose work tends to be read as if their own racial status and that of their white characters has no significance, his intricate depictions of dominant American racial identities and the social dynamics that have both formed and destabilized them have gone relatively unexamined. John N. Duvall's description of DeLillo's most commonly acclaimed "postmodern" novel, *White Noise* (1985), as "a meditation on postmodernity—what it *feels* like to live in the age of media saturation" holds true for many of DeLillo's other novels as well.[6] In *Underworld*, DeLillo provides his most extensive dismantling not only of late-twentieth-century modes of American de facto white supremacy but also of white male individualism's interiorized machinations, especially the habitual denial and consequent nostalgic longings that simmered within the discontented core of hegemonic dominance.

In this time-hopping novel's narrative present of 1992, fifty-seven-year-old protagonist Nick Shay feels a nagging ontological uncertainty, a lonely sense of "quiet separation" from his "phony role as husband and father, high corporate officer."[7] DeLillo anchors shuttling narrative perspectives among a dizzying array of characters with a continual return to Nick, especially his nostalgic yearnings for a pre-whitened, more authentic and conventionally masculine version of himself. Nick seeks to assuage his uncertainty about who and what he has become partly by figuring it as a sort of spiritual homesickness; wistful memories of his younger self reestablish him as an Italian American descendant, in both familial and cultural terms, and he reaffirms as well direct ties with the remaining estranged members of his immediate family, including his wife, mother, and brother as well as his own son.[8] However, although DeLillo does embed various decidedly modernist themes and aesthetics in this novel (which he has described as perhaps "the last modernist gasp"),[9] he often dismantles Nick's longings for lost time in what became traditional ways for postmodern theory and fiction by exposing them as heavily mediated fantasies—partially self-made myths that respond to quasi-historical events that to a large extent are also mediated fantasies, mostly generated in the interests of increasingly globalized capital. As with several of his other backsliding white male protagonists, DeLillo confronts and counterposes Nick with characters who embody the projected raced and gendered otherness that initially helped erect the pinnacled role of constitutively dependent white male autonomy that has contributed to his malaise.[10] In these and other ways, DeLillo dissects in *Underworld* the individualism fetish most fully embodied by mainstreamed white American masculinity; he diagnoses as well both the external circumstances that have accounted for this elevated identity status and the commonly resultant emotional states that not only drive his representative protagonist to wallow in denial-induced nostalgia while rejecting his current life and self but also lull him back into quiescent acceptance of the "phony role" it constitutes (*U*, 796).

THE RELATIONAL UNDERPINNINGS
OF COLD WAR WHITE MASCULINITY

In sociohistorical terms, *Underworld* registers how a collective white male identity was reconstituted over several decades, in part by the continually morphing ways in which that identity depended on countervailing conceptions, and consequent abuses, of racial others. As noted in this study's earlier chapters, nationalistic unity during the Second World War spurred integration among workers at home and fighting forces abroad, and racial and ethnic minorities increasingly demanded equality during the subsequent Cold War era. Such challenges impelled not only the collective psychic burial of white masculinity's own incriminating and ongoing abuses but also consequently compensatory revisions of American history. Postwar celebrations of racial and ethnic reconciliation contributed to a feel-good façade for exceptionalist claims to an emerging American Century, but inequitable economic conditions and segregated residential and work spaces remained the unacknowledged reality. *Underworld*'s lengthy prologue, which depicts the eclipsing in the mainstream American imagination of the Soviet Union's successful testing of an atomic bomb by a riveting baseball game, establishes the novel as an ambitious assessment of American life during the ensuing Cold War context. By beginning in 1951 with a lengthy focus on Cotter Martin, a young, gate-crashing, and self-consciously black baseball fan, DeLillo establishes a probing, insightful depiction of not only a shift in American collective identity toward a relational self-conception via the emerging Soviet Union but also new formations of the dominant white masculinity that obstinately undergirded domestic demographic arrangements, and of the common, increasingly anxious denial of such realities.

As a roving attempt to capture psychic and emotional states particular to late-twentieth-century white American life, *Underworld* also diagnoses residents who were seduced by the well-advertised allure of racially purified suburbs. Depicted in a series of snapshot-like tableaux, the Demings are a family welcomed into a 1950s suburb, a place where the "trees at the edge of the lawn were new, like everything else in the area," including, in a racial sense, the residents themselves (*U*, 514). At various points, DeLillo highlights not only the artificiality of this setting but also subsequent, reality-obscuring memories of this supposedly better decade. The mid-twentieth-century American suburb was a deliberate racial formation, one characterized as explicitly fresh, pure, and clean not only by its positioning amidst shiny new products and hypoallergenic kitchens and bathrooms but also against the excluded conceptual impurity of urban ethnoracial otherness, a suburban element that by its very glaring absence functioned constitutively. DeLillo's emphasis here lies as much or more in depicting what it felt like to live in this dream, specifically as a middle-class white person who could thereby fit one of its appointed roles, as it does in satirizing the product-lust of emergent American hyper-consumerism. As the chapter opens in 1957, wife and mother Erica feels vaguely anxious while constructing Jell-O parfaits, and she realizes later that the source of her discontent is the looming awareness of Sputnik, the eminence-challenging satellite recently put into orbit by the Soviet Union: "Erica felt a twisted sort of disappointment.

It was theirs, not ours" (*U*, 518). DeLillo places the Demings in a "split-level suburban house," thematically signaling a split between the staged, superficial level of their quotidian lives and a denied subterranean psychic level, where new middle-class white anxieties, fears, and excitements about binarized otherness lurk (*U*, 513).

Young Eric Deming exemplifies budding corporate America's manipulations of particularly masculine feelings while hidden away in his bedroom, "jerking off" into a condom that incites him because its "sleek metallic shimmer" evokes "his favorite weapons system, the Honest John, a surface-to-surface missile that carried yields of up to forty kilotons" (*U*, 514). Also exciting for Eric is a photo of Jayne Mansfield, even though her depicted breasts seem too "real" to him. Eric shifts his desire from Mansfield's breasts to her face, then manifests the success of corporate advertising's efforts to implant in the middle-class white male psyche an attraction to artificially enhanced, product-oriented eroticism—what appears to be Jayne Mansfield's face, Eric realizes, "was put together out of a thousand thermoplastic things. And in the evolving scan of his eros, it was the masking waxes, liners, glosses and creams that became the soft moist mechanisms of release" (*U*, 515). Since the new suburban life is so heavily conceived and lived in terms informed yet censored by family-friendly movies, TV shows, and the advertising that both surrounds and suffuses such identity-forming entertainments, feminized sexuality is both present and sublimated. Accordingly, while father Rick is mesmerized in the act of stroking his new car in the breezeway, Mansfield's breasts remind Eric of "the bumper bullets on a Cadillac" (*U*, 517). Neither Eric nor Rick could feel as they do without being white and male—properly situated in their roles but also excited in response to external social narratives that include people "like" themselves. More to the point, those later Americans who wistfully miss the "Golden Era" of the 1950s have most often done so by imagining lives superficially similar to those of the Demings, failing to register not only the manufactured, heavily advertised racial whiteness of such American dreams but also the excluded, other-populated underworlds. Such longing has become a form of nostalgic denial that obscures its object's own foundational denial.

One apparent goal of DeLillo's lengthy prologue, set several years earlier and depicting Major League Baseball's "shot heard round the world," a home run which won the 1951 pennant for the New York Giants, is to undercut a seemingly innocuous form of particularly white male nostalgia. This is a skewering of the storied mythos of baseball as a relatively untainted realm of nobility and fair play, a form of nostalgia that already shaped the prologue's seemingly prelapsarian setting. Despite the cozy, border-crossing familiarity that felt possible in the otherworldly space of a ballpark, Major League Baseball remained highly exclusionary in terms of race (and, of course, gender). As Duvall notes, "Although the color bar in the major leagues officially had been broken by Jackie Robinson in 1947, African American players [in 1951] are as much inter-lopers on the field as Cotter Martin is in the stands."[11] Robinson actu-ally played for the Dodgers in the famous game that *Underworld* depicts, and DeLillo carefully alludes to Robinson's game-changing status, refer-ring to him at one point as "brave Jack" (*U*, 44). Having introduced the subject of race relations on the novel's first page via a young black fan, who symbolically slips past barriers to join the experience of a live major league game, DeLillo chooses to puncture white male nostalgia about baseball's relatively early integration as an institution by focusing not on racial dynamics on the field but rather in the stands.

Within the temporary fraternal community of a packed baseball sta-dium, Cotter Martin can feel a tenuous cross-racial alliance with a mid-dle-aged white man, Bill Waterson, with whom he trades observations about the players and the game. However, a disciplinary, ever-hovering white gaze intrudes when a black peanut vendor works his way toward them: "Isn't it strange how their common color jumps between them? Nobody saw Cotter until the vendor appeared, black rays phasing from his hands. One popular Negro and crowd pleaser. One shifty kid try-ing not to be noticed" (*U*, 20). When Cotter later manages to wrench the winning home-run ball from the clutches of Waterson, he realizes, as a necessarily self-aware member of a subordinated race, that since the white imagination groups him with other automatically suspicious black people, running in a mostly white crowd would mark him as a thief. As Waterson then pursues Cotter outside of the stadium in an increas-ingly vicious chase for the ball, DeLillo allegorizes a question succinctly posed about Cold War domestic race relations by Leerom Medovoi: "how could the United States claim to defend human freedom against its totalitarian enemies abroad while it waged a totalitarian race war at home every time it terrorized its own black (and other minority) pop-ulations?"[12] In terms of racialized allegory, as Thomas Heise writes, DeLillo's focus on ownership of the ball itself "immediately precip-itates racial tension over the right to property at a pivotal moment in history when the city is about to fall into a period of steep decline."[13] A subsequent section depicting Cotter's family and home life is encased within pages printed entirely black on both sides, a graphic acknowledgement not only of "white flight," which proportionally darkened so many American cities in the years following the Dodgers-Giants game, but also of white America's defilement-fearing and self-aggrandizing consignment of darker American populations to increasingly underfunded, deindustrialized urban settings.[14] Thus, among the novel's many literal and figurative subterranean territories is that to which white America's darker others have been shuttled and contained, the racialized wastelands later occupied by such make-do figures as *Underworld*'s graffiti artist Ismael Muñoz and his minions, who in turn become romanticized by white urban-wannabes such as Nick's teenaged suburban-raised son.

As part of a quartet of celebrity baseball fans together attending the game that became legendary, Frank Sinatra thinks of America as "a country that's in a hurry to make the future," a place where "the names attached to the products are an enduring reassurance" (*U*, 39). A common feeling prompting this particularly white middle-class need for reassurance was not only an ongoing postwar sense of instability but also the fear of upcoming change; as the nation seemed to hurtle into the future, many white Americans had a racially informed sense that national stability and security were under threat, not only by the Soviet Union and the communism it represented but also by an increasingly restive domestic African American population. Later memories expressed by various characters in the novel express nostalgia not only for this past that constitutes a particularly white set of longings; as Damjana Mraović-O'Hare points out, they often miss as well the early Cold War's peculiar combination of a broadly optimistic, vividly portrayed sense of the future and the equally pervasive sense of fear and dread about a potentially imminent nuclear apocalypse. In a scene set in 1992, Nick's long-ago lover, the artist Klara Sax, explains that during the Cold War, political power seemed less diffuse: "Now that power is in shatters or tatters and now that those Soviet borders don't even exist in the same way, I think we understand, we look back, we see ourselves more clearly, and them as well.... And it held us together, the Soviets and us" (*U*, 76). As Mraović-O'Hare writes, such characters "are nostalgic—despite all of the attempts of denial—because the approaching end of the world seemingly stabilizes in their view the global order. In other words, they are nostalgic for the time during which they dreaded the apocalypse."[15] Amidst the more free-floating and vague uncertainties of the post–Cold War era, the missing "us versus them" superpower binary—a binary that DeLillo repeatedly highlights as a product of dichotomized white male thinking—at least felt tangible and thus more paradoxically reassuring.

As DeLillo's Sinatra recognizes, the urgent futurism of the 1950s was promulgated largely through advertising but also through movies, radio, and television, which effectively denied full-fledged citizenship to non-white people like Cotter, who returns to his predominantly black neighborhood. The South Bronx is soon to become a further underworld-ed "ghetto," and DeLillo directly counterposes the novel's depiction of the Martin family with the later portrait of the implicitly white, and thus right for the era's new suburban dream, Demings. In addition, during a scene in which Nick's brother Matt shares memories of the 1950s that differ from those of a coworker, the adult Eric Deming, DeLillo acknowledges that while whiteness, Italian American or not, could well have helped families like those begun by Nick and Matt into a "fun" and exclusively white suburban setting, certain formations of whiteness were excluded from popularized notions of all-American-ness. As they sit in a lunchroom exchanging memories, Eric says to Matt, who has just been depicted remembering a childhood visit to a "great Italianate" movie theater,

> "The placid nineteen-fifties. Everybody dressed and spoke the same way. It was all kitchens and cars and TV sets. Where's the Pepsodent, Mom? We were there, so we know, don't we?"
> "You know. I don't know," Matt said.
> "You were there. We both were there."
> "You were there. I was somewhere else." (*U*, 410)

As DeLillo frequently suggests, acknowledging such realities as how ethnoracially different people experienced the era, and how an effectively manufactured version supplanted others as the "all-American" version, would significantly dispel the wistful 1950s nostalgia later felt by many white Americans. Such understandings could also help modulate the compensatory memories of pulsating youth indulged in by men like the middle-aged Nick, for whom a period of his life is remembered as all the more vibrant because of its Italian American (and thus, supposedly, non-whitened) flavorings.

By setting *Underworld*'s lengthy prologue at the outset of a new phase of collective American self-fashioning, DeLillo emphasizes not an impending shift from some actual reality but rather the beginnings of certain heightened feelings—especially as experienced by white men—that the American past was somehow more real. As newspaper and magazine advertisements, feature articles, and photos rain down on the crowd and playing field, DeLillo registers the beginnings of a media-fueled nostalgia, a longing that many white American men were already beginning to feel for times when life didn't seem "phony," as the older Nick says of his own circumstances.[16] Having paid $34,500 for what he wants to believe is the home-run ball from the game, which he listened to on the radio at the age of sixteen, part of Nick's particularly white male nostalgia is his casting of the game, and of his own ethnic past, in glowing terms. Unlike the white American writers analyzed by Toni Morrison in *Playing in the Dark*, who typically use an "Africanist presence" in the form of stereotypically black characters, whose narrative purpose is to serve merely as foils for white characters, DeLillo works to unveil the fundamental dependence of white masculinity on figurations of blackness, and thus "the parasitical nature" of white male freedom.[17] *Underworld* continually depicts American Cold War forms of binarized thinking, including the mutually constitutive black-and-white simplifications of racism and masculinity. As FBI Director J. Edgar Hoover muses while watching the game, there "is that side to him, that part of him that depends on the strength of the enemy.... And what is the connection between Us and Them, how many bundled links do we find in the neural labyrinth? It's not enough to hate your enemy. You have to understand how the two of you bring each other to completion" (*U*, 28, 51). As exemplified by Hoover's tortured, apparently homosexual double entendre, DeLillo repeatedly highlights the masculinized competition that fixates on conceptions of "Us and Them." DeLillo depicts individualized white masculinity's denied ontological symbiosis by depicting Cotter's "American" story as a parallel to Nick's that is more than merely random. Indeed, DeLillo immediately announces one project of the novel, that of undercutting the traditional American equating of idealized independent agency with white masculinity, in *Underworld*'s opening sentence, which describes a black teenager, Cotter: "He speaks in your voice, American, and there's a shine in his eye that's halfway hopeful" (*U*, 11). In effect, DeLillo's depictions of black characters amidst a cast of mostly white ones differ in a crucial way from those Morrison critiques in that, in a subdued metafictional mode, DeLillo's very point—that "black" completes "white" in both social and literary senses—is basically the same as hers.[18] As I will explain, DeLillo later depicts another agential black character, Simeon Biggs, who points out more directly that the purportedly all-American nostalgia exemplified so expensively by Nick's purchasing of the game-winning ball is a specifically white male form of memory construction.

As critical whiteness studies scholars often emphasize, centuries of overt American white supremacy morphed in the twentieth century into more veiled, denied forms of hegemony, to the point where the racial status of many white Americans, let alone its guiding influences on their own perspective, feelings, and behaviors, rarely ever registered for them.[19] These were the Americans firmly ensconced in what DeLillo's version of Jewish American comedian Lenny Bruce refers to as "the invisible middle": "My name is Leonard Alfred Schneider. What was I doing when I took the name Lenny Bruce? I was moving toward the invisible middle" (*U*, 592). A common result of such membership for many white men was paradoxical reactions and behavior, many of which were guided by raced and gendered emotions that went unrecognized— feelings that in turn could warp the formation and reiteration of individual and collective memories. Having joined a current and historically resonant white movement westward into "the white parts of the map" (*U*, 422), the older, putatively successful Nick demonstrates this warping effect on his memories when he longingly remembers a version of himself that is not only youthfully impetuous and bluntly masculine but also specifically Italian.[20] Having moved away from that heritage to assume the role of corporate "waste manager," Nick has tried to contain, bury, and forget his own psychic garbage, much like Erskine Fowler, the tightly contained protagonist of Wright's *Savage Holiday*. However, like the methane gas that must escape from the landfills that Nick helps to construct, certain unresolved memories resist containment.

In a way that registers both irony and sincerity, Nick imitates Italian gangster speech for his colleagues, but according to coworker Brian Glassic, anything actually Italian in his background is imperceptible to others (*U*, 165). Having been influenced in part by media-generated portrayals to conceive of Italian ethnicity in aggressively masculine terms, Nick mythologizes the disappearance of his father as a likely mob hit, downplaying the equally plausible story of disgraceful abandonment by a selfishly negligent father and husband. Like many descendants of European immigrants, Nick's ways of clinging to his ethnic heritage actually reveal his stronger whitened tendencies. "I've always been a country of one," he says at one point, "There's a certain distance in my makeup, a measured separation like my old man's, I guess..." (*U*, 275). Having again raised the specter of his lost Italian American father, Nick then evokes an Italian word (which, in his muddled reconstruction of his past, he also thinks might be Latin) "that explains everything" about his own aura and feeling of detachment: "*lontananza*. Distance or remoteness, sure. But as I use the word, as I interpret it, hard-edged and fine-grained, it's the perfected distance of the gangster, the syndicate mobster—the made man" (*U*, 275). Although emotional remoteness is a common characteristic of those who follow the dictates of conventional masculinity, in terms of Nick's racialized identity, the irony is that the greater individualizing "distance" from others that he feels and enacts springs less from his Italian heritage than from his whitening residential and vocational movement away from it.

At the same time, the depressed Nick sometimes does see his current self as flaccidly de-ethnicized and dis-located, as evinced by a self-description he reports having often used by way of introduction: "I live a quiet life in an unassuming house in a suburb of Phoenix. Like someone in a Witness Protection Program" (*U*, 66). DeLillo depicts Nick performing this line with wry self-effacement, likely because it registers how Nick misses a more impressive, less whitened version of himself and perhaps as well because it echoes the ending of a then-recent Hollywood movie about another discontentedly suburbanized mafia romanticizer, Henry Hill, the protagonist of Martin Scorsese's *Goodfellas* (1990). In the film's closing scene, the character, played by Ray Liotta and based on the actual "half-Irish, half-Sicilian" Henry Hill, opens the door of a suburban ranch house to retrieve a newspaper.[21] In voiceover, Hill bemoans having been placed in the Witness Protection Program for testifying against Italian American gangsters because he will have to live the rest of his life "like an average nobody." The parallel becomes even stronger upon realizing that Nick is "half-Irish" as well—his last name is Shay because his Irish American mother reverted to her maiden name in response to her husband Jimmy Costanza's abandonment. As I will explain, having moved continually westward and landed in Arizona, Nick enacts what historian David Roediger and others have identified as a general movement for

Southern and Eastern European descendants of immigrants, a movement toward a seemingly blank middle-class whiteness that also specifically and ontologically retreats from vividly imagined figurations of both ethnicity and blackness. By moving his protagonist in a decades-long trajectory from the formerly Italian-dominated, early-twentieth-century Bronx, DeLillo effectively evokes and traces the historical mobility of such whitened descendants, an ever-expanding "white" group whose collective, fearful, identity-forming movement has always entailed a negatively relational ontology, conceiving of themselves less as white and more as "those who are not non-white."[22] A common emotional result of such a seemingly bland existence for men who felt like flaccid "nobodies" was to long for the supposedly enlivening thrills of that which was left behind.

As a middle-aged father, Nick ironically perceives this particularly white masculine form of emotional compensation in his teenaged son Jeff, who in response to the racially enflamed riots in 1992 Los Angeles adopts various contemporary signifiers of urban blackness: "an L.A. Raiders hat and an ultralong T-shirt that had a pair of sunglasses slung from the pocket… the same shy boy but physically vivid now, a social being with a ghetto strut" (U, 104–5). When Jeff tells his parents about a website describing the brutal Bronx death of a young girl (whom readers later learn is Esmeralda Lopez) and a crowd's reaction to it, Nick describes his son in terms that implicitly mark Jeff's suburban whiteness by instead marking his feelings about racialized inner-city otherness:

> Jeff is shy about the Bronx, shy and guilty. He thinks it is part of the American gulag, a place so distant from his experience that those who've emerged can't possibly be willing to spend a moment in a room with someone like him.… He doesn't feel he has the credentials to relate a tale of such intensity, all that suffering and faith and openness of emotion, transpiring in the Bronx. (U, 808)

As an unremarkably white resident of suburban Arizona, Jeff appears to be an indistinctly normal boy to any similarly normalized white beholder, such as his father, who thinks of the Midwestern upbringing of his wife Marian in similarly relational terms—not merely as normal, and thus only implicitly white, but also and more explicitly as different from urban and black, and feeling incomplete as a result: "Marian in her Big Ten town, raised safely, protected from the swarm of street life and feeling deprived because of it—privileged and deprived, an American sort of thing" (U, 344).

The parallel DeLillo draws in both cases is to Nick's own whitened masculine nostalgia, which prompts him to contrast his current, seemingly lifeless suburban life with what he remembers as his more vivid, urban, and ethnic—and supposedly more authentic—past.

Despite this frequent implicit marking of whiteness by marking instead that from which it differs, the reality of a common ethnic past like Nick's is that, as a group, Italian American immigrants quickly assumed a status that was more "white" than it ever was non-white; indeed, the first were, in historian Thomas A. Guglielmo terms, already white on arrival. Although Italian immigrants like Nick's paternal ancestors were at times perceived by other white Americans in terms that resembled racial animus, "they were white just the same. They were so securely white, in fact, that Italians themselves rarely had to aggressively assert the point."[23] While Nick accurately remembers the fact itself of ethnic difference, his training into late-twentieth-century suburban and anti-urban whiteness causes him to nostalgically gloss over not only the white privilege that he and his father always enjoyed but also its conceptual reliance on figurations of an inferior yet threatening blackness. His memory of punching a black interloper in the 1950s Bronx is more revealing of the obedience he already paid as a teenaged male to the dictates of whiteness than of any allegiance he felt to Italian neighborhood solidarity; his action signals how any such solidarity was already informed by white masculine denigration and fear of the supposed threat of black masculinity, and thus by an Italian American striving for full-fledged whiteness that formed itself against, and in many ways acted against, the specter of denigrated blackness. This raced and gendered conglomeration of fears and anxieties only became a more explicitly motivating force when ethnic descendants joined anti-urban expansion, as "the white suburb's need to imagine a black, anti-neighborly, and uninhabitable city structured perceptions, even as it added to the allure of the often shoddy and drab suburban working-class subdivision and hastened the forgetting of who—and what—was left behind."[24] As Nick moves westward from the ethnoracially rich Bronx and into suburban and corporate white masculinity, his middle-aged dissatisfaction with who and what he is takes shape as a regretful, ultimately failed effort to recover who and what he has left behind. As readers first meet Nick, the fifty-seven-year-old version of himself might seem to be seeking recuperative connection with others when he finds his long-ago lover, Klara Sax. However, Nick's motives prove largely solipsistic, and DeLillo portrays Klara as an artist whose work, if not her personal interactions, encourages more reflective and potentially healing uses of the past.

REFLECTIVE NOSTALGIA AND COMMUNAL ART

From the beginning of his career as a novelist, DeLillo has displayed a fascination with artists and the artistic process. Most of his fictional artists spend time curling inward into a meditative state, then springing back outward—or feeling ready to do so—as their stories end. David Bell is a budding filmmaker in *Americana* (1971) who ends up writing a manuscript that is the novel we're reading; Bucky Wunderlick is a rock star-turned-recluse in *Great Jones Street* (1973) who eventually decides to face his fans again; Bill Gray is a reclusive author of Salinger-like proportions in *Mao II* (1991) who emerges in an attempt to confront terrorists; and Lauren Hartke is a performance artist in *The Body Artist* (2001) who recoils inward in response to the death of her husband and then emerges to perform again. Perhaps because DeLillo often writes against destructive forces that insidiously shape individual identities and proclivities and because, in a hierarchical parallel with race, destructive proclivities tend to be engendered more in men than in women, DeLillo figures the reflective processes and resultant actions of his male and female artists differently. In *Underworld*, DeLillo describes the work, and often the ruminative, work-related thoughts, of several artists, the most prominent being Klara Sax, whose story parallels and dovetails with that of Nick in many ways. However, as with Carol Shields's depiction of quilting artist Brenda Bowman, Klara's artistic intents and practices purposefully deploy nostalgic memories for regenerative purposes, actions that contribute to the novel's thematic undercutting of restorative white male nostalgia.

That Klara could be read positively may seem unlikely, given her treatment of others in her personal life. When she and Nick first meet—she at thirty-two and he at seventeen—they betray her kindhearted husband Albert with a torrid affair. An indifferent mother, Klara repeatedly refers to her offspring Teresa not by name but as "the child" and "the daughter." Like Lenny Bruce and like a kid Nick remembers named Alfonse who insists on being called Alan because he wants "to be an actor in the movies," Klara nominally erases her ethnic origins by changing Sachs to Sax, apparently in order to gain acceptance in the establishment art world (*U*, 735). Later in life, Klara allows a man, Miles Lightman, to demonstrate extensively his devotion to her, only to suddenly marry another. Nevertheless, while still married to Albert, Klara chafes less against him than the confines of traditional marriage: "She didn't want more, she wanted less.... Solitude, distance, time, work. Something out there she needed to breathe" (*U*, 747). The personal side of Klara, like that of many artists, differs from the professional side and from the apparent intentions and messages of her art. In these terms, Klara's actions with Nick can be read as a movement toward escape as much as a betrayal; more to the point, she uses solitude and distance profession-ally to produce work that counters broad oppressive forces and affirms human connection and interdependency.

After depicting Klara and Nick's brief desert reunion in 1992, DeLillo spends extensive space on a summer in 1974, mostly relaying the aes-thetic musings of not only Klara but also Ismael Muñoz and a young black artist befriended by Klara, Acey Green. As DeLillo describes the reflections and work of these latter two artists, of another in Los Angeles, and then (in chronological terms) of Klara herself in the desert, a favored form of art emerges. As with *Underworld* itself, this is art that uses a broad thematic canvas, reflecting on the circumstances and fate of groups and thereby countering large-scale power, including the domineering and hyper-individualistic tendencies of white masculinity. Such an artistic praxis also counters the era's institutionally sanctioned art, which Klara characterizes as "heroic, American art, the do-it-now, the fuck-the-past— she could not follow that [by making] some furious now, some brilliant jack-off gesture that asserts an independence" (*U*, 377). In a similar vein, Ismael works with the tag Moonman 157 and an admiring crew of aspir-ants, painting trains in order to assert not only himself as his imagery assaults various urban spaces but also others. Whitman-like, Ismael seeks to "get inside people's heads and vandalize their eyeballs" in order to validate the presence and agency of the subjugated and ignored: "The whole point of Moonman's tag was how the letters and numbers told a story of backstreet life... this is the art of the backstreets talking... you can't *not* see us any more, you can't *not* know who we are..."[25] Similarly, Acey Green fills largely wide-populated gallery space with images of the Black Panthers and then with humanized images of idealized blonde beauty, emphasizing (as DeLillo does again in Eric Deming's masturba-tion scene) the contrast between media-generated nostalgia for figures like Marilyn Monroe and Jayne Mansfield and the actual, denied women behind them.

During a trip to Los Angeles, Klara visits another work of unsanctioned demotic art, one that DeLillo has already highlighted by having Nick visit it, the Watts Towers. An actual work built over several decades by an Italian immigrant commonly known as Simon Rodia (whom DeLillo identifies with his unassimilated name, Sobato Rodia), the "Towers" consist, as does Klara's desert project, of recycled garbage, or as Nick puts it, "steel rods and broken crockery and pebbles and seashells and soda bottles and wire mesh, all hand-mortared..." (*U*, 276).[26] When Klara also tours the Towers (a counterpart in the novel to the blunt, anonymously corporate and repeatedly featured World Trade Center towers), they make her feel rapturous, "a depth of spirit [and] delectation that took the form of near helplessness" (*U*, 492). What especially impresses Klara about Sabato's work is a "splendid independence this man was gifted with, or likely fought for..." (*U*, 492). In his analysis of historical elements in *Underworld*, Paul Gleason provides a common thematic interpretation of such moments in DeLillo's work: "For Klara and DeLillo, art is an assertion of freedom, a way in which humanity can reject and survive an American culture whose mass-market capitalism and weapons of mass destruction threaten individualism and human life."[27] However, given the narrative context, in which DeLillo frequently highlights communally oriented work produced outside the sanctifying confines of the era's New York City art world, this is not the personalized and illusory independence of the sort sought by adherents to the dictates of white masculinity. Aptly referred to in terms of Watts, the Los Angeles community in which it resides, Rodia seems to have built his work for a community of others more so than for elevation of himself. In his analysis of containment and counterhistory in *Underworld*, Mark Osteen points out that Rodia's project represents how demotic public art "can turn waste into wealth and bind the private to the public.... Watts Towers thus epitomize how art can become an 'agent of redemption,' reconstructing hope and beauty out of the wreckage of history; as such it offers a model for all post-Cold War artists."[28] DeLillo makes this point by describing Rodia humbly leaving his finished project to die in obscurity, without adding what would have provided further thematic support—Rodia's original named for the project, "Nuestro Pueblo" (Spanish for "Our Town").[29]

For DeLillo, as Paul Giaimo writes, the successful artist "must be concretely, socially engaged," and producing work that reflectively recycles the past, instead of trying to bury and deny it, is one way of being so.[30]

Decades later, as an artist who has achieved international fame, Klara reflects (while Nick listens) on the motivations behind her own monumental work in progress. *Long Tall Sally* is a desert-sited installation consisting of 261 painted (or soon-to-be-painted) decommissioned B-52 bombers. Echoing her earlier efforts with her gallery owner to find a producer of unsanctioned art, the elusive graffiti artist Moonman 157, Klara describes that which drives her current team's efforts, using a plural pronoun to include her team as she does so: "we're trying to unrepeat, to find an element of felt life, and maybe there's a sort of survival instinct here, a graffiti instinct—to trespass and declare ourselves, show who we are. The way the nose artists did, the guys who painted pinups on the fuselage" (*U*, 77). Klara dwells at length on the nose artists and on who an original Sally might have been, perhaps "a waitress, bedraggled you know, hustling a ketchup bottle across the room, and never mind the bomb..." (*U*, 78). "The bomb" here is both the literal nuclear weapons that some of these planes once carried and the entire set of political and cultural shifts effected during the Cold War by the new, overshadowing possibility of catastrophic nuclear devastation. Klara does not blithely brush apocalyptic fears and awareness aside; rather, like Ismael, Rodio, and Acey Green, she confronts the bomb as a form of impersonalizing power in order to highlight and revive that which it threatens to obliterate. As Klara puts it, this is "the ordinary thing, the ordinary life behind the thing," as represented by the demotic nose art she is so reluctant to paint over (*U*, 77).

Klara adds in regard to the nose art, as well as to those who made it and the women for whom they yearned, that "We may want to place this whole business in some bottom pit of nostalgia..." (*U*, 77). But to do so with such forms of publicly minded art, DeLillo implies, would be to dismiss it as kitsch or perhaps as folk art, and thus as something "beneath" the sort of internationally renowned art that artists with the fame Klara has achieved normally produce. A significant irony here is that Klara's artistic intentions and methods fundamentally rely on and deploy nostalgia, restoring and recycling not just actual discarded objects but also their culturally bound associations. A primary point that thus emerges from her ad hoc artist's statement for a French journalist is that collective memories, including nostalgic ones, can be repurposed, creatively shaped into inspiring, future-oriented, and multiform expressions of hope. In Svetlana Boym's explication of reflective nostalgia, she points out that, by contrast, nationalist memory—consisting of hegemonic conceptions of a collective past that are largely driven and shaped in the United States by its white male leaders—is insistently singular in its domineering orientation toward the future: "Nationalist memory tends to make a single teleological plot out of shared everyday recollections."[31] In keeping with the novel's pervasive garbage motif, DeLillo offers several artists, including himself, who creatively recycle discarded bits from the past in pursuit of a more egalitarian future, a direct contrast with the common white male tendency to disregard or bury the past because various facts and episodes from the nation's history would challenge white men's claims to justifiable eminence.

WHITE-MALE PATTERN DEAFNESS

By the early 1990s, the ever-shifting contours of de facto white supremacy continued to produce not only new racial attitudes, beliefs, and behaviors but also new residential and workplace patterns. The latter included patterns of white flight *from* suburban areas, often in response to new forms of middle-class labor and to increased economic viability among non-white homeowners. As many of the latter began moving into suburbs, some of the white residents who could afford to leave repeated the pattern of fearful or disdainful white flight. Although some of this movement took the form of "reverse white flight" back into urban areas, it was also for many a movement, yet again, into exurban areas, spaces often nostalgically conceptualized as bucolic, trouble-free (trouble having come to be associated with the inner city), and relatively empty.[32] A conceptual geographic emptiness is represented in *Underworld* in part by Nick's westward relocation of his family to another "white space on the map," an oft-repeated phrase in the novel (*U*, 529). In her study of the "new American literature of place," Wendy Harding examines literary depictions of the spatial conceptions held by those who occupied a fully "American" status, many of which constitute a particularly United States American "myth of emptiness." I would add that such citizens can only be conceived of as embodied most fully by members of a particular collective, that is, white men. In the hegemonic "cultural imagination," Harding writes,

> enjoying the full status of an American does not signify just inhabiting a city or belonging to a region; it means enjoying mobility and transience, being able to travel and migrate across the American continent,

entertaining cultural expectations within the national territory but also cherishing the dream of unattached, unfettered existence.[33]

In this sense, and as Nick demonstrates in his shift from a Bronx-located, Italian American identity to a suburban white one, the hyper-individualism of normalized all-American masculinity is ironically tied to a geographical setting, a landscape that is perceived as relatively empty in order to enable active performance of such an identity. As Carol Shields also demonstrates with her depiction in *Happenstance* of Jack Bowman's sense of himself in relation to geographical space, conceiving of the American landscape (or, later, portions thereof) as empty, or in DeLillo's terms as "white space on the map," enables the morality-assuaging conception of oneself as unfettered by history, particularly by conscious awareness of the abuses to which one's dominant collectivity has subjected others. Indeed, in order to quell feelings provoked by such guilt-inducing, reparation-demanding facts, one must bury the actual past and construct a false one. As Harding writes, "[I]nasmuch as it was held to be undiscovered, the land offered a site of invention and of creation. Rather than the site of the nation's memory, it was (at least imaginatively) the blank medium upon which its dreams could be projected and materialized."[34] In effect, the white male conception of geographical space as empty—a conception largely brought about by a felt emotional need to bury the abuses of one's collectivity and by the desire to embody one's nation-defining "freedom" by acting in ways that seem unencumbered—continued to be both a consequence and enabler of avaricious white male abuse.

Of course, the past lives in many ways in the present, and awareness of a past that includes abusive interaction with subordinated others cannot be completely buried, especially in a nation that proclaims pluralistic values and the supposed extension of full rights and opportunities to all. In *Underworld*, the pervasive motif of garbage and other forms of waste, especially forms that keep returning, often signals the resurgence of white masculinity's "garbage"-laden past. Having been abandoned by his father and having impulsively shot a man as a teenager, Nick has personal reasons for attempting to bury his personal past, but as a member of the middle-class, ever-westward, and non-white–fleeing collective, Nick enacts garbage-burying tendencies that are common among members of that collective. Since white masculinity's past generally stinks, as it were, contemplation of it can induce guilt and shame in any generation; in response, mainstream institutions and thus most white men cover it over, and as they "recycle" selected parts of the past for necessary self-constitution in the present, they sort through it, sanitizing, organizing, and burnishing chosen scraps. In the residential setting in which Nick and his wife meticulously sort their literal recyclables, he drives through a neighborhood where vanquished Native Americans are acknowledged only via street names. At another point, he and his family travel to an "ancient ruin," where even the park ranger serving as a guide seems oblivious not only to any accurate sense of who the land's former inhabitants were but also to the part that racialization of indigenous people as "savages" (and thus of white people as "civilized") may have played in their erasure.

The novel's somber acknowledgment in that scene of a common white conversion of subordinated otherness into touristic spectacle is earlier satirized more pointedly. While Sisters Edgar and Grace are handling out food in the South Bronx, the narrator asks from Gracie's perspective, "What's this, do you believe it? A tour bus in carnival colors with a sign in the slot about the windshield reading *South Bronx Surreal*" (*U*, 247, emphasis in original). As "thirty Europeans" disembark to gawk and snap photos, Gracie takes offense at the conversion of the urban setting into something like a wild-life theme park, calling attention, as DeLillo so often does, to blurred boundaries between some apparent reality and the dislocated fixation on representations of it: "This is real. The Bronx are real" (*U*, 247). Nevertheless, as DeLillo illustrates, boundaries between white consciousness and the ongoing realities of white supremacist disenfranchisement persisted. Accordingly, as Nick listens to the hired guide at the site of Native American remains, he finds himself more interested in the "protective canopy" than the ruins themselves. As with Shields's historian Jack Bowman, any genuinely interested and morally consistent sense of who indigenous peoples were and the part that white supremacy played in their decimation has been either figuratively or literally paved over, landscaped into what amounts to a successfully disguised landfill that appears pleasantly palatable (*U*, 342–43).[35]

Like another troubled white male protagonist, Jack Gladney in DeLillo's *White Noise*, Nick is fascinated by literal garbage and, by way of symbolic extension, the figurative waste of his own past.[36] Most of the meanings that Nick imposes on his personal recollections are just that— imposed and rarely accurate reflections of actual circumstances. DeLillo suggests that like the historical recollections of nearly any American white man, Nick's are inevitably contaminated by gross abuses and by the nationalistic fantasies that gloss over and erase them. By incorporating more racially astute characters of color, DeLillo also acknowledges that in broader, collective terms, historical memory reported from a minority perspective is often not only different but also more accurate. That Nick's white male perspective is a typically resistant one as well is also suggested by his occasional conversations with a black colleague, Simeon Biggs, whom Nick calls Sims. In 1978, Nick visits Los Angeles, where Sims works as a "landfill engineer" (*U*, 278), and the two of them spend an evening barhopping, idly chatting, listening to music, and avoiding, in a traditionally masculine way, intimate conversation about Sims's current marital difficulties. Having explained for Nick during a visit to his office the racially conformist demands of his corporate role ("I go to sleep black every night and come back white in the morning" [*U*, 303]), Sims repeatedly tries to discuss racial matters, only to be derailed by Nick. Recalling a photo of the black jazz artist Charlie Parker, Sims suggestively highlights Parker's "white suit," but Nick stubbornly wonders instead what the shoes Parker was wearing were called (*U*, 326). Sims also tells Nick about being frequently harassed as a black male driver, his "life held in some cop's bent finger because I resemble a suspect or my tail-light's out," and then adds, "You want to be my friend, you have to listen to this" (*U*, 327). Again, though, instead of listening attentively, Nick looks away at a wall decorated with jazz album covers and then changes the topic to his own graying hair. Later in the evening, when Sims recalls rumors about a barge full of garbage currently cruising the American coast and repeatedly facing refusals of entry, DeLillo's stagings of the common white male refusal to address the ongoing manifestations of the waste and abuses of collective neglect and abuse come full circle.

This former young tough who once hit a black kid for wandering into his "Italian" neighborhood is later quite willing, in 1992 during his middle-aged existential crisis, to have dinner at a baseball game with this black colleague. Nevertheless, Nick fails to register the significance to his nostalgic groping toward solace of Sims's more racially cognizant assessment of the collective fantasy that has arisen around the earlier famous ball game. As a black man, Sims the "landfill engineer" has spent a lifetime confronted by that which goodhearted, mildly liberal white men like Nick prefer not to bring to the surface, let alone listen to a more experienced person explain, that is, the ongoing workings and abuses of their social order's overtly white supremacist legacy. As Sims, Nick, and two other companions discuss the celebrity touring that a pair of players from that game have been doing for decades, Sims points out the significance of their whiteness, noting insightfully that even the losing pitcher can be redeemed by the collective white male nostalgia that reveres and mythologizes baseball lore: "'Because he's white,' Sims said. 'Because the whole thing is white. Because you can survive and endure and prosper if they let you. But you have to be white before they let you'" (*U*, 98). Sims also marks the whiteness of the other men at the table by referring to them, perhaps playfully, as "fellows" (and, later, "chaps"), and he proceeds to tell them about Donnie Moore, another actual professional ballplayer, a man who, like 1951's Ralph Branca, pitched a losing home-run ball in a playoff game. Unlike Branca's, Moore's life spiraled downward until he shot his wife three times and then killed himself in front of his son. The significant difference for Sims is that Moore was black (as was that game's home-run hitter) and thus quickly forgotten; as the narrator, Nick says he remembers nothing of this story, not even Moore himself. Their white dinner companion Brian Glassic dismisses Sims's claims by stating that the Branca pitch is remembered simply because it happened in simpler times, "decades ago when things were not replayed and worn out and run down and used up before midnight of the first day" (*U*, 98). However, although Nick doesn't tell us so, Moore's death actually took place just three years or so before this conversation, in July of 1989. Nick, who narrates this section, asserts—ironically, given his own extreme taste for the collective white male nostalgia for baseball lore—that Moore's story is not remembered because its relatively recent occurrence renders it "unhistorical" (*U*, 99). What Nick fails to realize here is how, as a white baseball fan, he actually proves Sims's point about the racial disparities of baseball fandom and reminiscence, by never having even heard of Donnie Moore, let alone the winning home run or the shootings.[37]

As in his earlier comments about assimilationist pressures on the job, Sims again addresses a broader white supremacist context that his companions seem unable to see, much less acknowledge: an extant ideology that infiltrates even such mundane leisurely activities as the fondling of baseball lore and memorabilia. In his extensive ethnographic study of what amounts to a late-twentieth-century subculture, that of collecting baseball cards, John Bloom writes regarding its pervasive whiteness, "very few baseball card collectors were [racial] minorities, and only one of the collectors in my interview sample was not white. This man was an African American who at one time was the president of the local sports' collectors club. His leadership, however, generated deep and bitter resentment, which he saw largely as the result of racial bias."[38] As Bloom also notes, the nearly monolithic whiteness of the participants speaks as well to how the mainstream nostalgic casting of baseball lore is driven by an anxious desire to shore up white masculinity, particularly in response to challenges aimed at its prerogatives by those still commonly denied them. Accordingly, as Nick departs from his dining companions, he enacts the common white male tendency to resist the puncturing of racialized nostalgia by harsh truths uttered by one of America's subordinated, experienced others when he remembers instead a vision of racial harmony—Sims's earlier reported memory that, as a child, he too succumbed momentarily to the cozy fantasy of borders obliterated by baseball fandom, by running down a street "waving his arms and shouting that he's Bobby Thomson," 1951's victorious white home-run slugger (*U*, 100).

Masculinized Isolation and Feminized Community

In such ways, DeLillo taps into what it often felt like to live as a middle-class, heterosexual white American man in the late twentieth century, thereby exposing root causes of an ironically obstructed, abusive form of privileged agency that encourages denial. In Wanda Vrasti's examination of the difficulties that those who oppose the abuses of late capitalism face in mounting effectively collective critique, she asks the following pertinent questions: "How do individuals become emotionally invested in social formations that betray an obvious propensity towards socio-economic and ecological crises?... What kind of moral legitimating structures does capitalism rely on to make critique look ridiculous or exasperating?"[39] Ultimately, DeLillo's fiction proffers an anti-individualist critique similar to that offered by Vrasti: "Before we can learn how to live-in-common, we first need to take a moment to examine our deepest attachments and remember how easily all the things we do to improve ourselves and the world around us are absorbed back into moral regulations and/or consumerist modalities."[40] In a moment that initially promises an affective rapprochement, Nick effectively demonstrates that in working through his mid-life crisis, he has not managed to examine the masculine and ethnoracial regulations that have governed and shaped his emotions, thereby failing to extricate himself from their influence. Nick seeks a revival of his conventionally masculine vitality by attacking Brian Glassic, the colleague having an affair with his wife, but the effort is half-hearted and unfulfilling. A rumbling conglomeration of powerful feelings continues to roil within Nick, and like the underground nuclear explosion of post-nuclear waste that they've travelled to the former Soviet Union to witness, Nick's slapping around of Brian fails to result in an above-ground, cathartic release. As a white male "waste manager," a role that metaphorizes his gendered and racialized training, Nick's emotional "waste" remains internalized and denied, its release thwarted.[41] When he ponders and relishes the chance to wreak vengeance upon Brian, he more explicitly contrasts an earlier, ethnic version of himself with the current middle-class and white version; he imagines he could "crush" Brian's face "with five earnest blows" while emphasizing the phenotypically "white" features of his colleague and then thinks, "But we don't do that anymore, do we? This is a thing we've left behind. Five dealt blows to the pinkish face with the paling hair" (*U*, 796). Nick's use of the collective pronoun "we" here instead of the singular "I" is striking, given that the social collective to which it refers is middle-class white men. At times, Nick briefly marks "a certain furtive sameness, a planing away of particulars" that provides membership in the paradoxically individualizing group that he has joined by moving away from an ethnic past crowded with people he knew (*U*, 786). DeLillo's scenes set in that community, into which he too was born and raised, depict it as vibrant *in terms of* community—as a place where people knew and cared for each other. However, because middle-aged Nick also sees himself flagging in masculine terms, he instead misses, in his last words as a first-person narrator, a brashly macho version of himself: "I long for the days of disorder... the days when I was alive on the earth, rippling in the quick of my skin heedless and real... when I walked real streets and did things slap-bang and felt angry and ready all the time, a danger to others and a distant mystery to myself" (*U*, 810). Again, the primary impetus for his visit to Klara is similarly vain—he travels to her desert worksite because he misses his virile seventeen-year-old self, not Klara and what they had together.

As Nick roams his house, sardonically located in Phoenix, he fondles his gathered relics, enacting again his deeper investment in objects than in people: "I rearrange books on the old shelves and then I stand there looking.... [I] look at the things we own and feel the odd mortality that clings to every object. The finer and rarer the object, the more lonely it makes me feel, and I don't know how to account for this" (*U*, 804). Nick's efforts to reestablish restorative emotional and psychic connections from his past have failed because the "waste" of his past that he sorted through was a fantasized version, an interpretation that he imposed on it: "They are making synthetic feces in Dallas," he repeatedly thinks (*U*, 805). In this sense, Nick's identity is also exposed as that of a constructed, script-following white American man; his fealty to mediated constructions of the stage set of his life, and of his role in it, has meant attaching more meaning and value to props and well-acted roles than to any human connection that might feel more genuine and intimate, in part because it could be more recognized as such by its participants.

At the same time, Nick ponders a "desperate crisis, the intractability of waste" and, more specifically, how "conference reports and newspapers," interpretations not unlike those he imposes on the waste of his own past, fail to account for the real thing and to deal with it adequately; the sheer global mass of human waste "is not otherwise touchable somehow, for all the menacing heft and breadth of the material, the actual pulsing thing" (*U*, 805). As Renato Resaldo has pointed out, history perceived from a privileged perspective often "makes racial domination appear innocent and pure."[42] Such an understanding of historiography's necessarily subjective nature appears on *Underworld*'s opening page, where the narrator of the prologue intones, "Longing on a large scale is what makes history" (*U*, 11). Yet Nick's awareness at times that memory tends to be warped by the inevitably subjective experience of loss does not stop him from wistfully casting his younger self—who, after all, slugged and ejected a black kid, had sex with the wife of a man he knew, and impulsively shot and killed another—as a version of Nick Costanza Shay that wasn't already tainted by the same sorts of raced, gendered, and geographically tribal influences that currently weigh on him. Like many middle-class white American men who follow the social training that encourages "containment" of realities that would challenge a sense of self as disconnected from its others and innocent of their abuse, Nick fails to see through the fantasy of his own autonomy and the injury and divisions that he inflicts by maintaining such tight "containment" of both his emotions and his sociohistorical awareness. However, although Nick is the closest character *Underworld* has to a protagonist, the novel does not end with him; instead, DeLillo switches his focus to another recurring female character and then ultimately to everyone and everything, with a view toward the future that suggests better ways of reconciling the past.

In this postmodern dramatization of numerous forms of reconstituted Cold War American subjectivity, DeLillo animates not only the mutually constitutive binaries that initially formed racialized and gendered identity constructions but also the emotions that prompted the deflection and denial of such social realities by those who benefited the most from them as a group. In these terms, DeLillo depicts *Underworld*'s urban-dwelling nun, Sister Alma Edgar, achieving a better resolution than does Nick, an opposing sense of human connection which echoes that of Klara Sax's artistic praxis, and that constructed by Carol Shields, with her reflective feminine makers of connective historical and personal relations between themselves and others. During an inner-city charity visit by Sister Edgar and her workmate Sister Grace, they learn of the gruesome death of Esmeralda Lopez, the elusive, seemingly feral twelve-year-old girl whom they have long been pursuing in the hopes of helping. DeLillo has por trayed Sister Edgar throughout the novel as similar to the novel's nearly eponymous J. Edgar Hoover, including her obsessive disdain for contact with anything biologically exterior to her own body, especially the bodies of other people. Archaically stalking through neglected neighborhoods in full nun's habit while wearing the protective rubber gloves of medical personnel, Sister Edgar is obstinately resistant as well to the notion that the work she and Gracie do is really helping anyone and indeed to any sort of hope for better conditions for those suffering the elite-benefiting ravages of late capitalism. However, the horrific news about the rape and killing of Esmeralda changes something inside Edgar, and her action of uncharacteristically laying a comforting, commiserative, and ungloved hand atop grieving Gracie's hand provides a clue to what sort of change this will become.

In a tableau of sorts that resembles the gendered and racially indic- ative moment when *Gray Flannel*'s Tom Rath gazes at an anonymous black women beneath a billboard's vision of a sunbathing white woman, DeLillo stages a climactic scene of communal ecstasy with the symbol- ically complex image of another billboard. This one depicts merely a woman's hand, holding a glass of orange juice in which, when struck by the lights of nightly trains, Esmeralda is said to appear. Significantly, DeLillo is careful to mark here that which his novel's version of Lenny Bruce earlier terms the "invisible middle"; the woman whose hand the billboard depicts is described as "a female caucasian of the middle sub- urbs" (*U*, 820). As during *Gray Flannel*'s much shorter scene in Harlem, the perceived impurity of the inner-city unwashed whom the Sisters join—while their roles reverse in terms of skepticism—is thus clearly marked in terms of class, race, and ethnicity. When a train appears and Edgar glimpses what indeed does appear to be a girl's face, DeLillo describes her reaction this way: "Sister is in body shock" (*U*, 821). For the first time, a one-word reference to "Sister Edgar" appears as Sister instead of as Edgar. The difference matters because, like Sister Edgar's sudden willingness to touch Sister Gracie's hand, the term "Sister" marks a relational status whereas "Edgar" individualizes. As the billboard-watching crowd erupts into something approaching a communal paroxysm, Sister Edgar takes off her disinfectant gloves and embraces the urban residents from whom she has been physically and emotionally distancing herself (*U*, 822). This dramatic opening of herself to othered people is foreshadowed much earlier, when we hear of her teaching practices: "Edgar stopped hitting kids years ago, even before she grew too old to teach, when the neighborhood changed and the faces of her students became darker. All the righteous fury went out of her soul. How could she strike a child who was not like her?" (*U*, 238)

Again, DeLillo echoes in this scene an alternative, traditionally feminine conception of self in relation to others also proffered by Carol Shields, and the similarity grows when *Underworld* virtually changes protagonists. Sister Edgar soon dies, and instead of going to heaven, her afterlife form enters the internet, where, as opposed to the white masculine imposition of innumerable, self-interested divisions, "There are only connections. Everything is connected," especially people to other people (*U*, 825). In her critique of scholarship on DeLillo's earlier novel *White Noise*, Sally Robinson points out a remarkably masculinized critical consensus, one that continually misreads key gendered moments in the narrative. Robinson writes, for example, that critics have tended to see in that novel's shopping scenes a depiction of consumerism as a feminized threat to an implicitly masculine mode of generalized postmodern subjectivity. Such binaries are wrongly imposed on the novel, Robinson argues, betraying a scholarly nostalgia, "which wittingly or unwittingly reproduces a modernist logic equating masculinity with authentic culture and femininity with consumer culture."[43] In the process, these mostly male scholars have tended to overlook the novel's inclusion of more positive instances of not only shopping and commodified consumption but also other aspects of quotidian experience in late capitalist life. The novel's general depiction of the latter is instead continually understood as a set of threats to some "real," and ultimately to some unmediated form of genuine experience and meaning: "The 'real' in this line of argument is not the 'real' of material objects, but the 'real' of some more abstract value having to do with independence from mediation, commodification and exploitation, and with 'being' not determined by commercial interests."[44] The numerous, countervailing positive interactions in *White Noise* between male and female characters, and between both members of both genders and the acts of shopping and consumption, have been largely ignored. I would argue, in agreement with Robinson's interpretation of DeLillo's interest in valorizing less conventionally masculine and more communal modes of being, that DeLillo's shift of focus at the end of *Underworld* from Nick to Sister Edgar also conveys a message that, while we should indeed remain wary of the threats to autonomy posed by the latest encroachments of multinational capital, effective resistance need not entail assertion of the kind of delusional white masculine independence clung to by Nick. The hyper-individualism most fully performed by middle-class heterosexual white American men becomes evident as a self-serving form of denial when contrasted with what amount to understandings, conventionally cast as feminine, of necessarily interdependent human relations.

Accordingly, the novel's final section offers a secular prayer of sorts, poetically recommending agential embrace and usage of connectivity, as represented by the connections now available online. In addition to merging with both the blasts of atomic bombs and with their victims, Sister Edgar "joins the other Edgar," a union again described with relation-marking pronouns that transcend socially imposed, identity-confining nomenclature: "Sister and Brother. A fantasy in cyberspace and a settling of differences that have less to do with gender than with difference itself, all argument, all conflict programmed out" (*U*, 826). Sister Edgar's sympathetic connection with the victims of bombing blasts echoes DeLillo's commentary throughout the novel not only on the disturbingly faded fear in late capitalism of nuclear Armageddon but also on the furthered global advance of self-directed materialism apparently brought about by the fall of Soviet communism and, by historical extension, on the "big winner," hyper-individualized white masculinity (*U*, 793). Earlier, as Nick and Brian Glassic wait in Kazakhstan for a horrifically ouroboros-like blasting of nuclear waste with a nuclear weapon, Nick belatedly asks Viktor Maltzev, the former Soviet historian-turned-waste management entrepreneur, whether, like other atomic blasts, this one is banned by international agreement. Viktor replies ambiguously, "Banned, not banned. We are exception" (*U*, 795). No matter the technical legality, let alone the potential environmental and demographic consequences, the blast proceeds. Nick and the guests gorge themselves on a sumptuous array of viands, and Nick spends more time wondering how to confront Brian about the affair than worrying about the aftereffects of this blast (a lack of concern he demonstrates even when Viktor takes him on a tour of "misshapens," preserved and living bodies horrifically disfigured by numerous previous explosions). In a mode that anticipates the bleakly hyper-neoliberal landscape depicted in Margaret Atwood's *The Heart Goes Last*, DeLillo emphasizes here an alarming shift in human-induced apocalyptic danger—from the mutually assured destruction of superpower nations that threatened each other with nuclear weapons to individualistic pursuit of profit via the use of such weapons for environmental- and population-damaging, blithely profit-seeking purposes. When Viktor asks Nick how it feels as an American to be the "Big winner" (793) of the Cold War, the moment reads as a Russian speaking to a United States American, but it reads as well as a question directed toward those who occupy perhaps the most individualism-inducing status on earth, that of a financially successful middle-class white American man. Nick does not feel like a winner; he feels nearly ravenous, in a physical sense, but also empty in ways that can be termed both social and spiritual.

Having banished himself to an emotionally deserted wasteland in the western desert, Nick also feels, in bleak contrast to Sister Edgar's bliss, "a loneliness, a loss" (*U*, 808). Although he frames this loss largely in terms of a father whose likely abandonment he continues to deny, the emotion is clearly about something more immediate. While also feeling haunted by the "long ghosts" of his mother and other people he once knew intimately, ghosts he imagines "walking the halls" of his house, Nick recalls touring a waste management facility with his granddaughter (*U*, 805). He then muses, "Maybe we feel a reverence for waste, for the redemptive qualities of the things we use and discard. Look how they come back to us, alight with a brave kind of aging" (*U*, 809). As Nick demonstrates, members of his era's subsumed white male collective commonly sought both refuge and restorative redemption in self-serving, identity-bolstering nostalgia, and as they did so, they tended to repress awareness of the potentially remedial truths of the history that is self-serving white supremacist dominance, exclusion, waste, and slaughter. Having receded into a state of numbed acquiescence to isolation that contrasts sharply with the communal ecstasy experienced in cyberspace by Sister Edgar, Nick remains representatively lonely in more ways than one. His enduring sense of longing and loss renders him an emotional exile who continues to deny, and thus fails to nourish and appreciate, his intricate connections to others.

NOTES

1. "Jerusalem Prize."
2. Begley, 88. Relatedly, DeLillo has also said, referring specifically to *Underworld*, "What a writer does—a writer from a certain background— is write himself out of his neighborhood and into the broader culture.... To a degree, this is what I did, you know, this is how I wrote myself out of the Bronx and into America" (Chénetier and Happe, 107).
3. In some of the early short stories that DeLillo published in the 1960s, he did include overtly Italian American characters and settings. See, for example, DeLillo, "Spaghetti and Meatballs" and "Take the 'A' Train." For studies of ethnicity or race (or both) in *Underworld*, see Duvall, "Excavating," Gardaphé, Gattuso, Giaimo, Heise, Hendin, Lauret, Noon, Pardini, and Russo.
4. The walk home through city streets of *Americana*'s protagonist, David Bell, also echoes that of Carol Shields's Jack Bowman, particularly when Bell suggestively tells readers, "I liked to walk home from the office because it made me feel virtuous" (DeLillo, *Americana*, 29). In *Americana* and *Happenstance*, both DeLillo and Shields examine the perceived need of a white American man (who has been trained into normative a white masculine epistemology and ontology) for seemingly appropriate open geographic spaces in which to enact his identity. Doing so provokes a certain set of empowering feelings, both about oneself and about the self-serving, as it were, space in which one is both acting and enacting.
5. Traber, 2. In his study of "straight white male" American protagonists "who choose otherness to divorce themselves from a dominant 'white' culture," Traber explicates a common pattern in American literature, that of depictions of identity construction via rebellion. This is a pattern in which protagonists ironically seek individualizing marginalization by identifying with racial otherness, thereby replicating prevailing ideologies of the dominant order from which they seek escape.
6. Duvall, "*White Noise*," 117, emphasis added.
7. DeLillo, *Underworld*, 796. Hereafter cited as *U*. In regard to Nick Shay's central position as protagonist, Paula Martín Salván writes,

DeLillo "privileges" Nick's story among those of the novel's many other characters:

> DeLillo foregrounds Nick's story by means of two narrative devices: first, the sections devoted to him are narrated in the first person so that Nick's voice is highlighted over the rest of the characters; second, the plot advances toward the unveiling of Nick's past, in a reverse chronological sequence. (339)

8. For extensive treatment of other forms of nostalgia in *Underworld*, see Ladino and Mraović-O'Hare. For analysis of the emotional casting of the past by several of the novel's characters in terms of loss, see Marshall. As noted more fully at the end of this chapter, Sally Robinson offers in "Shopping for the Real" an insightful analysis of what amounts to unwarranted white male nostalgia in the common scholarly response to another DeLillo novel, *White Noise*.

9. A *Guardian* feature on *Underworld* quotes DeLillo saying, "I don't see *Underworld* as post-modern. Maybe it's the last modernist gasp. I don't know" (Williams, "Everything under the Bomb").

10. For studies of unwitting white male subjectivity and its consequences in previous DeLillo novels, see Engles, "Who are you, literally?"; Engles, "DeLillo and the Political Thriller"; and Engles, "I know you must be somebody."

11. Duvall, "Excavating the Underworld," 268. In addition, although the gradual integration of Major League Baseball did constitute racial progress within a realm that remained white-dominated, it also had enormous consequences for other black players, fans, and communities, as popular Negro Leagues and many of the black-owned businesses and institutions they supported gradually fell apart. As baseball historian John Holway notes,

> The real significance of the Jackie Robinson Revolution was that it got the black owners and black fans out [of professional baseball]. Now the great black players played for white owners. Now, the great black players played for white fans. They entertained whites. They used to entertain blacks. Now if you go to the game you very rarely see a black person in the grandstand. (As quoted in Ruck, *Raceball*, 116)

12. Medovoi, 177.
13. Heise, 233.

14. As Eric Avila explains regarding new postwar racial formations and consequently altered conceptions of race and geography, "black" grew increasingly synonymous in the collective white imagination with "urban" or "inner city." The overt racial casting of the boom in suburban development as "white" was a concurrent process and result:

> [A]s a racial privilege sustained by redlining, blockbusting, restrictive covenants, and municipal incorporation, as well as by outright violence, federally sponsored suburbanization removed an expanding category of "white" Americans from what deteriorated into inner-city reservations of racialized poverty. The collusion of public policy and private practices enforced a spatial distinction between "black" cities and "white" suburbs and gave shape to what the Kerner Commission, a presidential commission appointed to assess the causes of the 1965 Watts Riots in Los Angeles, identified as "two societies, one black, one white—separate and unequal." (5)

15. Mraović-O'Hare, 213.
16. 1951 also included publication of Salinger' s *The Catcher in the Rye*, a milestone novel in the literary depiction of American white male identity formation, in which a signature expression of the narrating protagonist is also the word "phony" (Salinger, 55).
17. Morrison, 6, 57.
18. *Underworld*'s opening challenge of white racial presumptions to embodiment of genuine American-ness also echoes Morrison in *Playing in the Dark*, particularly her objection to the traditional racialized casting of national identity: "American means white, and Africanist people struggle to make the term applicable to themselves with ethnicity and hyphen after hyphen after hyphen" (47).
19. As Woody Doane explains, "The central component of the sociology of whiteness is the observation that white Americans have a lower degree of self-awareness about race and their own racial identity than members of other racial-ethnic groups" (7). For further discussion of the common white American lack of self-awareness qua "white," see Frankenberg and Chambers.
20. DeLillo portrays Nick's longings for an earlier version of himself as much more complex, particularly in gendered, ethnoracial terms, than the nostalgia that many of us feel for younger versions of ourselves. The latter, simpler feeling is summed up well by David Lowenthal:

> Life back then seems brighter not because things were better but because we lived more vividly when young.... Now unable to

experience so intensely, we mourn a lost immediacy that makes the past unmatchable. Such nostalgia can shore up self-esteem, reminding us that however sad our present lot we were once happy and worthwhile. (8)

21. As Hill's *New York Times* obituary notes, "A native New Yorker of half-Irish, half-Sicilian parentage, Mr. Hill was involved with the Luchese family, considered the most powerful of the city's original five Mafia families, from his youth in the 1950s until 1980" (Fox).

22. Haney López, 20. In his examination of a series of court cases in which immigrants sought United States citizenship—a status limited until 1952 by the 1790 Naturalization Act's clause requiring that one be a "free, white person"—Haney López demonstrates that in the juridical setting as well, the way to become "white" was not to match criteria in some (apparently nonexistent) list of white racial qualities; it was instead to prove that one did not match criteria for any non-white ones.

23. Guglielmo, 6. As David R. Roediger also explains, mid-twentieth-century Italian American descendants who sought upward social mobility were encouraged by racially preferential housing loans and job openings to leave "stigmatized 'mixed race' areas" in favor of exclusionary suburban spaces. While descendants of Italy and other (from a white American perspective) provisionally white European nations did face relatively muted forms of discrimination while living and working in urban areas, when they joined mass movements into new, "fun" suburban houses of the sort that *Underworld's* Bill Waterson's company would have built, they became de facto white people, with ethnic identity an increasingly and merely personal option (231).

24. Guglielmo, 234.

25. *Underworld*, 435, 436, 440, emphasis in original.

26. For clarification regarding variations on the first name of Rodia—variously identified as Sam, Simon, Sabato, and Sabatino—see Del Giudice, 157.

27. Gleason, 140.

28. Osteen, 255.

29. Del Giudice, 167. Del Giudice adds that "'Nuestro Pueblo' represents more than just a village or town but perhaps an entire people—the Italians" (167).

30. Giaimo, 14.

31. Boym, 53.

32. As Murray Forman writes in regard to the effects of such changes on the production and reception of rap and hip-hop culture, the 1990s saw the beginnings of a raced and classed demographic reversal that is also commonly termed "gentrification," that is, the "reclaiming of urban

zones that had previously been abandoned to urban dwellers with the onslaught of white flight" (46). As Forman adds, "This [reclaiming] has produced an interesting boomerang effect, as it repositions those returning to occupy chic apartments or high-security urban condominiums as new pioneers, active revanchists whose newfound economic prosperity positions them in a unique relationship to exploitable space. Such trends have redefined the inner city as the next frontier of American capitalist conquest..." (46). In the 2010s, such racialized spatial opportunism has become well known enough to acquire a demotic label, one that wryly recognizes nostalgic overtones of conquest, territory, and the oblivious conception of such spaces as empty: "Columbusing." The lingering white-supremacist underpinnings and attendant associations of such a common white middle-class disposition apply perhaps even more strongly to opportunistic movements away from both cities and suburbs to seemingly emptier "white spaces on the map," in Nick's terms. On the phenomenon of Columbusing, see Salinas, "Columbusing."

33. Harding, 4.
34. Ibid., 4.
35. For an argument that takes DeLillo to task for being unable in *Underworld* "to fully imagine the consequences of the cold war for... Native American communities in the nuclear West..." (183), see Noon.
36. DeLillo, *White Noise*, 258–59.
37. For more on Donnie Moore's career and suicide, see Christopher Bell's *Scapegoats: Baseballers Whose Careers Are Marked by One Fateful Play*. For an alternative view on the validity of Sims's claims about the impact of racism on memories of Moore, see Bérubé, 137–38.
38. Bloom, 83, 84.
39. Vrasti, n.p.
40. Ibid.
41. As Marni Gauthier writes, Nick "maintains his personal life by containing his past and maintains his professional life by containing... the poisonous past of the nation. The novel's archeological excavation of the underworld of American history and culture, as well as of Nick's self, reveals the persistence and indissolubility of these national and individual histories" (67).
42. Rosaldo, 107.
43. Robinson, "Shopping for the Real," n.p.
44. Ibid.

Bibliography

Avila, Eric. *Popular Culture in the Age of White Flight: Fear and Fantasy in Suburban Los Angeles*. Berkeley: University of California Press, 2004.

Bell, Christopher. *Scapegoats: Baseballers Whose Careers Are Marked by One Fateful Play*. Jefferson, NC: McFarland, 2002.

Bérubé, Michael. "Plot Summary: Motives and Narrative Mechanics in *Underworld* and *White Noise*." In *Approaches to Teaching DeLillo's White Noise*, edited by Tim Engles and John N. Duvall. New York: Modern Language Association Press, 2006: 135–43.

Bloom, John. "Cardboard Patriarchy: Adult Baseball Card Collecting and the Nostalgia for a Presexual Past." *Hop on Pop: The Politics and Pleasures of Popular Culture*, edited by Henry Jenkins, et al. Durham: Duke University Press, 2003: 66–87.

Boym, Svetlana. *The Future of Nostalgia*. New York: Basic Books, 2002.

Chambers, Ross. "The Unexamined." In *Whiteness: A Critical Reader*, edited by Mike Hill. New York: New York University Press, 1997: 187–203.

Del Giudice, Luisa. "Sabato Rodia's Towers in Watts: Art, Migration, and Italian Imaginaries." *Sabato Rodia's Towers in Watts: Art, Migrations, Development*, edited by Luisa Del Giudice. New York: Fordham University Press, 2014: 155–82.

DeLillo, Don. "Take the 'A' Train." *Epoch* 12, No. 2 (1962): 9–25.

———. "Spaghetti and Meatballs." *Epoch* 14, No. 3 (1965): 244–50.

———. *White Noise*. New York: Viking, 1985.

———. *Americana*. 1971. New York: Penguin, 1989.

———. *Underworld*. New York: Scribner, 1997.

———. "An Interview with Don DeLillo." Interview with Marc Chénetier and François Happe. *Revue française d'études américaines* 87 (2001): 102–11.

———. "The Art of Fiction CXXXV: Don DeLillo." Interview with Adam Begley. *Conversations with Don DeLillo*, edited by Thomas DePietro. Jackson, MS: University Press of Mississippi, 2005: 86–108.

Doane, Woody. "Rethinking Whiteness Studies." *White Out: The Continuing Significance of Racism*, edited by Ashley W. Doane and Eduardo Bonilla-Silva. New York: Routledge, 2003: 3–20.

Duvall, John N. "Excavating the Underworld of Race and Waste in Cold War History: Baseball, Aesthetics, and Ideology." In *Critical Essays on Don DeLillo*, edited by Hugh Ruppersburg and Tim Engles. New York: G. K. Hall, 2000: 258–81.

———. "*White Noise*, Postmodernism, and Postmodernity." In *Approaches to Teaching DeLillo's White Noise*, edited by Tim Engles and John N. Duvall. New York: Modern Language Association Press, 2006: 116–25.

Engles, Tim. "'Who Are You, Literally?' Fantasies of the White Self in *White Noise*." *MFS: Modern Fiction Studies* 45, No. 3 (1999): 755–87.

———. "DeLillo and the Political Thriller." In *The Cambridge Companion to Don DeLillo*, edited by John N. Duvall. New York: Cambridge University Press, 2008: 66–76.

———. "'I Know You Must Be Somebody': White Masculinity in Don DeLillo's *Americana* and *White Noise.*" In *Don DeLillo: Contemporary Critical Perspectives*, edited by Katherine Da Cunha Lewin and Kiron Ward. London: Bloomsbury (forthcoming, October 2018).

Forman, Murray. *The 'Hood Comes First: Race, Space, and Place in Rap and Hip-Hop.* Middletown, CT: Wesleyan University Press, 2002.

Fox, Margalit. "Henry Hill, Mobster and Movie Inspiration, Dies at 69." *New York Times*, June 13, 2012. http://www.nytimes.com/2012/06/14/nyregion/henry-hill-mobster-of-goodfellas-dies-at-69.html. Accessed 10.25.2016.

Frankenberg, Ruth. *White Women, Race Matters: The Social Construction of Whiteness.* Minneapolis: University of Minnesota Press, 1993.

Gardaphé, Fred L. "The Gangster as Public Intellectual: Anthony Valerio and Don DeLillo." *From Wise Guys to Wise Men: The Gangster and Italian American Masculinities.* New York: Routledge, 2006: 129–48.

Gattuso Hendin, Josephine. "Underworld, Ethnicity, and Found Object Art: Reason and Revelation." In *Don DeLillo: Mao II, Underworld, Falling Man*, edited by Stacey Olster. New York: Continuum, 2011: 99–115.

Giaimo, Paul. "Confronting Unspeakable Evil: DeLillo's 'Filming' Italian Americans." In *Appreciating Don DeLillo: The Moral Force of a Writer's Work.* Westport, CT: Praeger, 2011: 117–38.

Gleason, Paul. "Don DeLillo, T.S. Eliot, and the Redemption of America's Atomic Waste Land." In *UnderWords: Perspectives on Don DeLillo's Underworld*, edited by Joseph Dewey, Steven G. Kellman and Irving Malin. Newark: University of Delaware Press, 2002: 130–43.

Guathier, Marni. *Amnesia and Redress in Contemporary American Fiction: Counterhistory.* New York: Palgrave Macmillan, 2011.

Guglielmo, Thomas A. *White on Arrival: Italians, Race, Color, and Power in Chicago, 1890–1945.* New York: Oxford University Press, 2003.

Haney López, Ian. *White by Law: The Legal Construction of Race.* New York: New York University Press, 2005.

Harding, Wendy. *The Myth of Emptiness and the New American Literature of Place.* Iowa City: University of Iowa Press, 2014.

Heise, Thomas. "White Spaces and Urban Ruins: Postmodern Geographies in Don DeLillo's *Underworld*, 1950s–1990s." In *Urban Underworlds: A Geography of Twentieth-Century American Literature and Culture.* New Brunswick: Rutgers University Press, 2010: 213–54.

"Jerusalem Prize." *Jerusalem International Book Fair.* http://www.jbookfair.com/en/346-2/. Accessed 5.25.2018.

Ladino, Jennifer. "Don DeLillo's Postmodern Homesickness: Nostalgia After the End of Nature." In *Reclaiming Nostalgia: Longing for Nature in American Literature.* Charlottesville: University of Virginia Press, 2012.

Lauret, Maria. "DeLillo's Italian American: The Early Short Stories and *Underworld*." In *Don DeLillo: Contemporary Critical Perspectives*, edited by Katherine Da Cunha Lewin and Kiron Ward. London: London: Bloomsbury (forthcoming, 2018).

Lowenthal, David. *The Past Is a Foreign Country*. Cambridge: Cambridge University Press, 1985.

Marshall, Alan. "From This Point on It's All About Loss: Attachment to Loss in the Novels of Don DeLillo, from *Underworld* to *Falling Man*." *Journal of American Studies* 47, No. 3 (2013): 621–36.

Medovoi, Leerom. "The Race Within: The Biopolitics of the Long Cold War." In *American Literature and Culture in an Age of Cold War: A Critical Reassessment*, edited by Steven Belletto and Daniel Grausam. Iowa City: University of Iowa Press, 2012: 163–86.

Morrison, Toni. *Playing in the Dark: Whiteness and the Literary Imagination*. 1992. New York: Vintage Press, 1993.

Mraović-O'Hare, Damjana. "The Beautiful, Horrifying Past: Nostalgia and Apocalypse in Don DeLillo's *Underworld*." *Criticism* 53, No. 2 (2011): 213–39.

Noon, David. "The Triumph of Death: National Security and Imperial Erasures in Don DeLillo's *Underworld*." *Canadian Review of American Studies* 37, No. 1 (2007): 83–110.

Osteen, Mark. *American Magic and Dread: Don DeLillo's Dialogue with Culture*. Philadelphia, PA: University of Pennsylvania Press, 2000.

Pardini, Samuele F. S. "From Wiseguys to Whiteguys: The Italian American Gangster, Whiteness, and Modernity in Don DeLillo's *Underworld* and Frank Lentricchia's *The Music of the Inferno*." *Critique* 57, No. 3 (2016): 254–67.

Robinson, Sally. "Shopping for the Real: Gender and Consumption in the Critical Reception of DeLillo's *White Noise*." *Postmodern Culture* 23, No. 2 (2013): n.p.

Roediger, David R. *Working Towards Whiteness: How America's Immigrants Became White: The Strange Journey from Ellis Island to the Suburbs*. New York: Basic Books, 2005.

Rosaldo, Renato. "Imperialist Nostalgia." *Representations* 26 (1989): 107–22.

Ruck, Rob. *Raceball: How the Major Leagues Colonized the Black and Latin Game*. Boston, MA: Beacon Press, 2012.

Russo, John Paul. "Don DeLillo: Ethnicity, Religion, and the Critique of Technology." In *The Future Without a Past: The Humanities in a Technological Society*. Columbia: University of Missouri Press, 2005: 211–42.

Salinas, Brenda. "'Columbusing': The Art of Discovering Something That Is Not New." *NPR Code Switch*, July 6, 2014. http://www.npr.org/sections/codeswitch/2014/07/06/328466757/columbusing-the-art-of-discovering-something-that-is-not-new. Accessed 10.25.2016.

Salinger, J. D. *Catcher in the Rye*. Boston: Little, Brown, 1951.

Salván, Paula Martín. "'Of Childhoods and Other Ferocious Times': Traumatic Reverberation in Don DeLillo's *Underworld*." *Amerikastudien* 59, No. 3 (2014): 335–55.

Traber, Daniel S. *Whiteness, Otherness, and the Individualism Paradox from Huck to Punk*. New York: Palgrave Macmillan, 2007.

Vrasti, Wanda. "'Caring' Capitalism and the Duplicity of Critique." *Theory and Event* 14, No. 4 (2011): n.p.

Williams, Richard. "Everything under the Bomb." *The Guardian*, January 10, 1998.   http://www.theguardian.com/books/1998/jan/10/fiction.dondelillo. Accessed 10.25.2016.

CHAPTER 6

Possessive White Male Nostalgia: Louis Begley's *About Schmidt*

Louis Begley is a Jewish American Holocaust survivor who emigrated from Poland to the United States in 1947 at the age of fourteen. As an adult, Begley worked his way through anti-Semitic barriers into Harvard College and then into a successful career in a top-tier (or "white shoe") New York City law firm.[1] While doing so, Begley undoubtedly found it necessary to carefully scrutinize the ways and mores of the northeastern white elite, especially those of the men who primarily formed his clients, colleagues, and competitors. Given the barriers faced by mid-twentieth-century Jewish professionals and the acumen regarding human psychology and behavior required to overcome them, who better than a successful and literarily inclined Jewish American professional to dramatize the subtle attitudes and feelings of those whose ranks he successfully fought to join? Born in 1933 as Ludwik Begleiter, Begley did not begin publishing fiction until the age of fifty-seven. His first novel (with Alfred E. Knopf, which has published nearly all of his subsequent novels), the award-winning *Wartime Lies* (1991), describes a young Holocaust survivor who avoids Nazi persecution by pretending to be Catholic, a story that echoes Begley's own early travails. Begley has since turned primarily to American scenes and characters, and his fourth novel, *About Schmidt* (published in 1996 and the basis for Alexander Payne's eponymous 2002 film), which examines the late-life crisis of a retired lawyer who self-identifies as a WASP, is an acute, deeply observed portrait of privileged, late-twentieth-century white masculinity in crisis. Begley's novel thus joins the ranks of numerous besieged-white-male narratives of

© The Author(s) 2018   185
T. Engles, *White Male Nostalgia in Contemporary North American Literature*, https://doi.org/10.1007/978-3-319-90460-3_6

the 1990s, yet, like DeLillo's *Underworld*, it crucially distinguishes itself from most of them by exposing the emotional states commonly inculcated by the construction of whiteness typically depicted in this brand of fiction as reactionary rather than justified. Thus, the novel can be read as a counternarrative to the era's more standard depictions of white masculinity as a normative yet besieged status since it reveals instead the costs to self and others of the obdurate persistence with which many middle-aged men clung to outmoded codes for white masculine behavior. More to the point of this chapter, the protagonist's persistent enactment of a received script for proper WASP masculinity reflects a steady undercurrent of longing for an earlier era, a social setting in which entitled, grasping, competitive behavior was conducted at the expense, and with the seemingly subservient acquiescence, of gendered and ethnoracially subordinated others.

Some of Albert Schmidt's depicted internal states, which other white-male narratives of the time also illustrate ad nauseam, include anger, grief, and despair, emotions often felt by the privileged when confronted with a changing social order. As Sally Robinson explains in *Marked Men: White Masculinity in Crisis*, her landmark study of an array of '80s and '90s novels written by white American men, such narratives gave voice to an emerging conviction that the rise of identity politics among disempowered groups, and the consequent highlighting of hegemonic white masculinity, constituted an unwarranted attack on white men. Such responses coalesced into a new "identity politics of the dominant," as expressed by such cultural narrative producers as literary authors, filmmakers, TV show writers, and politicians, all of whom frequently cast the supposedly "disenfranchised white man" as a "symbol for the decline of the American way."[2] This widely reiterated narrative ironically appropriated the liberationist claims of the minoritized, reformulating "what had once been an unquestioned privilege … into a liability" and casting the average white male in essentialist terms as a newly restrained repository of imminently and justifiably violent sexual energy.[3] One common reaction among the era's white men, including fictional portrayals created by white men, was to continue feeling and behaving in abusive ways that were once more condoned and even encouraged. A contingent reaction was to reflect nostalgically not only on the actions and apparent virility of younger versions of themselves but also on earlier times and settings, in which their hegemonic status and their possessive prerogatives did not seem under fire.

Writing amidst the popularity of such narratives as a Jewish American achiever of elite access and stature, Begley critiques in *About Schmidt* a particular sector of the white masculine collective, the entitled leaders among those who (as explained in Chapter 2) once openly declared themselves White Anglo-Saxons but who by the late twentieth century had largely been subsumed into less ethnoracially self-conscious whiteness. This chapter examines Begley's psychological appraisal of his protagonist, Albert Schmidt, as a figure who displays emblematic feelings and reactions commonly induced by a salient white supremacist legacy in the era's empowered denizens of insular elite enclaves. Aside from depicting xenophobic and paranoid responses to ethnic and racialized others perceived as intruding into previously exclusive WASP spaces, Begley dramatizes more submerged feelings, including ethnoracially inflected sensations of repression and entitled possessiveness.

As noted in previous chapters, any era's manifestations of racial whiteness are formed and shaped by both regional and national influences. In *About Schmidt*, elite workplaces, families, and neighborhoods receive insightful and at times satiric scrutiny, particularly the legal profession and one of the depicted region's most exclusive districts of respite and social interaction, the Hamptons on New York's Long Island. These locations, along with broader sociohistorical contexts, comprise the extant yet changing structures that encourage Schmidt in new ways to repress many of his emotions and, when they resurface, to channel them into gendered and ethnoracialized reactions and behaviors. My analysis is thus aligned with Jonathan Flatley's study of depictions in earlier modernist literature of potentially productive melancholic states, a scholarly effort to map sociohistorical forces that shape emotions in order to better grasp "the lived, affective and very unfixed, half-articulated way that most of us experience our lives most of the time."[4] Socially constructed whiteness and masculinity are, of course, two such intertwined shaping forces, and reading *About Schmidt* as a diagnostic portrait of a particular, historically contextualized form of whitened masculine subjectivity can illuminate the emotionally driven reactions of such privileged people, who often feel beleaguered by growing numbers and demands of racial or ethnic others (or both) and by the increasing insistence of women to equitable treatment and access. Schmidt ultimately does achieve release from forces that he perceives as being arrayed against himself, in part by reviving a sense of himself that reflects nostalgically glorified memories of his younger days. However, discerning readers can see that his personal losses, including that of his daughter's affection, are greater than he realizes. Begley portrays his protagonist's liberation not as the inevitable and legitimate result of undeserved impositions on elite white men like Schmidt but rather as another destructive symptom of a gendered, sociopolitically situated whiteness—the obstinate elite, northeastern, white masculinity that influences and prompts Schmidt's revanchist reveries and thus his current psychological and emotional reactions.

ENTITLED WHITE MASCULINITY

In interviews and much of his non-fiction work, Begley has expressed admiration for the themes and methods of various modernist writers, many of whom deployed deeply psychological modes of storytelling and character development.[5] Unsurprisingly, *About Schmidt*'s third-person narrative relates events from deep inside the perspective of its protagonist, Albert Schmidt, a sixty-year-old man who instructs seemingly everyone but his daughter to call him by the ironically suggestive diminutive "Schmidtie" but whom the third-person narrator simply calls Schmidt. As the novel opens, Schmidt has recently retired from corporate finance work for Wood & King Associates, and his wife Mary, a relatively high-profile fiction editor, has died several months earlier.[6] Having sold off a large Manhattan apartment, Schmidt now lives in a Bridgehampton house that is technically owned by his deceased wife—more soon on how that important financial arrangement came about. His daughter, Charlotte, who lives in New York City, has recently informed him of her plans to marry Jon Riker, a young Jewish American lawyer at Schmidt's former firm. In a conventionally restrained white Anglo-Saxon Protestant manner, Schmidt recoils from such a supposedly mixed union. Upon meeting Jon's parents, Schmidt recoils further, hastening his plans to flee from the house that Charlotte and Jon had hoped to share with him on their weekends and vacations and pursuing a relationship with Carrie (or, as we later learn, Caridad Gorchuk), a half–Puerto Rican waitress who is one third Schmidt's age. Other significant characters include Jewish American Gil Blackman, who is Schmidt's former Harvard College roommate, current confidant, and lifelong best friend (at least in Schmidt's mind), and Mr. Wilson, or "the man," as Schmidt continually calls him, even after learning his name. This character is a wildly animated homeless white man who, doppelgänger-like, repeatedly shadows and pesters Schmidt.

Primary questions driving the novel's plot include just who "the man" is; whether Schmidt will settle into amicable relations with his daughter and future in-laws; why he reacts as he does to his new situation and to the people he knows; and whether Schmidt will change enough to accept and embrace the life that could be his, that of a respected, successfully retired professional and proud, supportive, and loved father. In a reaction to the 2002 film version of his novel published in the *New York Times*, Begley summarized his novel's intended themes: "Schmidt's frightful and, I believe, lifelong loneliness; the devastating realization that we can botch a relationship that matters to us above all others—in the event, that between Schmidt and his daughter—even though we have worked hard to make it succeed and believe with some reason that we have done a good job; [and] the way in which our fears of the Other and prejudices against the Other imprison us."[7] I would add that Begley also offers an insightful analysis in fictional form of psycho-sociohistorical forces that shape, confine, and guide a representative character's emotions and memories, and thus his self-serving and often abusive treatment of others.

In the novel's opening section, Schmidt struggles with his daughter's engagement announcement and with new living arrangements in the Bridgehampton house. These early domestic scenes establish this protagonist as a geographically and sociohistorically situated exemplar of certain white masculine feelings and proclivities, particularly a presumptive sense of ownership. Sherrow O. Pinder points out that "At the beginning of American history, the distinction between who could *have* property and who could *be* property was paramount."[8] As many other historians have also explained, the social script for respectable, successfully performed white American masculinity long called for property ownership, in terms of both land and people. The latter included not only slaves but also wives and children. Although people are no longer a legally sanctioned form of property, remnants of the perceived perquisites of paternal ownership linger in the habits and feelings of a self-declared WASP like Schmidt, who clearly views his daughter's impending marriage to a Jewish American in terms of loss—the loss of "his" daughter—instead of as a gain of more family members.

On the novel's first page, Charlotte tells her father during breakfast of her decision to get married. At this news, Schmidt openly sheds tears, something he remembers not having done since learning of another imminent loss, that of his wife Mary several months earlier to cancer. As Charlotte strokes his hand, Schmidt tells her that he cannot explain his uncharacteristically emotional display and then attributes it to "happiness. Or because you are so grownup. I'll stop now, I promise."[9] Schmidt's embarrassment about a momentary release from emotional restraint evinces an ethnoracial context. By the time Schmidt had become a successful lawyer for Wood & King, the term "WASP" had gained widespread currency as a descriptor for white Anglo-Saxon protestants. Prior to the twentieth century, "Anglo-Saxon" and "white Anglo-Saxon" had been self-declarations of a dominant ethnic group that harkened back explicitly to English lineage, culture, and traditions. In the early twentieth century, with its influx of increasingly varied European immigrants, the term WASP gained salience, describing less people of Anglo-Saxon descent and more those in the northeastern United States who were not, especially, Catholic or Jewish. By the mid-twentieth century, with the ascent of Dwight D. Eisenhower, a man of German descent, to the presidency, WASP increasingly became a descriptor, largely used by those outside the group, and largely in a disparaging sense, for those who still took pride in having come from, and in still possessing, "old money."

By the dictates and mores of this demographic, crying and other open displays of emotion were rarely acceptable forms of behavior, and the emotions that provoke them were to be squelched or hidden when they arose. As Tad Friend writes in *Cheerful Money: Me, My Family, and the Last Days of Wasp Splendor* (2009), his probing memoir about his own declining WASP family, "I am fiercely but privately emotional.... I ended up spending my inheritance and then some on psychoanalysis. I was in trouble, but it was nearly impossible for anyone who didn't know me well to tell, and I made it nearly impossible for anyone to know me well" (13–14).[10] At one point, Schmidt explicitly self-identifies as a WASP, and it occurs during another emotionally vulnerable moment involving Jon's mother, Renata. As Schmidt writes a diary entry included in the novel about a day that he spent lying sick in bed, he recalls admitting to Renata, "I love my daughter," and then adds in an aside to his diary, "I keep all note of pathos out of my voice. It helps to be the last of the Wasps" (*AS*, 143). As Schmidt processes his daughter's news of her decision to wed, his professed confusion about his emotions may seem sincere. However, as the novel progresses, Begley gradually suggests that the array of conflicted feelings prompting Schmidt's outburst have their roots in common WASP conceptions not only of the supposed value of suppressed emotional display but also of an admirable man's superordinate relations to others. In particular, these mores dictated that the primary mark of male propriety is a relationally heightened level of success, and the primary mark of heightened success is possession, not only of material property but also of people.

As Charlotte enters the kitchen, Schmidt is immersed in figures listed in the *New York Times* related to his financial holdings. Upon hearing Charlotte's announcement, Schmidt "put aside the paper [and] looked at his daughter, so tall and, it seemed to him, painfully desirable in her sweat-soaked running clothes..." (*AS*, 2). For a daughter to seem not only desirable to her own father but "painfully" so strikes an odd note, but Schmidt's twinge of desire for a far younger woman becomes more characteristic of him as the novel progresses. In a particularly perceptive review of this novel, Thomas R. Edwards makes a relevant point about the similarity of the names of three young women whom Schmidt finds desirable: "'Charlotte' sounds just a little like 'Corinne,' the name of the French-Asian *au pair* girl with whom he went to bed [during his forties], and quite a lot like 'Carrie,' the young woman he gets deeply involved with as the book goes on."[11] Although Begley may seem to be depicting with these three "C's" a latent incestuous desire on Schmidt's part, this opening moment, with its conjunction of Schmidt's money, "his" daughter, and perceived threats to both, establishes him more pointedly as a protatgonist whose very identity is grounded in an ethnoracially informed, masculine possessiveness. And, of course, the younger and more conventionally attractive the possessed woman, the more the possessive man feels that those features reflect similarly on himself. These are the terms in which the impending "loss" of Charlotte to marriage means losing instead of gaining for Schmidt, making him feel a self-affirming possessiveness that prompts something akin to unrequited lust. Possession itself, Begley suggests, is a source of excitement for Schmidt, one with a resemblance to sexual excitement that becomes more apparent when that to which Schmidt feels a proprietary right is a woman.

Schmidt's possessive conception of his daughter is further established as a manifestation of an animating disposition when he feels resentment over not having been asked by Charlotte's fiancé for her hand in marriage: "couldn't Riker have gone to the trouble of coming to Charlotte's father to ask for her hand?" (*AS*, 10). Schmidt feels disrespected as a father because he wishes for enactment of a ritual that would have struck most Americans of Charlotte and Jon's generation, if they had even thought of it, as archaic. Indeed, Schmidt's unrequited expectation actually does resonate historically and, in terms of gender and ethnicity, by echoing a particularly Anglo-Saxon tradition of marriage. In the medieval era, these mores dictated that a daughter's prospective husband approach her father in a courtly manner and request the daughter's "hand" in marriage. The request was not merely an effort on the suitor's part to seek paternal approval of himself; it was also a financial transaction since a daughter was a form of paternal property destined to become another man's property, as a wife. As Carl Holliday noted in 1919, in his study of Anglo-Saxon marital customs, "The etymology of the very name 'wedding' betrays the character of the second stage in the development of matrimony. The 'wed' was the money, horses, cattle, or ornaments given as security by the Saxon groom and held by trustees as a pledge and as proof of the purchase of the bride from her father.... [A] handsome daughter has always been considered a decidedly marketable product."[12] Recalling these mores is not to deny, of course, that many other cultures have also treated daughters as transferable property in marriage rituals. Rather, in this particular tradition, and as Schmidt's feelings illustrate, remnants of the Anglo-Saxon conception of impending marriage as a masculinized exchange of property lingered with greater-than-average salience among the entrenched American elite, given their occupancy in the upper realms of a social hierarchy that resembled feudal English stratification in more ways than one. Here and elsewhere, then, Begley depicts the WASP masculinity of his era as a lingering, increasingly besieged ideology with myriad status-related manifestations, including nostalgic yearnings for the restoration of marital traditions that have become outmoded because they strike most people as absurdly patriarchal.

Throughout the novel, Schmidt's latent anti-Semitism functions similarly, as an anxious effort to maintain a pure, entitled sense of class-inflected WASP ethnicity, for himself as well as for his future progeny. Accordingly, certain thoughts and feelings on Schmidt's part suggest that he resents what he sees as an impending loss of his daughter not only to another man but also to a Jewish man and to his Jewish family. Schmidt falsely believes that he succeeds in keeping such feelings to himself. While other characters indicate at times their awareness of Schmidt's genteel bigotry, only his daughter eventually becomes fed up enough to confront him about it directly. In her study of attitudes and mores among the members of exclusive country clubs in the northeastern United States, sociologist Jessica Holden Sherwood notes, "Polite indirection is characteristic of the WASP style of interacting..."[13] In her discussion of Jewish experiences in WASP-led "white shoe" law firms, Martha C. Nussbaum relays the reported preference of a young lawyer for work in a Jewish-led firm: "I went to a Jewish firm partly because I like people who are straightforward and do not hide their emotions.... People used to say, that if you did something wrong in a Jewish firm the partner would jump up and down and scream at you whereas in a white shoe firm they would treat you very nicely and after 7 or 8 years deny you a partnership with no warning."[14] Begley's portrayal of Schmidt's obstinate denial of his own anti-Semitism goes further, suggesting that evasive indirection may even be characteristic of the WASP style of interacting internally *with oneself*, especially about one's own less-than-admirable traits. Although Begley depicts Schmidt interacting with many other characters, he spends most of the narrative on his protagonist's internal divagations and avoidances. As Sherwood also notes of wealthy, northeastern elite values, "a family is conventionally expected to be ethnically homogenous," and a persistent thorn in Schmidt's psyche is his daughter's impending marriage to Jon Riker.[15] Again, a WASP of Schmidt's generation was likely to feel such a union as the "loss" of a daughter, and an attendant feeling is that since she must be released into adulthood, she should at least marry someone "like us," or as Sloan Wilson describes WASPs in the mildly ironic title of a novel in which he attempted to assess them as a demographic, *All the Best People* (1971).[16]

Schmidt's declared identity as "the last of the Wasps" is a grudging recognition that in terms of race and ethnicity, his insular, monochromatic milieu has changed (*AS*, 143). One irony of the novel is that with a name like Schmidt, his own family's entrée into White Anglo-Saxonism is technically tenuous as well as quite recent (as is his wealth). Indeed, although Schmidt has thoroughly adopted the WASP masculine mores of his younger days, his claim to Anglo-Saxonism ultimately proves little more genuine than claims to such a status by a Jewish American would be. Nevertheless, although Schmidt has worked extensively with Jewish colleagues, his daughter's impending marriage still *feels* like an incursion, and Schmidt doesn't quite know why. "Decidedly there was nothing wrong with Jon Riker," the narrator says at one point in Schmidt's internal voice but without directly stating that Schmidt somehow senses the marriage is wrong (*AS*, 10). Rather than admit, even to himself, that his feelings are both anti-Semitic and paternally possessive, Schmidt instead focuses on certain characteristics he remembers being displayed by Jon.

In effect, his nearly unconscious efforts to revive dominant ethnic mores function to reassert his fading sense both of possessive ethnic privilege and of his masculine virility, which feels under attack because of his recent retirement and merely because of his advanced age.

Recollection of actual Jewish American forays into elite northeastern United States settings reveals that although Schmidt thinks he is judging Jon's candidacy for son-in-law by a list of objective criteria, what he actually manages to resuscitate are stereotypes that entrenched elites had come to associate with Jewish Americans, especially the men who worked their way into spaces traditionally owned, both literally and figuratively, by the white Anglo-Saxon protestant elite. These stereotypes constituted an exclusionary strategy of WASP entitlement as it reproduced itself within institutional structures. As Karen Brodkin explains in her study of Jewish American assimilation, exclusive colleges and universities of the mid-twentieth century were converting from finishing schools and sites of social connection for the elite to a "newer professional training mission": "Pressures for change were beginning to transform the curriculum and to reorient college from a gentleman's bastion to a training ground for middle-class professionals needed by an industrial economy."[17] As Begley illustrates in his later novel *Matters of Honor* (2007), which traces the adulthood path of a professionally successful Jewish immigrant much like himself, competing well academically became a viable mode of advancement for Jewish Americans (particularly those of Ashkenazi descent and thus lighter-skinned), who lacked the generationally transferred social capital of elite whites and often as well the nuanced manners, interests, vocabulary, and other markers of insider status. An attendant and greater barrier was the prevailing perception of Jewish people; as Brodkin writes, "The Protestant elite complained that Jews were unwashed, uncouth, unrefined, loud, and pushy."[18] As Nussbaum writes, in addition to laughing out loud and telling jokes, "Above all, [Jewish men] were more emotional about everything, and they simply did not comprehend that emotion, like humor, is itself vulgar and must be carefully concealed, particularly at the dinner table, in order that society should roll on smoothly."[19] Such perceptions of a Jewish other led to de facto forms of discrimination in educational institutions, including admissions applications that asked for religious affiliation as well as "a fixed class size, a chapel requirement, and preference for children of alumni..."[20] In the face of such barriers, doing all that one could do to develop and prove one's suitability for a professional field, especially in academic terms, was a common strategy on the part of ambitious Jewish students. An unfortunate consequence was that such hard work reinforced the elite white perception of Jewish people as fundamentally different—as "pushy" but also as too driven and too narrowly focused to fit in well with the more "well-rounded" Protestant elites.

Begley spends several early pages depicting Schmidt's efforts to sort out his feelings against Jon. His protagonist's rationalizations reflect with finely grained precision several preconceptions that were commonly held against Jews by northeastern white elites during the mid- to late-twentieth century, dramatizing in the process ways in which hegemonic whiteness has become normalized for most of its bearers as a set of proper, practical mores and values. Accordingly, Schmidt's thoughts and feelings on this matter often demonstrate a common lack of self-awareness regarding one's own ethnoracial biases, which white Americans often characterize instead as reasonable, supposedly accurate perceptions of mere differences from an unspecified (though, actually, specifically white) norm. At the same time, the reactions of other characters to Schmidt's obstinate bigotry help to demonstrate, again, that he deploys it in the service of a particularly WASP male sense of entitled possessiveness that has been outmoded for decades.

Schmidt's first ethnoracially tinged demurral regarding Jon is that although he is certainly "an excellent young lawyer, almost certain to become a partner … he works much too hard" (*AS*, 10). After discerning what amounts to a perception of Jewish pushiness, Schmidt dwells further on this supposed characteristic of his future son-in-law, recalling that when he and Jon traveled together for their firm, Jon continued working during night flights while Schmidt "struggle[d]" to stay awake over "some contraband belles lettres" (*AS*, 13). Schmidt often finds time for classic European novels but he does so more dutifully than enthusiastically; the suggestion is that Schmidt regards the habit of reading literature as a distinguishing mark of a conventionally genteel, polished man like himself. Accordingly, Jon's apparent uninterest in such supposedly edifying and broadening fare constitutes a mark against him, and Schmidt recalls Jon reading only one book, "the first volume of Kissinger's memoirs" (*AS*, 13). As the noteworthiness for Schmidt of Henry Kissinger's surname suggests, what clearly makes this supposed uninterest in the arts more risible for Schmidt, and even noticeable, is Jon's Jewishness; because he sees Jon primarily in terms of his ethnicity, especially since Jon has been dating his daughter, his feelings against the young man's encroachment upon Schmidt's familial property of sorts are channeled through the lens of anti-Semitic sentiment. At other points, Schmidt recalls himself having worked excessively hard to achieve prominence in his profession, and the long hours he spent working away from home are identified as another source of estrangement from his daughter; given this contrast to his judgment of Jon's apparent work habits, readers can easily imagine Schmidt ironically overlooking or even embracing such traits in a non-Jewish suitor.

Consideration of the broader context of the legal profession helps to discern the more nuanced details of Begley's portrait of these inclinations in Schmidt. By the late twentieth century, with law firms like Schmidt's former employer of Wood & King having (according to him) "filled up with Jews since the day he had himself gone to work there," elite resistance to Jewish incursions into educational, professional, and social spaces had greatly lessened (*AS*, 14). In a study of the rise and fall of exclusionary WASP law firms and of Jewish firms that arose in response, Eli Wald shows that widespread anti-Semitism was quickly jettisoned in the northeastern legal profession, largely in response to the unprofitable loss of young talent and of clients, Jewish or otherwise, who resented anti-Semitism.[21] As Nussbaum writes of the effects of Jewish success in legal settings, by the 1970s, common Jewish cultural mores had heavily influenced those of WASP-led legal firms and might even be said to have supplanted them:

> what happened was not the triumph of assimilationist WASP manners. It was, instead, the marginalization, indeed the virtual disappearance of those manners. Nobody thinks, any longer, that the behavior of the 1950s country club is formative for law firm success. Guts, emotion, robust humor, talking loudly, using the hands—all these are normal or even normative. It wasn't a merger, not at all. It was a hostile takeover.[22]

Such changes in the ethnic makeup and mores of the legal profession, which occurred during Schmidt's career, render his prejudicial judgments of Jon remarkably old-fashioned. Other moments suggest that although he appears to have harbored bigotry toward Jewish colleagues throughout his career, it lessened over time in response to such changes; he currently thinks, for example, in a rather muted mode: "To the best of his recollection, no matter how deeply or far he looked, Schmidt was sure he had not once in his life stood in the way of a Jew" (*AS*, 13). As a self-professed adherent to a fading WASP heritage as well as a man who now feels that his masculinity is flagging, Schmidt appears to become more anti-Semitic in response to his daughter's impending marriage as he focuses more sharply on the seemingly Jewish traits of not only Jon but also Jon's mother, who tries to cajole Schmidt into embracing new family members. Schmidt is a self-conscious adherent to an elite though faded WASP status and ideology, a man who feels the slipping away of possessions that mark his status; consequently, resurgent anti-Semitism becomes a weapon of sorts in his battle to reassert that status.

Nevertheless, Schmidt can never fully admit, even to himself, that he harbors these culturally instilled prejudicial feelings. His anti-Semitism becomes less genteel as the novel progresses, and his denial of these feelings leads not only to the severance of relationships that could have been positive for him but also to the channeling of those feelings into other possessive, ultimately injurious relationships, all in an effort to restore a sense of individualistic, independent masculinity.

SOVEREIGN WASP MASCULINITY

The complexities of Schmidt's possessive stake in the Bridgehampton house, or his technical lack thereof, are worth spelling out since they serve to flesh out another vestigial sector amidst his socially structured feelings—a long-standing white American male sense that one should stand alone, unencumbered by others, despite needing markedly subordinate others to help establish that status. Early in the novel, having initially sorted through his resentment against Jon as he strolls about the house's yard and ending up little more than angry in the process, Schmidt descends into the cellar, where he makes a momentous decision. A long-standing aggravation has been the fact that this house does not technically belong to Schmidt. Rather, his wife Mary inherited it from an aunt, who had to be persuaded against leaving it to Charlotte, who was only four years old at the time. The aunt nevertheless instructed Mary to leave it to Charlotte when Mary died. As a result, Mary left Schmidt a "life estate" in the house, meaning that when he died, Charlotte would then legally inherit it (*AS*, 18–19). This decision was reached because Charlotte would not be able to afford taxes incurred by inheriting the house but would be able to pay them with money inherited from him when he dies. The upshot for Schmidt of this convoluted plan is the expectation that he continue living in the house and maintaining it,

"a slave to a house that would never be his own" (*AS*, 19). While brood-
ing in the cellar and feeling that he cannot quite be his own man without
owning his own home, Schmidt decides to move out and set up his own,
smaller "shack" in Sag Harbor. He makes this dubious domestic decision
with Charlotte and Jon continually in mind, despite the emotional distance from them it would inevitably create and despite fears of financial
insecurity due to the loss not only of a large amount he would pay for
Charlotte's gift taxes but also of the annual interest income from that
money and of the money to be spent on a new home.

Schmidt goes through these tortuous financial and residential calcu-
lations for two reasons, both resulting from his self-perceived declining
status as a member of a dominant, elite, and thus extensively proper-
tied, ethnoracial group. The first reason is, again, that Schmidt resents
the intrusion into his family life of a Jewish man as well as the expectation that he and his daughter form a marital union with a Jewish family.
The second is that Schmidt considers such a situation even less tolerable
because he cannot commandeer it from the ground base of a home that
he himself actually owns:

> Damn the taxes and the loss of income. He would give the house to
> Charlotte and move out. Living under the same roof with Jon Riker mar-
> ried to Charlotte during vacations, all summer weekends, and however
> many other weekends in the year they would want to use it might have
> been contemplated if it were on his own terrain, in a house that was really
> his, where he made the rules. But never in a fake commune, where he felt
> the obligation to consult those two about calling the plumber, repainting
> the house blue, or ripping out a hedge! (*AS*, 23)

Schmidt attributes his feelings to the potential living situation, which he
disparages as a "fake commune," but what he also exhibits is an instantia-
tion of his locale's lingering dominant ethnoracial habitus. To own one's
home outright upon retirement has, of course, been a long-standing and
central component of the (United States) American Dream, for people
of all races and ethnicities. Nevertheless, Schmidt's feelings and decision here also reflect the shaping influences of a lengthy history of class-
bound ethnoracial formation that exacerbates such common possessive
white male presumptions.

As numerous historians of racial formation have explained, the sense
of achievement that white American men have felt in owning their own

home and land has arisen within a gendered, racialized national context. In terms of material property, early contact between Native Americans and those who later dubbed themselves "white Anglo-Saxons" soon melded with religious conceptions of humanity's responsibility for using what they saw as the God-given gifts of land, flora, and fauna to form colonial conceptions of proper usage of land as just that—usage, via farming especially, a practice which white elites and other "settlers" accused Native Americans of failing to perform (despite abundant evidence to the contrary).[23] White appropriation of land thus became a collective racial responsibility. As Cheryl Harris notes in her groundbreaking work on whiteness as itself a form of property, "being white automatically ensured higher economic returns in the short term, as well as greater economic, political, and social security in the long run."[24] As George Lipsitz and others have demonstrated, numerous subsequent methods of limiting land and other forms of ownership primarily to white men has resulted in vast racial disparities in terms of material and financial possession.[25] In the 1800s, generationally transferred ownership of real estate became a distinguishing hallmark of white Anglo-Saxons, an affiliation that took on salience greater than mere whiteness, as an exclusionary nationalized identity, when waves of non-British European immigrants arrived, most of whom had to work their way gradually into whiteness. In the early 1900s, atomized homeownership became a naturalized ideology, and whether a family rented property, or lived in newly available public housing, or whether one could eventually afford it, in one's own home, became key markers not only of class difference but also of ethnic differences within the hierarchized category of whiteness.[26] A marker of elite Anglo-Saxon masculinity was, of course, a purposefully impressive "estate," consisting of not only a large house and extensive grounds but also enough "help" in the form of hired, decidedly non–Anglo-Saxon people to maintain them.

The century-long fading of an overtly dominant, white Anglo-Saxon ethnicity gradually muted direct expectations of rightful occupancy among what amounted to the nation's self-appointed version of England's landed gentry. However, as Begley's depiction of Schmidt's feelings about the Bridgehampton house illustrate, long-standing white Anglo-Saxon male conceptions and feelings about oneself in relation to significant real estate ownership have lingered.

A broader, contributing factor is that few contemporary white Americans feel disturbed by ongoing racial disparities in home ownership, let alone by their resonant historical roots. One reason that those who possess especially disproportionate amounts of unearned or more easily gained property fail to perceive such disparities as unjust is that ownership of land and housing, and the relative lack of such ownership by non-white Americans, still seems and feels right to them. In Shannon Sullivan's study of "whiteness as possession," she examines "the possessiveness of unconscious habits of white privilege," noting that such ownership habits "manifest an 'appropriate' relationship to the earth, including the people and things that are a part of it":

> The appropriate relationship is one of appropriation: taking land, people and the fruits of others' labor and creativity as one's own. Failure to embody this proper relationship with the world marks one as a subperson, as a quasi-thing that is then legitimately available for, seen in need of, appropriation by full persons…. Whiteness as possession describes not just the act of owning, but also the obsessive psychosomatic state of white owners…. The benefits accrued to white people through this process include not merely economic gain, but also increased ontological security and satisfaction of unconscious desires.[27]

In historical terms, what's of course missing from Sullivan's otherwise helpful analysis is the masculinity of such white people—very few women have been able to occupy the status of such "white owners."

As I will explain, several of Schmidt's possessive "unconscious desires" do indeed come to be satisfied, including that of "ontological security," and the structured racial order in which he lives helps focus his desires toward ultimately damaging pursuits. In the novel's early description of Schmidt's thoughts on the Bridgehampton house, he demonstrates more pointedly the desire for what geographer Steven D. Farough terms "the dominant standpoint of white men, sovereign individuality."[28] This perspective includes a sense of self in terms of socio-geographic spaces that seems to its bearers independent and non-racial: "To be sovereign, or free, means that only those who are in positions of privilege or 'supreme rank or power' may possess a consistent sense of self-determination. The outcome of sovereignty is a subjective sense of 'complete independence,' a distinct separation between the individual and the social world, where the person is self-governing and autonomous."[29] Yet to be a sovereign individual is not to be truly independent, because the very concept depends on self-defining conceptions of others, including, in the case of elite white American men, the conception of oneself as an owner of that which others—usually darker or ethnic others as well as women—do not own, as well as conceptions of other types of people living in less desirable spaces. In this identity-forming dynamic, and as Schmidt goes on to demonstrate, perceiving the egalitarian demands or incursions (or both) of subordinated others can constitute an anxiety-inducing challenge to one's own ontological security, bound up as it is with status, and thus induce a nostalgic longing and grasping for conditions and relationships that seem to resemble those of the past.

In this novel's socio-geographic setting, some of these other people leave their own places of residence in such communities as Sag Harbor to work for people like Schmidt. During his stroll around what amounts to an almost feudally conceived estate, Schmidt notes with satisfaction the "chattering Ecuadoreans" he has hired for yard work (*AS*, 6). Later, he repeatedly refers to a group of women who arrive for weekly housecleaning with the terms "Polish" and "Polacks," and as he ventures outside of the house's grounds, he continually surmises the apparent ethnicities of other people as well. Again, as a more or less landed, self-identified WASP, Schmidt's attention to ethnicity and to its seemingly appropriate residential locations as far from his own establishes the classed and raced differences of such others from himself, thereby asserting his own difference, and supposed superiority, in the process. Begley's attention to Schmidt's conception of hierarchically indicative geographical arrangements furthers the portrait of Schmidt's historically resonant, representatively elevated self-conception.

Schmidt enjoys his house's expansive yard because its meticulous orderliness strikes him as aesthetically pleasing but also because its size provides "the feeling of open space" (*AS*, 5). This feeling of owned openness enhances Schmidt's sense of achieved individualism, but again this is a "sovereign" individualism because his open space exists primarily as such for him not merely because it is relatively empty, but also because that expansive and expensive emptiness constitutes a barrier between himself and other, supposedly lesser people. When Schmidt recalls, for instance, that his neighbor might sell some land for subdivisions and that developers could "put up two or three houses," thereby destroying his feeling of open space, he soon hits upon a solution for maintaining his individualized sense of spatial isolation: "it would not be difficult to plant out whatever monstrosities they might build" (*AS*, 5). As cultural geographers Nancy and Jack Duncan point out, "aesthetic appreciation of residential landscapes is an issue that primarily preoccupies the affluent."[30] However, such appreciation is not merely a matter of aesthetics: "A seemingly innocent pleasure in the aesthetic appreciation of landscapes and efforts to maintain and protect them can act as subtle but highly effective excluding mechanisms for reaffirming class and race identities."[31] In sum, Begley's interiorized portrait of Schmidt dramatizes how keeping other, lesser people out of one's residential space and sightlines is a common, largely unconscious elite white male desire, a sense of landed possessiveness that indicates habitual conceptions of others in subordinated relation to oneself, and thereby one's own vaunted, supposedly independent self-conception as well.

Nostalgic White World-Traveling

Prior to depicting Schmidt in full flight from his daughter and future in-laws and toward a self-involved and ultimately numbing relationship with sexually abused, twenty-year-old Carrie, Begley further cements the elite, white male underpinnings of the sociohistorical and geographically resonant context in which Schmidt is situated by temporarily sending him into an allegorical idyll of privileged, pampered exile. After spending Thanksgiving and another evening with Charlotte, Jon, and his parents, Schmidt declines an invitation to spend Christmas with them, falsely indicating that it feels too soon after the death of his wife to spend a family holiday with anyone but himself. He then visits best friend, Gil, and his wife, Elaine, who help him decide how to spend the holidays. They hit upon the idea of sending Schmidt to "our Amazon island," a small patch of ground in Brazil containing an air strip, a guest house, and "silent" native servants who move "like polite shadows" (*AS*, 156–57). What all three characters demonstrate in this conversation, and by their visits to this island, is described well by Sullivan as a racially informed "ontological expansiveness," the same presumptive feeling in regard to physical space displayed by Shields's protagonist, Jack Bowman: "As ontologically expansive, white people consider all spaces as rightly available for their inhabitation of them."[32] Sullivan elsewhere describes a specific example of this unconscious white way of being and acting as "white world-traveling," an entitled sense not only that all spaces should be entirely available for one's touristic consumption but also that the inhabitants of non-white communities should be hospitably adaptive to white middle-class ways of being, rather than the reverse.[33]

Readers are prompted to think of Schmidt's Brazilian idyll in allegorical terms when Gil twice refers mistakenly to the German ex-patriot who
oversees the island—a man whose name Elaine says is "something like
Oskar Lang"—as "Herr Schmidt." "My Doppelganger," Schmidt replies
in a metanarrative mode (*AS*, 158). As I will explain, another character,
Mr. Wilson, or "the man," better fills the novelistic role of Schmidt's
ontologically suggestive double; nevertheless, when Schmidt later arrives
and settles into the house as the island's only guest, the parallels between
"Oskar Lang" and Schmidt become significant. According to Elaine,
Lang has an unnamed "native" wife whom he appreciates with a paternalistic combination of sexism and racism. "He kept on pointing out to
Gil that white women's breasts fall as they get older," Elaine says, "while
his Indian woman has boobs that stayed small and hard. Like *mein* fist,
only nice, so nice and small, was how he put it!" (*AS*, 158). Schmidt
has also been engaging in increasingly vigorous appreciation of a darker
woman, the half–Puerto Rican waitress Carrie, whom he too finds especially alluring because of the racialized differences between her body and
those of most of the (white) women he has known.

Schmidt, Gil, and Elaine clearly share a collective ideology that structures their conceptions of themselves in relation to racialized others,
both those who live in their environs and nation and, in a more nostalgic sense, some others who live elsewhere. Because white supremacy has
largely morphed into a hegemonic ideology, they register no understanding of how their privileged ability to enjoy such a vacation is enabled by
their positioning within an ongoing colonialist set of relations, between
people who became "white" and in many settings "white Anglo-Saxon"
and those whom they declared inferior and exploitable because of their
darker differences. These hierarchical relations are echoed by the very
arrangement of this island and its "Caboclo servants, very silent, moving like polite shadows. You only see them when you want something,
and they seem to know it without being called" (*AS*, 157). That such
people would have other lives apart from their work for wealthy white
people, and would likely understand much about such visitors because
they need to watch them carefully, never seems to occur to these three
people, the sort who would likely label themselves "Americans," thereby
placing themselves at an empowered, normalized center and ignoring the
fact of other Americas. Upon arrival in Brazil, Schmidt does make some
effort to assess the local context of his vacation by reaching into a more
overtly colonial past for Joseph Conrad's novel *Nostromo* (1904) "since

he decided that if he were going to South America he might as well test his theory that Conrad had fixed in it completely and forever the essence of that continent ..." (*AS*, 173). Aside from fatuously believing that anyone, let alone a Westerner, could capture some singular "essence" of such a highly variegated continent, Schmidt never considers consulting the insights of South American authors. His attempts to analyze the place (though not his own current relation to it) via Conrad apparently fail; as he basks in the sun on the island house's deck, his concentration on the book wanes because he "has been overcome by intense, rather stupid happiness. He feels good all over.... Nature is beautiful and good..." (*AS*, 173).

In spite of this stupefying comfort, and like in other moments in the narrative, pangs of something like privileged, Western white guilt also arise here for Schmidt, along with a twinge of interest in probing within himself for the source of that guilt. Earlier, on the way to a Thanksgiving dinner with Jon's parents, such feelings also arise when Schmidt stops at the exclusive Harvard Club, where he makes his way to a restroom, adjusts his hair and clothing, and then leaves for the Rikers' apartment. As he approaches their home, Schmidt has no particular conscious reason for stopping at the club. That this WASP male has an underlying need to bolster himself, precisely as a racially sanctioned member of the Ivy League–educated elite (one who at the moment resents the paternal loss threatened by the incursion into his family and world of Jewish people), is suggested by his self-assessing pause in front of the restroom mirror. The mirror tells him that he "looked worse than even the sour person wearing his own clothes he had glimpsed returning his own stare from a Fifth Avenue window" (*AS*, 91). Of course, time changes everyone fortunate enough to reach Schmidt's age of sixty, but this brief Harvard Club visit itself and what drives Schmidt to make it suggest just how this man does not know himself. Since readers know by this point that Schmidt looks down, as it were, on the Rikers merely because they are Jewish, he clearly pauses at this bastion of elite privilege not to partake of its amenities but rather to reassert his position in relation to the Rikers as a member of the WASP elite who once in effect owned elite northeastern culture and spaces.

That Schmidt's continual need to shore up his self-conception is the point here, and that it is ever ironically relational in a sense that became fixed in him decades earlier, become more evident when thoughts of less privileged others very briefly occur to him: "There's enough fancy stuff on me to lodge and feed a homeless family for a month" (*AS*, 93). Another pang of this sort arises as Schmidt basks in his stupor of "happiness" on the Amazonian island when he idly imagines "barefoot, brown boys and girls tirelessly playing soccer in the village perhaps half a mile away with a bundle of rags tied with a string [who] will never get to kick a leather ball or learn to read" (*AS*, 173).[34] At these moments, such thoughts, not only of perceived others but also of his highly privileged positioning in relation to them, subside quickly, as Schmidt performs habitual internal retreats from a better understanding of his social positionality and from his emotions (in this case, something like sympathy) into a numbed, isolated distance from others. Accustomed to thinking of his subordinated others, especially women and ethnic or darker people, in an increasingly archaic sense, as the emotional ones and thus of himself as rational and controlled, Schmidt continually retreats from the possibility of a more mature understanding of his own highly raced and gendered emotions. He instead pursues internal numbness, especially during encounters in which he is confronted with those he persistently perceives as vaguely threatening or inferior others or both, through such palliatives as a pampered vacation, alcohol, and, later in the novel, sex and money.

THE WHITE MANCHILD

Since Begley depicts his protagonist as a representative white male who lacks self-awareness, Schmidt serves as an ostensibly respectable, successful insider who in a sense is not yet a fully mature adult. Not only does he make remarkably selfish and immature choices in his relationships, he does so because the broader structures of feeling in which he operates, and in which he has been raised, have stunted his emotional capacities and responses.[35] As with other aspects of his psyche, his obstinate adherence to early relational constructions of white masculine identity account for much of this problem. As white men developed their collective self-conception in relation to others, a European claim of limited emotional capacities in non-white people arose. In these terms, *About Schmidt* initially reads as a sort of late-life bildungsroman, and it's worth noting that this term is commonly understood as having two primary components: a "novel that recounts the development (psychological and sometimes spiritual) of an individual from childhood to maturity, to the point at which the protagonist recognizes his or her place in the world."[36] A key character in this regard is the seemingly minor figure of a person whom Schmidt continually refers to as "the man" even after learning his name. Deployed by Begley as Schmidt's doppelgänger, this person represents the "darker" racialized and sexualized aspects of Schmidt's psyche, and he also functions, like other traditional doppelgängers, as the potential bearer of a message to Schmidt about these deleterious sides of himself. That Schmidt ultimately fails to receive this message, and thus to mature emotionally, has much to do with his self-conception as the "last of the Wasps" (*AS*, 143).

Schmidt first encounters this man after falling asleep on a bus while trying to read another European classic, Trollope's 1855 novel, *The Warden*.[37] Significantly, Schmidt is on his way home after the Thanksgiving dinner at which he has met Jon's parents for the first time. Jon's mother, Renata, is a psychiatrist, and she has pulled Schmidt aside for a long, inquisitive chat. As Renata asks Schmidt increasingly personal questions, she warmly takes his hand. Schmidt is unaccustomed to such open intimacy with women, except in sexual encounters. Accordingly, he considers trying to fondle Renata's breast and then tells her, "I want to kiss you" (*AS*, 117). She rebuffs him, apparently uninterested in sex because her actual goal—acceptance and affection from Schmidt toward her son and his union with Charlotte—occurs at an emotional level, a realm from which Schmidt habitually flees. Having had his masculinity bruised yet again by the rejection, Schmidt abruptly ends the conversation by telling Renata of his plans to give his life estate in the Bridgehampton house to Charlotte as a wedding gift and of moving into his own house, thereby withdrawing, both literally and symbolically, from the newly formed family that would include the Rikers. Schmidt, then, is briefly attracted to Renata not as a friendly and caring future fellow parent-in-law but rather, in a more adolescent manner, as a sexualized and exotified (because of her Jewishness) female. The stage set that is Schmidt's internal emotional landscape has thus been arranged for the entrance of "the man," a doppelgänger who immediately emerges as if from Schmidt's dreaming unconscious.

On an otherwise empty bus that evening, this shambolic white man invades Schmidt's personal space, and indeed his personhood itself, by sitting right next to him. Both this man and Schmidt have fallen asleep when the latter is awakened by a "stench" (*AS*, 118). In their study of racialized aesthetics in suburban New York settings, geographers Duncan and Duncan note that in such ostensibly tolerant settings, "the Other is not so different from me as to be an object.... But at the level of practical consciousness they are affectively marked as different."[38] Because tolerating racial difference (if not embracing it) had become a polite white norm by Schmidt's time, racial difference is no longer perceived in essentialist terms, and explicitly naming it has become censured as well. An affective result is that members of other racialized groups "threaten to cross over the border of the subject's identity because discursive consciousness will not name them as completely different.... The face-to-face presence of these others, who do not act as if they have their own 'place,' a status to which they are not confined, thus threatens aspects of my basic security system, my basic sense of identity, and I must turn away with disgust and revulsion."[39] Similar responses in Schmidt are evoked by this man, but in order for him to function more clearly as Schmidt's abjectified doppelgänger, his difference from Schmidt is marked in terms of class rather than race. As Begley depicts Schmidt confronting the reality of the person slumbering noisily beside him, he underlines the man's flagrant corporeality to comedic, satiric effect:

> He shifted in his seat and broke wind. It was expelled in ample bursts, followed by a liquid rumbling in the stomach.... The cloacal odor was unbearable, but different from the stench that had interrupted Schmidt's sleep and continued to nauseate him. Was the man hiding a piece of carrion in his pocket, had he a suppurating wound on his feet or somewhere under his clothes? It seemed impossible that an accumulation of dirt and sweat alone could account for such fetor. (*AS*, 119)

Humor arises in this scene, not from the man's rank corporeality but rather—as emphasized by such recondite vocabulary as *cloacal, carrion, suppurating,* and *fetor*—from Schmidt's appalled reaction to it. Again, as an apparent "hobo," this man is othered with disgust in classist terms, but Schmidt's revulsion also springs from a literal invasion of himself, via his senses, by humanity abjectified as filth. Schmidt's rising panic as he awakens the man and tries to get past him is thus a reaction to the breaching of his "basic security system," and the man also represents a threat to Schmidt's "basic sense of identity," a threat that grows as Schmidt repeatedly encounters this character during a time in his life when events and the desires of others seem to be undercutting his possessive masculine WASP sense of himself. Eventually, this man's blatant violation of genteel WASP decorum renders him a signaling foil for the novel's protagonist, an indicator, should Schmidt be willing to see "the man" in such self-reflecting terms, of his own refusal to relinquish that which is causing his excessive possessiveness, that is, his internal and thus behavioral "filth."

Begley emphasizes this mirroring possibility of self-recognition by detailing this character's suggestive physical similarities to his protagonist. Schmidt is wearing his dead father's tweed jacket, and this man, who is "as tall" as Schmidt, is "dressed in a threadbare tweed suit of the same shade" (AS, 119). Schmidt, a self-declared WASP with a discordantly German name, is also mirrored in his perception of this man's "good English or German face"; the man also wears a tie and carries a cane, with which he swaggers foppishly at other points in the novel, a mocking echo of Schmidt's own rather pompously inflated masculinity and class status.[40] In such ways, this man's seemingly parodic appropriation of genteel masculinity, despite his othered "hobo" status, threatens to disrupt the brittle identity that Schmidt has been trying to shore up. As a traditionally deployed doppelgänger, "the man" represents resurgent sides of Schmidt that he actively represses from his own conscious awareness; accordingly, Schmidt presses past this person with an excuse about having "to go to the can this very minute," takes another seat far from the man, and then scurries to his car and locks himself inside (AS, 120).

Schmidt goes on to encounter this person several more times. In one scene, while Schmidt chats with Carrie in O'Henry's, her place of employment, this man appears outside the restaurant's window. He winks at Schmidt, gives him the finger when Schmidt doesn't respond, and then leaves obediently when Carrie shakes her fist and waves him away. At another point, after dining with Gil and Elaine and hearing their suggestion of a trip to Brazil, Schmidt drives home with Gil. As his headlights shine on the house, he notices a figure on the porch, "like a melting snowman, squatting on top of the steps. Its exposed buttocks were fat and exceedingly white" (AS, 162). Schmidt recognizes this figure, who pulls up his pants and scurries away, as the same man. What he does not recognize is the symbolic import of that which the man has left literally on his doorstep, "the fruit of the white buttocks" (AS, 164). Significantly, Schmidt scoops up the feces, throws it away, and continues to more or less ignore both this person and the question of why he has taken an interest in Schmidt, paralleling his disavowal of all the disturbing clues about himself and his structurally informed emotions that this figure does deliver to alert readers.

Those attuned to common usages of the doppelgänger figure will be primed by these encounters with "the man" to watch for an internal change in Schmidt, which would manifest as him recognizing, and then grappling with, that which this abject figure represents, that is, the unacknowledged content that has backed up, as it were, in his own constipated psyche. These parts of himself—his adamant and antiquated sexist and ethnoracial bigotry—are not components of self that a late-twentieth-century WASP male faced with a changing social order is likely to acknowledge, perhaps even to himself. As Thandeka writes in her analysis of common modes of white shame, "Experiences of shame are self-exposures that lower one's own sense of personal esteem and respect. They are snapshots of embarrassing features of the self. Looking at these uncomplimentary mug shots, one feels shame, as in the feeling 'I am unlovable.'"[41] Yet, as Schmidt continually demonstrates, shame, disgust, and other ugly feelings about himself nevertheless arise, provoking his actions in ways that the more conscious and socially sanctioned side of himself guiltily recognizes at times as reprehensible. When interpreted in this light, "the man" represents the man performing behind the social imposture of "Schmidtie," and whether Schmidt will recognize this mirrored image of himself, thereby advancing in maturity—by dealing better with the egalitarian demands of others and with his own circumstances instead of longing for times in which WASP male perquisites and mores seemed securely ascendant—becomes the novel's central question.

Repressed White Male Shame

After discarding the mess on his porch, Schmidt enters the house with Gil and tells him about having seen the same man at O'Henry's and about odd feelings that this man has repeatedly triggered in him, including "revulsion," "panic," and a suspicion that this man is trying to "terrorize" him (*AS*, 168). After Gil leaves, Schmidt, who often imbibes heavily, pours himself another drink as he ponders what to do about the man and the odd feelings that this person inspires. "Shame and paralysis!" he thinks, as he ponders whether to call the police (*AS*, 168). Were Schmidt to analyze his strong yet confused reactions to the man more fully, he might wonder why these feelings arise. Readers, of course, are invited to perform this analysis themselves. Given the hints here of connections made in traditional psychoanalysis between abject bodily functions and shame, as well as the probing conversations that Schmidt twice endures with Jon's psychiatrist mother, Renata, an interpretation of "the man" as the bearer of a message about the denied parts of Schmidt's self—his bigotry, possessiveness, and misdirected, exotifying sexual desire, especially—becomes appropriate. In rather traditional Freudian terms that resemble those deployed by Wright in *Savage Holiday*, qualities and behavior displayed by "the man" function symbolically as the return of Schmidt's repressed. Schmidt has spent a lifetime denying to both himself and others his own destructive, possessive feelings and characteristics. That he may well continue to ignore his occasional, resultant shame is suggested here, and elsewhere, by his habit of anesthetizing himself whenever budding sensitivity arises within him, in this case with alcohol, which clouds and diverts his thoughts about "the man" onto other subjects. Schmidt also turns to sex and money for similar reasons, reasons that inspire in him falsely restorative modes of nostalgia.

A more direct connection between Schmidt and this man arises one night when Carrie unexpectedly arrives at Schmidt's house for the first time. As Schmidt begins a sexual relationship with her, Carrie reveals that she met the apparently homeless man when she was fourteen years old and that he has been following her ever since. The topic arises when Schmidt asks Carrie who the love of her life is, and she reveals that this man was once a chemistry teacher named Mr. Wilson: "An old guy like you. He broke me in" (*AS*, 212). Mr. Wilson (we never learn his first name) began having sex with Carrie after he walked in on her during a sexual encounter with a fellow student in a classroom. Whether Carrie is attracted to Schmidt because she now simply prefers "old guys" or because, like many people who have been sexually abused, she unconsciously seeks reminders and repetition of her abuse is a question the novel does not answer.[42]

Within the framework of Begley's anatomization of Schmidt's culturally induced and outmoded inclinations, it is significant that Schmidt never questions Carrie's attraction to himself. He has pursued her for several months by dining at O'Henry's, where Carrie always serves him, and now that she has arrived literally at his doorstep—the same place where Mr. Wilson left his abjectified message of sorts for Schmidt—he instead revels in the feeling that he now possesses her. When Carrie asks what he likes about her, he replies, "It's what you said, you belong to me" (*AS*, 199). Begley underlines how strongly the urge to possess drives his representative WASP male protagonist when Schmidt also ponders to himself at this moment how his life has changed: "Here was an aspect of unemployment and nearly total loneliness he had not previously examined, let alone apprehended: they set one free! … There was [only] Charlotte's wedding reception to be held in June, and the need, which was turning into a wish, to move into another house" (*AS*, 198). The "need" Schmidt had felt to move into another house, and away from one that he did not technically own, is weakening into a "wish" because he now feels that he possesses Carrie. This feeling compensates for the possessive lack Schmidt had felt before as he considered the looming "loss" of his daughter and the expectations that he live in and be "a slave to a house that would never be his own" (*AS*, 19).

Begley's primary point about the culturally induced inclinations and feelings instilled long ago in Schmidt because of his social positionality as an older, unregenerate WASP male is that his clinging to them steers him toward further loss and destruction. At this point in the narrative, because at this stage in his life he especially objects to "losing" his daughter to a Jewish husband, Schmidt is gradually alienating and driving away both his daughter and his future in-laws. Similarly, the satisfaction he now takes in believing that he possesses Carrie, while concurrently feeling a rejuvenated sense of domineering masculinity, blinds him not only to what he really sees in her—an objectified entity for him to "own"—but also to who she is and to the significance of who else she shares her life with, especially Bryan, a young man who lives in nearby Sag Harbor: "I've kind of been with him since I got this job [at O'Henry's]" (*AS*, 210). This news "[goes] through Schmidt like an icicle," but he ignores how this relationship may well be more significant to her than the one she has with Schmidt, continuing to insist that she still "belongs" to him: "Nothing mattered. He had to keep her body. She said she belonged to him" (*AS*, 210). Indulging this narcissistic desire distracts Schmidt from thinking about what Bryan really means to Carrie and thus about what he himself could mean to her.

Nevertheless, Schmidt's relationship with Carrie is not portrayed as an entirely negative manifestation of his self-absorbed WASP male possessiveness, and Begley clearly does not cast a disapproving authorial eye merely because of the socially inappropriate age gap. To the contrary, Begley has stated that he meant for the union to represent a possibility for Schmidt to break out of his numbed loneliness. In his commentary on the film based on his novel, Begley writes of the filmmakers' decision not to include Carrie: "I missed the theme of the redemptive and regenerative power of Eros, embodied in my novel by Carrie, the personage

I care for most among all that I have created.... her love for Schmidt, and the torrid sex between them, ripen him and open the possibility that he will become a freer and wiser man."[43] By emphasizing here both a pent-up sexual force in his protagonist and the potential of a sexist, one-dimensional caricature of a conveniently available female to provide release, Begley would seem to echo in this regard other American "male liberationist" writers of his time. As Robinson notes, these writers typically portrayed a dominant white masculinity in crisis, in the form of central characters who are "wounded by their power, their responsibilities, and indeed, by patriarchy itself."[44] A problem with many such texts is that, unlike Begley in *About Schmidt*, their authors lose sight of how social relations nevertheless both influence and empower white men. Schmidt does revel in sexual release with Carrie, and he does become temporarily enlivened by it, but his primary interest in her—ego-boosting, possessive sex—soon becomes but another palliative, which both numbs him and distracts him, especially from the impending severance of any positive connection with his daughter Charlotte.

As a representative middle-aged male WASP who continually represses powerful feelings, Schmidt has battened down the complex emotions provoked by the loss of his wife Mary and by Charlotte's engagement. Begley highlights Schmidt's anesthetic use of both alcohol and Carrie during a telephone conversation with Charlotte about her wedding plans, including the expected services of a rabbi. Carrie has quietly situated herself in his lap, but as Schmidt struggles to express his objections to a Jewish wedding and as his emotions rise accordingly, he notices that the warm glow of sex and a nap is fading: "The novocaine was wearing off. He nudged Carrie off his lap" (*AS*, 203). Carrie then prepares a drink for Schmidt, and as Charlotte presses her father on the prejudice that he is again obliquely but obstinately expressing, he thinks, "The effect of one hundred proof bourbon on an empty stomach was marvelous" (*AS*, 205). Confronted with an emotional eruption that pushes him to acknowledge, just as his daughter is doing, his own bigoted and possessive self, Schmidt's habitual repression asserts itself. After offering the evasive (and common white) assertion that he cannot be harboring discriminatory feelings against Jews because he has openly socialized with many of them,[45] Schmidt abruptly ends the conversation and then turns immediately to Carrie for condolence and then for more sex, this time on the kitchen table. His refusal to acknowledge certain emotions, let alone to consider their sources, continues, as does his compensatory drive to possess others, and the gap between himself, his daughter, and the possibility of wider familial contentment increases. Thus, where Begley differs from the essentialist politics of many of his era's white male storytellers is by maintaining a critical focus on broader forces that influence common white male feelings. Although a man in Schmidt's situation might find some sort of life-affirming release in a new sexual relationship, Begley's protagonist remains sadly responsive to earlier sociohistorical forces that have shaped his emotions and actions, warping how he regards and reacts in a newer social order toward not only Carrie, his daughter, and his future in-laws but also himself and his own general future.

As the novel approaches its conclusion, Schmidt again meets with Jon's mother, Renata. He requests that they meet at "his club," the Harvard Club, a spatial choice that suggests how being energized by Carrie has solidified not into a new appreciation for life and the people around him but rather into his habitual mode of privileged and possessive white masculinity. Prior to consummating his relationship with Carrie, Schmidt had vacillated between finding Renata bearable and alluring, but he now thinks of her as a "meddling witch" (*AS*, 216). As they talk, it becomes clear that Charlotte is quite happy to join their Jewish family and also to move further from what remains of her own family, that is, her father. Renata relays to him Jon and Charlotte's proposal, that contrary to his own idea regarding the Bridgehampton property—that he pay her gift taxes so the house will be hers right away rather than when he dies—he instead buy out her portion and keep the house himself. Schmidt agrees, reasoning to himself that he can quickly sell it and that he "wouldn't be selling the Schmidts' ancestral homestead. Someone must have sold that long ago" (*AS*, 229). Charlotte and Jon are instead thinking of buying property north of New York City, and they will also hold the wedding reception at a restaurant in Manhattan instead of in Bridgehampton, where Schmidt had hoped it would be. That he has lost all shreds of his daughter's affection seems obvious to all but Schmidt, who suppresses, beyond even his own awareness, his sense of loss in order to focus instead on being sure that he understands the financial matters at hand and what the various arrangements will cost him in those terms. When he later reads a letter from Charlotte that further explains her wishes regarding the house and the wedding, he quickly writes back, mostly to assert again his own financial agreements and refusals, the latter including a notice that he will keep the family

silverware that Charlotte has requested. His own curtness is clearly further prompted by Charlotte's explanation in her letter that she will likely
convert to Judaism. When Schmidt finishes his letter, his masculine
and ethnoracialized tendency to suppress his feelings results in another:
"Shouldn't I send a copy of the letter to Renata? … In the end, he didn't
do it; he felt too ashamed" (*AS*, 242). Once again, Schmidt does not
understand his sense of shame, let alone examine it. Readers can surmise
that for a moment he feels something akin to disgust with his actions,
and ultimately with himself, not only because he has driven away his
daughter but also because he let his possessiveness, and thus his resurgent
anti-Semitism, cause that to happen.

Begley suggests in these moments that although the feelings of paternalistic, ethnoracial shame are often confusing, searching for their roots
can prove enlightening, particularly in regard to how one conceives of
oneself. Schmidt's ultimate failure is his refusal to take the opportunity
for personal understanding and growth provided by a more egalitarian social order and thus by the provocation of the surprising emotions
it evokes in him. Were such a person to do so, he might uncover the
sources of his anti-Semitism in his early training as WASP male status and
its attendant mores, which have no doubt included disdain for and fears
of Jewish people, effectively embedding such feelings within him and
creating an illusory psychic split between "his" people and "them" that
he refuses to suture.

That Schmidt will continue refusing as well to face the roots of his
own emotional confusion is conclusively suggested in what I read as
the climax of this novel's largely internal drama—Schmidt's killing of
the person he only ever refers to as "the man." After attending a party
thrown by fellow Hamptons residents who are no longer, and clearly
never really were, his friends, Schmidt races home toward Carrie. He hits
a lengthy patch of dense fog, "an immense, unending bottle of milk,"
out of which rises none other than the man (*AS*, 266). Like a deus ex
machina, the car kills this message-bearing adversary, freeing Schmidt
from an irritating and vaguely frightening presence and freeing him as
well, at a symbolic and subliminal level, from the various forces that have
been pushing him to confront the repressed, rigidly maintained characteristics within himself that this mirroring double figure represents. Just
as Schmidt has refused to recognize this person with his name, "Mr.
Wilson," he also refuses to recognize the actual "man" that he himself

remains. In this sense, then, this novel's protagonist refuses to grow up; he remains the "Schmidtie" of yore instead of becoming Albert Schmidt.

By portraying the inner workings of a recalcitrant United States American who feels that his status is under threat, Begley exposes the effects of masculine, white supremacist forces that commonly animated the more traditional members of an elite demographic. These are ongoing sociohistorical forces that also bolster an inequitable social order and discourage recuperative human connection. In the novel's denouement, after the car accident, Schmidt finds himself being nursed at the Bridgehampton house by Bryan, the young man whom Carrie has said she is "kind of seeing." Schmidt remembers his plans to sell the house after buying out Charlotte's share since the cost of upkeep would be beyond his remaining means. It becomes clear that Bryan and Carrie are involved in illegal drug trafficking, and when they smoke hashish in front of him, he refuses to partake, preferring his own habitual anesthetics. He remains largely unconcerned about what the true relationship and motives of this pair might be and fixated instead on Carrie's continued claims that she actually "belongs" to him. In the novel's final pages, Schmidt receives a letter regarding the death of his stepmother, who had been living in Florida. In a traditional O'Henry twist, the letter reveals that she has left him a great deal of money, both from his long-dead father and from her own deceased family members.[46]

Schmidt now has no need to sell the Bridgehampton house, and having just acquired another one in Florida, he instantly sees a way to vanquish this young man, whom he can't help but think of as a rival for Carrie's body and affections. Bryan has portrayed himself as something of a jack-of-all-trades, so the novel closes with Schmidt offering to hire him for extensive renovations on the Florida house, a move that would leave Carrie with Schmidt. Thus, while Begley provides an ostensibly happy ending, careful readers will deduce that, as Victoria N. Alexander writes, "Schmidt's world, like King Lear's, is presided over by irrational gods."[47] Given the course of Begley's penetrating, incisive depiction of both his protagonist's representatively distorted WASP-male emotional inclinations and an obstinate refusal to explore and alter them, Schmidt seems likely to go on harming himself and others. He remains stubbornly influenced by an earlier era's racially influenced inducements toward enactment of material and corporeal possessiveness and thus into continuing to assert a using, abusing, and narcissistic version of himself.

Notes

1. Hepburn, 380 and Begley, "Louis Begley, The Art of Fiction," 111.
2. Robinson, *Marked Men*, 3, 2.
3. Robinson, *Marked Men*, 5.
4. Flatley, 25. As noted in this study's introduction, see also Frederik Tygstrup, who writes that if we understand the self as socially situated in such a way that discernible structures like whiteness and masculinity tend to provoke predictable emotional responses, then "we can study the self in different historical situations and chart different historically contextualized emotions," and we can also trace "how [such] subjectively felt emotions taint the perception of outer stimuli..." (195).
5. Begley's explicitly admired modernists include Henry James, Marcel Proust, F. Scott Fitzgerald, Hemingway, Joseph Conrad, Thomas Mann, and Franz Kafka (Begley, "Louis Begley, The Art of Fiction," 126–27). Begley has also written a biography of Kafka, *The Tremendous World I Have Inside My Head: Franz Kafka: A Biographical Essay* (Atlas & Co., 2008).
6. When pronounced aloud, the firm's name sounds like "wooden king," suggesting Schmidt's lack of human emotional display as well as his elevated but rickety pose of self-assuredness. In Alexander Payne's 2002 film version of the same name, Schmidt's job is changed to actuary at an insurance company with an equally suggestive name, "Woodman of the World" (*About Schmidt*).
7. Begley, "My Novel," n.p.
8. Pinder, 33, emphasis in original.
9. Begley, *About Schmidt*, 4. Hereafter cited as *AS*.
10. Friend, 13–14.
11. Edwards, 65.
12. Holliday, 9, 11.
13. Sherwood, 43.
14. Nussbaum, 180.
15. Sherwood, 43.
16. Begley again assesses this group as a demographic, particularly its wealthier members, in his novel *Memories of a Marriage*, in which the protagonist remarks on the city of Salem, Massachusetts as the place "where my ancestors have lived since before the witch trials" (Begley, *Memories*, 187).
17. Brodkin, 31.
18. Ibid., 30.
19. Nussbaum, 165.
20. Ibid., 31.

21. Wald, "The Rise and Fall of the WASP and Jewish Law Firms."
22. Nussbaum, 180.
23. See Dunbar-Ortiz, *An Indigenous Peoples' History of the United States*; Reginald Horsman, *Race and Manifest Destiny: Origins of Racial Anglo-Saxonism*; Charles C. Mann, *1491: New Revelations of the Americas Before Columbus*; and Ronald Takaki, *A Different Mirror: A History of Multicultural America*.
24. Harris, 1713.
25. See George Lipsitz's *The Possessive Investment in Whiteness: How White People Profit from Identity Politics* and Melvin Oliver and Thomas Shapiro's *Black Wealth/White Wealth: A New Perspective on Racial Inequality*.
26. Regarding the salience of race and ethnicity in residential terms, see David R. Roediger's *Working Toward Whiteness: How America's Immigrants Become White. The Strange Journey from Ellis Island to the Suburbs* and Richard Ronald's *The Ideology of Home Ownership: Homeowner Societies and the Role of Housing*.
27. Sullivan, *Revealing Whiteness*, 122.
28. Farough, 243.
29. Ibid., 244.
30. Duncan and Duncan, 160.
31. Ibid., 160. See also Eduardo Bonilla-Silva and David G. Embrick, "'Every Place Has a Ghetto…'"
32. Sullivan, *Revealing Whiteness*, 144.
33. Sullivan, "White World-Traveling," 303. Sullivan acknowledges her debt to María C. Lugones for the term and concept of "world-traveling."
34. As Timothy J. Lensmire writes, "People of color are central to the drama of White lives…. White people are *always already in relationships with people of color (even if imagined) and always already 'know' them*" (Lensmire, 26, emphasis in original).
35. It's worth noting here that when asked for recommendations of novels from his native region, Begley recommended—for the same reason—Polish novelist Witold Gombrowicz's *Ferdydurke* (1937): "Gombrowicz is one of the greatest writers of the 20th century. … *Ferdydurke* [is] a haunting humorous and terrifying nightmare about *how society forces us into immaturity*. Whoever hasn't read it should drop all other occupations and plunge into it" (Charney, n.p., emphasis added).
36. Murfin and Supriya, 39.
37. As Begley suggests in his description of Schmidt as a man whose prejudices "imprison" him ("My Novel," n.p.), the Trollope title, *The Warden*, indicates Schmidt's figurative status as both prisoner and warden; as a WASP male, he has usually followed dictates for a person like himself that

entail "proper" containment of perceived desires and impulses. Others are perceived in a binary mode as "other" because they supposedly fail to contain, or imprison, themselves in these ways.

38. Duncan and Duncan, 172.
39. Ibid.
40. Another repressed side of Schmidt's self, his family's forgotten ethnicity, is represented by both this doppelgänger with a "good English or German face" and the doppelgänger-like figure of the German Amazonian island proprietor, whom Gil mistakenly dubs "Herr Schmidt." As Russell A. Kazal notes in his study of formations of German ethnicity and assimilation in Philadelphia, "No other large immigrant group in the twentieth century saw its country of origin twice go to war with the United States; none, correspondingly, faced such sustained pressure to forego its ethnic identity for an 'American' one; and none appeared to mute its ethnic identity to so great an extent" (11). As Kazal also points out, degrees of German assimilation took different forms in different times and places and in accordance to differing affiliations within the German immigrant population. Those who were Protestant rather than Catholic, for instance, often assimilated into whiteness more readily, a difference that would help to account for the accelerated movement of German descendants like Schmidt's toward a self-declared WASP identity.
41. Thandeka, 12.
42. As Bessel A. van der Kolk notes regarding the repetition compulsion initially conceptualized by Freud, "Many traumatized people expose themselves, seemingly compulsively, to situations reminiscent of the original trauma. These behavioral reenactments are rarely consciously understood to be related to earlier life experiences" (389). See also M. S. Levy, "A Conceptualization of the Repetition Compulsion."
43. Begley, "My Novel," n.p.
44. Robinson, *Marked Men*, 130.
45. Schmidt echoes here a "standard semantic move" of defensive, white American "post-Civil Rights racial discourse," a move perhaps most commonly iterated in the phrase "Some of my best friends are black" (Bonilla-Silva, 99).
46. As Steven G. Kellman writes, "The fact that Schmidt dines regularly at a local Bridgehampton restaurant named O'Henry's should alert the reader to a reversal of fortune on the final page" (99). William Sydney Porter (1852–1910) published over 600 short stories under the pen name of O. Henry; their most remembered feature is surprise endings.
47. Alexander, 302.

BIBLIOGRAPHY

About Schmidt. Directed by Alexander Payne. 2002. Burbank, CA: New Line Entertainment, 2003. DVD.

Alexander, Victoria N. "Louis Begley: Trying to Make Sense of It." *The Antioch Review* 55 No. 3 (1997): 292–304.

Begley, Louis. *About Schmidt*. New York: Knopf, 1996.

———. "Louis Begley, The Art of Fiction No. 172." Interview with James Atlas. *The Paris Review* 162 (2002): n.p. http://www.theparisreview.org/interviews/392/the-art-of-fiction-no-172-louis-begley. Accessed 10.25.2017.

———. *New York Times*, January 19, 2003. http://www.nytimes.com/2003/01/19/movies/my-novel-the-movie-my-baby-reborn-about-schmidt-was-changed-but-not-its-core.html. Accessed 10.25.2017.

Begley, Louis. *Wartime Lies*. 1991. New York: Ballantine Books, 2004.

———. *Memories of a Marriage*. New York: Nan A. Talese/Doubleday, 2013.

Bonilla-Silva, Eduardo. *Racism Without Racists: Color-Blind Racism and the Persistence of Racial Inequality in the United States*. Lanham: Rowman and Littlefield, 2006.

Bonilla-Silva, Eduardo, and David G. Embrick. "'Every Place Has a Ghetto…': The Significance of Whites' Social and Residential Segregation." *Symbolic Interaction* 30, No. 3 (2007): 323–45.

Brodkin, Karen. *How Jews Became White Folks: And What That Says About Race in America*. New Brunswick: Rutgers University Press, 1998.

Charney, Noah. "Schmidt Is Back: Louis Begley: How I Write." *Daily Beast*, August 28, 2013, http://www.thedailybeast.com/louis-begley-how-i-write. Accessed 10.25.2017.

Dunbar-Ortiz, Roxanne. *An Indigenous Peoples' History of the United States*. Boston: Beacon Press, 2014.

Duncan, James, and Nancy Duncan. "Aesthetics, Abjection, and White Privilege in Suburban New York." In *Landscape and Race in the United States*, edited by Richard H. Schein. New York: Routledge, 2006: 157–75.

Edwards, Thomas R. "Palm Beach Story." *The New York Review of Books*, October 31, 1996: 65.

Farough, Steven D. "The Social Geographies of White Masculinities." *Critical Sociology* 30, No. 3 (2004): 241–64.

Flatley, Jonathan. *Affective Mapping: Melancholia and the Politics of Modernism*. Cambridge: Harvard University Press, 2008.

Friend, Tad. *Cheerful Money: Me, My Family, and the Last Days of Wasp Splendor*. New York: Little, Brown and Company, 2009.

Harris, Cheryl I. "Whiteness as Property." *Harvard Law Review* 106, No. 8 (1993): 1707–91.

Hepburn, Allan. "Lost Time: Trauma and Belatedness in Louis Begley's; The Man Who Was Late." *Contemporary Literature* 39, No. 3 (1998): 380–404.

Holliday, Carl. *Marriage Customs Then and Now*. Boston: Stratford, 1919.

Horsman, Reginald. *Race and Manifest Destiny: Origins of Racial Anglo-Saxonism*. Cambridge: Harvard University Press, 1981.

Kazal, Russell A. *Becoming Old Stock: The Paradox of German-American Identity*. Princeton: Princeton University Press, 2004.

Kellman, Steven G. *The Translingual Imagination*. Lincoln: University of Nebraska Press, 2000.

Lensmire, Timothy J. "White Men's Racial Others." *Teachers College Record* 116, No. 3 (2014): 1–32.

Levy, M. S. "A Conceptualization of the Repetition Compulsion." *Psychiatry* 63, No. 1 (2000): 45–53.

Lipsitz, George. *The Possessive Investment in Whiteness: How White People Profit from Identity Politics*. Philadelphia: Temple University Press, 2006.

Mann, Charles C. *1491: New Revelations of the Americas Before Columbus*. New York: Vintage, 2006.

Murfin, Ross, and Supriya M. Ray. *The Bedford Glossary of Critical and Literary Terms*. Boston: Bedford/St. Martin's, 2003

Nussbaum, Martha C. "Jewish Men, Jewish Lawyers: Roth's 'Eli the Fanatic' and the Question of Jewish Masculinity in American Law." In *American Guy: Masculinity in American Law and Literature*, edited by Saul Levmore and Martha C. Nussbaum. Oxford: Oxford University Press, 2014: 165–201.

Oliver, Melvin, and Thomas Shapiro. *Black Wealth/White Wealth: A New Perspective on Racial Inequality*. New York: Routledge, 2006.

Pinder, Sherrow O. *Whiteness and Racialized Ethnic Groups in the United States: The Politics of Remembering*. Lanham, MD: Lexington Books, 2011.

Robinson, Sally. *Marked Men: White Masculinity in Crisis*. New York: Columbia University Press, 2000.

Roediger, David R. *Working Toward Whiteness: How America's Immigrants Become White. The Strange Journey from Ellis Island to the Suburbs*. New York: Basic Books, 2005.

Ronald, Richard. *The Ideology of Home Ownership: Homeowner Societies and the Role of Housing*. Basingstoke: Palgrave Macmillan, 2008.

Sherwood, Jessica Holden. *Wealth, Whiteness, and the Matrix of Privilege: The View from the Country Club*. Lanham, MD: Lexington Books, 2010.

Sullivan, Shannon. "White World-Traveling." *Journal of Speculative Philosophy* 18, No. 4 (2004): 300–4.

———. *Revealing Whiteness: The Unconscious Habits of Racial Privilege*. Bloomington: Indiana University Press, 2006.

Takaki, Ronald. *A Different Mirror: A History of Multicultural America*. Boston: Little, Brown, and Company, 1993.

Thandeka. *Learning to Be White: Money, Race and God in America*. New York: Continuum, 1999.

Tygstrup, Frederik. "Affective Spaces." In *Panic and Mourning: The Cultural Work of Trauma*, edited by Daniela Agostinho, Elisa Antz, and Cátia Ferreira. Berlin and Boston: Walter de Gruyter GmbH, 2012, 195–210.

Van der Kolk, Bessel A. "The Compulsion to Repeat the Trauma: Re-enactment, Revictimization, and Masochism." *Psychiatric Clinics of North America* 12, No. 2 (1989): 389–411.

Wald, Eli. "The Rise and Fall of the WASP and Jewish Law Firms." *Stanford Law Review* 60 (2008): 1803–66.

CHAPTER 7

Epilogue: Margaret Atwood's *The Heart Goes Last* and the Futures of Domineering White Masculinity

As the once-futuristic dawning of the new millennium fades into the past, Margaret Atwood's depiction of a totalitarian, theocratic patriarchy in her 1985 novel, *The Handmaid's Tale,* has undergone a vibrant revival. During the summer of 2017, the online streaming service Hulu offered a popular ten-part adaptation, prompting massive amounts of commentary, some of it critiquing the narrative's ironically white perspective. Many observers also remarked on Hulu's timing, given that far-right populism in the United States had recently gained not only the presidency but also a Republican-led congress. As I write, Mike Pence, the new vice president, appears to be even more inclined toward the possibility of building a real-world version of Atwood's Gilead, given not only his evident enmity for birth control and all forms of abortion but also his stated refusal to dine alone with any woman other than his wife.[1] Shortly after the presidential election, hundreds of thousands of women marched in the nation's capital, some wearing the novel's signature red robes and others carrying signs that read "Make Margaret Atwood Fiction Again!," "NO! To the Republic of Gilead," and a slogan from the novel, *"Nolite Te Bastardes Carborundorum"* ("Don't let the bastards grind you down").[2] If the revival of Atwood's novel itself constitutes a form of nostalgia, it seems to have taken a reflective form, a communal-minded effort to resist current permutations of entrenched domineering white masculinity.

Although Atwood's warning about the danger of a possible Christofascist patriarchal tyranny is clearly pertinent to present

© The Author(s) 2018   223
T. Engles, *White Male Nostalgia in Contemporary North American Literature,* https://doi.org/10.1007/978-3-319-90460-3_7

conditions and threats, I will conclude this study by positing that she provides a closer analogue (albeit also a problematically white one) to current American realities in another novel, *The Heart Goes Last* (2015). As credible observers gauge the contours of the new century's social landscapes, "neoliberalism" has become an increasingly urgent descriptor, encapsulating as it does the declining material circumstances suffered by most people for the profiteering sake of a predominantly white male, increasingly distant elite.[3] In their analysis of masculinities under neoliberalism, Nancy Lindisfarne and Jonathan Neale point out that, as an economic model, neoliberalism is a "deliberate set of strategies to increase the share of profit going to capitalists and corporations."[4] While the euphemizing proponents of its policies tout trickle-down economics, austerity, deregulation, flexible labor forces, and so on as promises of greater prosperity for all, neoliberalism instead "produces more suffering. It does this directly by making work harder, increasing unemployment and shredding social safety nets."[5] As the extremely wealthy grow ever more so as well as more physically distant (and thus psychologically and emotionally distant), the rest of society in so-called developed nations grows more anxiously weary and worried about the future: "[Neoliberal] processes create anxiety that something—anything—might go wrong. This destroys confidence in the future."[6] In *The Heart Goes Last*, Atwood extends this recently reconfigured, increasingly bleak economic order into a potential future, where the history of white masculine tendencies results in commodifying possession and control of nearly everyone and everything, including nostalgia.

Although the five novels considered earlier in this study provide deeply interiorized portraits of white American masculinity, *The Heart Goes Last* takes Atwood's usual wider view. In this latest of her five speculative fictions (the others being *The Handmaid's Tale* and the three-volume MaddAddam series), Atwood, a Canadian, depicts a United States no longer united but ravaged instead by neoliberal policies. The novel effectively addresses a question that I asked at the outset of this study: Although nostalgia is often thought of as an emotion felt by individuals, how does it work to shore up entrenched collective power? In this novel's future, the elite have completely jumped ship to live offshore on barricaded artificial islands, while large swaths of the remaining landscape are wracked with desperation-inducing poverty. In this severely downsized America, most white people have been reduced to conditions long endured by many of their subordinated ethnoracial others, and white male nostalgia has become a commodified lure, used to attract those who seek escape from their bleak precarity in order to extract labor and money from them. The story opens with the car-bound existence of two mononymic thirty-somethings, Stan and Charmaine. Constantly fearing roving bands of people even more distressed than themselves, this married couple barely ekes out a fraught, anxiety-ridden existence. This state of being provokes them into jumping at the chance to work in, and permanently live in, Consilience, a corporate-owned gated community seemingly in the middle of nowhere. The catches are that Consilience contains within it a profit-generating, death penalty–inflicting prison and that joining it voluntarily means signing up for life. *The Heart Goes Last* takes a fast-paced, plot-driven form that combines stark realism with horror and farcical satire; nevertheless, by alternating between the perspectives of its two protagonists, the novel effectively illustrates potential future effects of the currently extant white masculine ideology that weaponizes nostalgia in its continual quest for security of its status and dominance of others.

Prior to winding up in their car, Stan and Charmaine had been "middle-of-the-road people," an implicit indication that they were middle-class white people.[7] Stan previously worked at a robotics company, and Charmaine at a nursing home, but a recent economic crash, which echoes the neoliberal paroxysm of 2008, has cost them not only their steady jobs but also their mortgaged home. Stan now feels acutely emasculated, and therefore more desirous of a traditionally dominant husband role, because Charmaine provides most of their income with dangerous work at a wretched bar-and-brothel. Financial constraints drive Charmaine to consider joining the brothel's sex workers, but an opportunity arises for steady work and security at Consilience, which contains the "experimental" prison named the Positron Project. Atwood satirizes corporate euphemisms by rendering *Consilience* a portmanteau term that combines "con+resilience": *con* denotes convict (and for readers, a second meaning regarding the con job that is the entire Consilience project/factory and, by extension, the neoliberal capitalist order itself), and *resilience* a regular, patronizing call to the workers/prisoners to applaud themselves for working hard (*HGL*, 41). In this setting, the residents swap places, performing prison labor one month and residing during the other in a simulated neighborhood consisting of 1950s-style suburban homes, complete with manicured lawns and piped-in music performed by that era's blandest white pop stars.

Given the hyperincarceration inflicted in the United States in the current neoliberal era on black and brown people as well as the police-state conditions in urban areas exposed and fought against by the Black Lives Matter movement, a fair question arises about this novel that extrapolates from the present in its depiction of a future American prison: "Where are the black and brown characters?"[8] By my reckoning, no one in the novel is identified as any particular race, which by the racial rule of thumb for American fiction probably still means that the characters are all white. Although the novel does show potential results for most United States citizens of current neoliberal policies, which do indeed weaponize what amounts to common modes of white male nostalgia, I can only wish that *The Heart Goes Last* did more to reference racialized disparities in the criminal justice system. Charges leveled in similar terms against *The Handmaid's Tale* further expose a broader thematic absence: the lack of explicit racial portrayals in *The Heart Goes Last*. As recent commentators on *The Handmaid's Tale* have pointed out, the experiences of its protagonist, Offred, echo all too closely those of black women subjected to slavery. Writing for *The Establishment*, Ana Cottle points out that

> Offred's name means literally "Of Fred," signifying the "commander" she "belongs" to, calling to mind the practice of African American slaves taking the surnames of their masters when they were emancipated; she's forbidden to read, a common provision in many slave codes; she needs a special pass to leave the house, a rule akin to the laws restricting the movement of slaves; and she is repeatedly raped by her master, as many slaves were.[9]

Although the depiction of such abuse of white women might seem defensible in a satiric warning about the potential teleology of contemporary state tendencies, the accusation of unwarranted appropriation from black experience becomes less so in light of the novel's inclusion of a network for smuggling women called "The Underground Femaleroad." There's also the extreme narrative marginalizing of black characters, most of whom have been shipped off to confinement in what used to be North Dakota. Such authorial acts of racial appropriation and elision make some sense in *The Handmaid's Tale* because it depicts a social order overtly grounded in fundamentalist Christian, white supremacist patriarchy. However, *The Heart Goes Last* is harder to defend in these terms, as the presumably white male leaders are also so far offstage that any motives they might have beyond economic exploitation are indiscernible.

Nevertheless, the novel does effectively depict and warn about common contemporary white male dispositions, including the ongoing allure that nostalgia has for many white men under siege. Instead of an imagined threat from women and ethnoracial minorities, who supposedly seek to emasculate and displace white men in a zero-sum social order, the real threat is economic, coming as it long has from the domineering elite, comprised largely of white men who stoke raced and gendered resentment in order to distract attention from entrenched class divisions. In Consilience, the fabricated neighborhood's clichéd stylings, which serve as the initial lure for voluntary residents like Stan and Charmaine, manifest a shadowy corporate commodification of white nostalgia. Operationalized as well, this nostalgia functions in the same way current politically deployed forms do, by evoking longings—which have been heightened in our time by both the steady rise of economic precarity and the increasing cultural, political, and workforce presence of racial minorities and women—for a time when white, masculine middle-class status seemed more secure and more promising. On the margins of the narrative, the unseen elite reside offshore in sequestered opulence, pulling the strings of both their minions and the cattle-like *hoi polloi* upon whom they prey. In our current neoliberal order, the elite already commodify white male nostalgia, pandering via advertising to the sense that things used to be better by promising, as both Donald Trump and Ronald Reagan did, to "make America great again," an implicit communal project in which citizens can supposedly participate by exercising their purchasing power and by agreeing that the real threat to widespread economic disparity is various groups of nonwhite people, who play only small roles in common white fantasises of postwar economic prosperity.[10] In Atwood's satiric future, the elite commodify nostalgia by peddling not only the chance of permanent residence in Consilience but also the sexually charged fantasies of Las Vegas, where some of those living outside the community can still afford to rent the prison's primary product, life-like Elvis and Marilyn sexbots, as well as living Elvis and Marilyn impersonators, who work as companions, party entertainers, and sex workers.

Another contemporary analogue in *The Heart Goes Last* is a more specific revival in our times of domineering white masculinity's de facto possession of others, the increasing privatization of prisons. One result is the hyper-exploitation of prison labor in profit-driven prisons sited in rural communities that have also been ravaged by several decades of neoliberal economic policies. Relatedly, the ever-growing scarcity of well-paying jobs already pushes many Americans into activities that the state increasingly deems criminal, while others are driven to work in prisons, places where the wages and working conditions are such that many realize how easily they could find themselves more literally imprisoned. For the immiserated populations in such locales, the resemblance to Consilience is already stark.

Although Atwood foregoes depiction of the racial disparities in the judicial system, the hidden ethnicity of Sloan Wilson's novel—in the cases of both author and protagonist, a resurgent Anglo-Saxonism obscured by the postwar expansion and normalization of whiteness—exists in Consilience in the form of a pervasive lack of racial and ethnic specificity. Again, because race is not specified, readers gather that everyone is white; both their whiteness and any lingering ethnic affiliations that such people might have go unspoken. By focusing on the precarity of formerly "middle-of-the-road" (middle-class white) people and by emphasizing the increasingly ubiquitous panoptic surveillance that helps to imprison residents of both Consilience spaces, Atwood warns readers about the potential endgame of those who enact a history of white masculine dominance and exploitation—a callous, rapacious elite, relentlessly bent on profit-seeking possession of all aspects of life among the subjugated. When Stan's brother, Con, organizes a kidnapping of Ed, the leader of Consilience, news reports expose perhaps its most vile function: "it was clear that after Management had gone through their stash of criminals and also realized what the going price was for livers and kidneys, they'd started in on the shoplifters and pot-smokers, and then they'd been snatching people off the streets because money talks, and once it had started talking to Positron it wouldn't shut up" (*HGL*, 285). Current conditions resemble de facto elite possession of others for the sake of profit closely enough that the novel's depiction of a prison industry that snatches people in order to sell their organs seems close to imminently plausible.

In the late twentieth century, white masculine anxieties about increasingly restive and resistant women, as examined most extensively in Wright's *Savage Holiday* and Begley's *About Schmidt*, often prompted a nostalgic desire for an earlier, supposedly more submissive and pliant femininity. Atwood immediately foregrounds this form of hegemonic power under threat in the opening epigraphs of *The Heart Goes Last*, which reference the Pygmalion myth and the complaints of a sex-toy reviewer about the difficulty of finding objects that feel like the real thing (that is, like the fetishized parts of an actual woman). Seemingly in response to his diminished circumstances, Stan's gendered objectification of Charmaine intensifies when he becomes bored with her supposed lack of passion for him during sex, thereby framing his boredom, and thus her, in terms of sexual desire. More broadly, sexual objectification takes on the form of restorative nostalgia with a product of the profit-driven community/prison complex, "sexbots" (the most popular models replicate Marilyn and Elvis, and Stan eventually escapes in a shipping box while pretending to be one of the latter).

Still feeling emasculated by his lack of autonomy while serving a life sentence in what is undeniably a prison, Stan longs for self-bolstering reflection in a subordinated other. This feeling is seemingly relievable by the acquisition of a lust-filled partner, preferably one whose beauty would make him the envy of other men. Stan's efforts to regain his self-esteem take the form of elaborate sexual fantasies about "Jasmine," his imagined name for the woman who functions as the wife of the pair that occupies Stan and Charmaine's house every other month, a pair of counterparts whom they are forbidden to meet. Stan's feelings for Jasmine arise from his masculine longing for control and apparent autonomy, a nostalgia that includes restoration of himself as head-of-the-home breadwinner; they're also a reminder on Atwood's part of the ultimately frustrating nature of this longing felt by many men amidst neoliberalism's expectation that both partners work full-time or longer in order to afford and maintain a suburban household. As Andrea Cornwall points out in her study of masculinities under neoliberalism, the reactionary ideology of "man as provider reduces available masculinities to a single idealized figure." In addition, Cornwall adds, with the exacerbating effects of neoliberal economic policies, "in which patterns of consumption and costs have been ratcheted up, being able to achieve the demands of [normative heterosexual masculinity] becomes an unattainable aspiration for most men."[11] I would add, as Atwood effectively does, that this ideology also objectifies the man's partner, creating a possessed status that Charmaine rejects when she enacts her own sexual agency by having an affair with the man who turns out to be the partner of "Jasmine." In terms of white patriarchal possessiveness, the novel portrays not only a potential future where masculine desire for sex with enthusiastic, conventionally beautiful women is a common impetus for self-affirming possession of them, but also compliant sexbots as a compensatory commonplace, a logical extension of economically bludgeoned white masculinity. The novel's sexbot metaphor suggests that Stan does not miss only passionate sex with Charmaine. As with Begley's recently retired protagonist Albert Schmidt, the emasculating diminution of Stan's economic circumstances plays a primary role in driving him to seek restoration of a sense of control via objectifying fantasies of masculine possession of a conventionally desirable and compliant woman.

In their distanced offshore locales, Atwood's offstage elite enact a logical extension of white masculine spatiality, the self-staging movement into seemingly empty places also dramatized by Carol Shields in the form of Jack Bowman's representatively white male conceptions of socio-geographic space. Such space is overlaid ideologically by the collective dominant white male psyche not only as effectively empty, except when selectively populated, but also as an appropriate stage for enactment of active, agential white masculine subjectivity. The recent efforts of entrepreneur Elon Musk toward colonization of Mars—for those who could afford it—again enact this fundamentally unquenchable thirst for conceptually empty yet usable land and its resources.[12] As Atwood's disengaged elite move offshore into conceptually unoccupied oceanographic space, they also pursue further opportunities for exploitation of another resource—the rest of humanity. One method for doing so is to evoke and deploy a seemingly restorative form of nostalgia, conjured in the guise of 1950s (middle-class white) Americana. Although patriotism does not explicitly appear in this novel's setting, a particularly whitened form of United States nationalism nevertheless is registered in Atwood's depiction of commodified nostalgia in the form of iconic dead living legends Elvis and Marilyn, the era's other white pop stars and music, its architectural and residential designs, and its domestic settings and accoutrements.[13] As social theorist Zygmunt Bauman points out in his recent analysis of permutations of nostalgia in the neoliberal era, *Retrotopia*, the fracturing and recently accelerated pace of global economic interaction has provided an increasingly denationalized elite the opportunity to deploy nationalistic sentiment as a diversionary rallying tool. As neoliberal globalization degrades a populace's sense of social stability, politicians and corporate advertising teams disseminate nostalgia-inducing representations of prior, seemingly more stable and homogeneous times, times that were "unambiguously 'ours,' unspoiled by 'their' obtrusive proximity."[14] Smaller, effectively tribal figurations—of picket-fenced neighborhoods, racially monochromatic small towns, and so on—are often nationalist at their core. Yet they can seem comforting, especially for those white men who feel, as does *Underworld*'s Eric Deming, that they once belonged in such settings and that their dominant status in them was secure and unchallenged. With the specular figuration of Consilience, Atwood satirizes the insular, backward-looking nature of the allure of such reactionary tribalism.

In these terms, the novel's conjoined town-and-prison arrangement is the satirically logical conclusion of a process brought about by the accelerated pace and constraints of twenty-first-century life under neoliberalism. As Svetlana Boym writes, one result is a "global epidemic of nostalgia, an affective yearning for community with a collective memory, a longing for continuity in a fragmented world."[15] For Boym, as for Atwood and all of the other novelists considered here, "nostalgia goes beyond individual psychology," as it "inevitably reappears as a defense mechanism in a time of accelerated rhythms of life and historical upheavals."[16] At the same time, as Bauman helpfully adds, advanced capitalism continues to promote and foster atomized individualism, a fabricated subjectivity that is figured most fully as middle-class white masculinity. Throughout United States history, this ironically collective white male fantasy has constituted a continual effort to shift the conceptual framework for "the prospects of human happiness"—from collectivist ideals and effort to the supposed freedom of the atomized agent, who is figured as "unfixed, untied from any particular *topos*... individualized, privatized and personalized."[17] As Bauman and the novelists considered here warn us, such ultimately immiserating and endangering notions of ideal citizenship and subjecthood have been "sold by the powers that be and embraced by most of their subjects as liberation: breaking free from the stern demands of subordination and discipline—at the cost of social services and state protection.... Annoyances of constraints [have been] replaced with no less demeaning, frightening, and aggravating risks that can but saturate the condition of self-reliance by decree."[18] Nevertheless, despite such atomization, a general zeitgeist persists, albeit one that has by now nearly relinquished hope for a more equitable and openly diverse, yet unified, national future. As stable social institutions and a sense of collective participation in them continue to disintegrate, wistful longings for earlier modes of supposed collectivity become both more attractive and easier to inspire as a mode of exploitative manipulation.

In terms of restorative nostalgia prompted more specifically in such a milieu by white masculine denial, what Stan tries to deny is another prison of sorts, that of work—that is, of the heightened *need* to labor, ever more and in ever-declining work conditions, unless one wants to run the risks that come with homelessness, as figured in the couple's previous car-bound life, or with life-sustaining crime, as figured in the activities of Stan's brother, the aptly named Con (short for Conor). The imprisoning labor that Stan performs in Consilience provides what feels somewhat more like a home, but it nevertheless parallels the declining fortunes, felt as emasculating, of today's middle-class white men. Stan's demotion from the cognitive work of software engineering to the manual labor of scooter repair references the circumstances of many putatively middle-class white men in an increasingly neoliberal order, men who continue to seek a sense of autonomy in labor while denying the reality of the relentless teleology of their economic circumstances, sometimes toward desperate precarity and at other times toward the same ennui and threatened autonomy that is depicted in the laboring lives of Wilson's Tom Rath and DeLillo's Nick Shay. Denial of such conditions, the awareness of which prods at one's consciousness like *Underworld*'s wandering garbage ship in search of a receiving harbor, can impel the search for restorative modes of compensation. To continue toiling happily in such a rigged setup, while still being as vaguely aware of the broader context of exploitation as Stan is, constitutes trying to live in denial not only of the declining personal fortunes afforded by one's own work but also of the exploitation of others in which one participates, and which helps to make one's relatively easier existence possible. By switching her characters back and forth monthly, from laboring de facto prisoners to relaxing faux-suburbanites, Atwood figures both sides of this contemporary psychic polarity.

Atwood also updates the critique of the moral destitution of white patriarchal ideology provided six decades earlier by Richard Wright in *Savage Holiday*, particularly its self-righteous and self-constituting exploitation of others deemed inferior. Neoliberal policies and practices continue to demand morally deadening labor, performed primarily for the ever-increasing benefit of distant elites who remain predominantly white male and who profit not only from increasingly exploitative labor conditions but also from the worldwide theft from and even greater immiseration of others. A difference from the postwar and Cold War eras for those currently living in the United States is that whereas formerly much of the exploitation took place overseas, now it takes place domestically as well. As Mat Johnson writes in a particularly perceptive review of *The Heart Goes Last*, its dystopian social order references "a middle-class existence that can be sustained only by economic oppression. Instead of a wealthy lifestyle made possible by sweatshops and slave wages in distant lands, the Positron Project's innovation is that now the exploited and those who benefit from the exploitation are the same people."[19] In Consilience, these inhumane conditions and relations are also represented by the "snatching" of people by shadowy forces (that is, operatives who actually function on behalf of the wealthy elite) for organ transplants and for neurological conversion to lovesick sex slaves. Whereas Stan's prison labor consists of the relatively benign task of scooter repair, Charmaine's job is to administer lethal injections to condemned (and essentially kidnapped) prisoners. Her organ-harvested victims are men further down the economic ladder, incarcerated (as in our times) for increasingly petty crimes. Laboring within a social order that deadens moral awareness of her own part in an overarching system of abusive exploitation, Charmaine squelches her compassion for these men, and thus her qualms about what she does to them, by telling herself that if she doesn't kill them, others will. The smiling mask worn by corporate profiteers and expected of its employees is also referenced, as Charmaine kills in ways that strike her as kindly (that is, by adding soothing words and parting kisses). As both Atwood and Sloan Wilson suggest, working in morally deadening conditions in the hopes of securing an increasingly unattainable, and thus nostalgic, domestic ideal pushes people to deny the broader realities and implications of their working lives, thereby numbing parts of themselves—including their sensitivity, their mental acuity, and their morality—in the process. In these terms, Charmaine's labor dramatizes the heightened psychological and emotional contortions that many of us perform in order to maintain a sense of ourselves as reasonably moral, ethical beings.

At the same time, like other novelists studied here, Atwood eventually manages to offer hope. As *The Heart Goes Last* closes, Stan believes that his possessive desire for a woman devoted in all ways only to himself has come true, in the form of a devoted, because neurologically altered, Charmaine. However, once the nefarious doings of the Positron Corporation have been exposed by an intrepid reporter (if only to be subsequently trivialized in corporate-owned news and social media), the novel's final plot twist is the revelation that Charmaine actually hasn't been altered; her devotion to Stan is an act, performed by her with a form of free will, in the sense that it was her in effect pretending to be a living robot. Escape is achieved from the neoliberal imposition of conditions approaching Agembenian bare life in camp-like abjectivity, and the novel's ending question, expressive of a larger hope, is whether Stan will go on to accept love from Charmaine that she would provide on terms that she plays an equal part in drafting. To do so, he would have to see her not as a de facto object but instead as an agential subject, free of his self-aggrandizing control. Faith in humanity's future remains, not only in the possibility for a genuinely loving relationship for Stan and Charmaine but also in the earlier heartfelt sympathy that drove Charmaine's soothing treatment of condemned prisoners. If the "heart"—that is, our desire for connection with other people—does in this sense "go last," finding ways to heighten sympathy, as literary fiction can do so well, remains an effective tool in the quest to build effectively resistant forms of solidarity.

The dominance of white men in the United States, which once seemed (especially to them) so everlasting, is currently under more fire than ever. In response, common late-twentieth-century white male emotions endure, including not only anger, frustration, and anxiety but also such complexes as a sense of collective victimhood and a compensatory turn to restorative nostalgia. These feelings animate increasingly anxious performances of white male identity, threatening the livelihood of both themselves and others. Because so many members of the white masculine collective persist in nostalgic efforts toward the resuscitation of self-bolstering gendered and ethnoracial hierarchies, a greater possibility of horrific actual futures continues as well. However, as demonstrated by five of the six novelists considered here who are otherwise positioned—some as women and some as Canadian, African American, Italian American, or Jewish American—with their engaging, provocative, and inspiring exposure of hegemonic power and of proclivities enacted by those who embody it, hope can be found in the obstinate resistance to power by those subject to it—and, we might also hope, in the ability of most domineering white men to take a more discerning look at themselves.

In *Frames of War: When Is Life Grievable?*, Judith Butler analyzes a relevant schism in the general post-9/11 culture and consciousness of so-called developed nations: the split between deaths widely considered "grievable" and the many more othered deaths that provoke no widespread Western grief. For Butler, the contrast between collective American paroxysms of anguish for those who died in the World Trade Center attacks and the relative American silence regarding the many hundreds of thousands more who have subsequently died in Iraq and

Afghanistan reveals a collective pathology. Wrought by the spread of dehumanizing hierarchical thinking, this collective conceptual contrast, between the valued lives of people like oneself and those of others who are disregarded because they supposedly differ from oneself, initially arises when "the subject asserts its own righteous destructiveness at the same time as it seeks to immunize itself against the thought of its own precariousness."[20] In response, Butler issues a reparative "call to interdependency," a transnational, and indeed contra-national, recognition and nurturing, not only of our common humanity but also of our mutual reliance and subjective, ontological constitution. In much the same manner, all of the novelists studied here intricately portray both the imposing power of extant white masculine ideological frameworks and the anxieties and fears that motivate common white male impositions. These obdurate forces can hamper efforts to move toward a heightened state of empathetic consciousness when white men are confronted with the costs of their collectivity's rampant use of their subordinated others for illusory modes of seemingly invulnerable self-assertion. On the other hand, neoliberalism's heightened, pervasive emphasis on individualistic, atomized thought and action is, after all, relatively recent. Indeed, the increasingly common turn for recompense to nostalgia, as opposed to the cynically commodified deployment of it, suggests an underpinning of powerful ideals and collective feelings that have yet to be extinguished. Literary fiction can play an effective part here. People still, of course, enjoy stories, and the novels considered here finally serve as a defense of the healing potential of narrative itself, exposing as it often does the interior machinations of those who have built our worlds, and thereby suggesting avenues toward the building of better ones.

NOTES

1. On Mike Pence's legislative efforts to restrict access to abortion and birth control, see Murray. Regarding Pence's personal, Christian-influenced dining (and drinking) rules in regard to women other than his wife, see Parker, who writes, "In 2002, Mike Pence told the Hill that he never eats alone with a woman other than his wife and that he won't attend events featuring alcohol without her by his side, either."
2. For photos of these signs and others based on *The Handmaid's Tale*, see Levine.

3. Regarding the membership of the domineering elite as predominantly white male, see Feagin and Ducey, who write,

> The central problem of the twenty-first century is elite white men. They long ago created what we term the *elite white-male dominance system*, a complex and oppressive system central to most western societies that now affects much of the planet. This small elite rules actively, undemocratically, and globally, yet remains largely invisible to the billions of people it routinely dominates. (1, emphasis in original)

4. Lindisfarne and Neale, 29.
5. Ibid., 43.
6. Ibid.
7. Atwood, *The Heart Goes Last*, 7. Hereafter cited as *HGL*.
8. Hyperincarceration is Loïc Wacquant's term for the current, decades-long slew of criminal justice policies and practices that primarily target African American men. As Wacquant writes, race and class are intertwined in this immiserating elite endeavor—an intertwining that fits Atwood's novel thematically but that she declines to dramatize:

> the stupendous expansion and intensification of the activities of police, criminal courts, and prison over the past thirty years have been finely targeted, first by class, second by race, and third by place, leading not to *mass* incarceration but to the *hyper*-incarceration of (sub)proletarian black men from the imploding ghetto. This triple selectivity reveals that the building of the hyperactive and hypertrophic penal state that has made the US world champion in incarceration is at once a delayed reaction to the Civil Rights movement and the ghetto riots of the mid-1960s … and a disciplinary instrument unfurled to foster the neoliberal revolution by helping to impose insecure labor as the normal horizon of work for the unskilled fractions of the postindustrial laboring class. (n.p.) For an accessible, highly influential analysis of the relatively recent hyper-incarceration of African Americans, see Alexander.

9. Cottle, n.p.
10. Regarding Ronald Reagan's use of the phrase "make America great again," see Margolin.
11. Cornwall, 16.
12. An American citizen with roots and experiences in numerous countries, Elon Musk was born in 1971 in South Africa to a Canadian mother. His

current net worth is commonly estimated at over $20 billion (USD). For analysis of Musk's currently perceived embodiment of "heroic masculinity," see Markus Giesler, who writes that Musk's "business credentials read like the biography of *Iron Man* alter-ego Tony Stark: after selling his PayPal venture, he became CEO of both Tesla and the space exploration company SpaceX in addition to being the chairman of innovative solar panel maker Solar City. And like Tony Stark, Elon Musk talks, seriously, about colonizing Mars and saving the human race."

13. The nostalgia-laden concept of a "dead living legend" arises during a disaster scene in DeLillo's novel *White Noise*, where evacuees listen as Babette Gladney reads predictions from a tabloid magazine: "From beyond the grave, dead living legend John Wayne will communicate telepathically with President Reagan to help frame U.S. foreign policy. Mellowed by death, the strapping actor will advocate a hopeful policy of peace and love" (146).

14. Bauman, 61.
15. Boym, xiv.
16. Ibid., xv, xiv.
17. Bauman, 4.
18. Ibid., 5–6.
19. Johnson, n.p.
20. Butler, 48.

BIBLIOGRAPHY

Alexander, Michelle. *The New Jim Crow: Mass Incarceration in the Age of Colorblindness.* New York: The New Press, 2012.

Atwood, Margaret. *The Heart Goes Last.* New York: Doubleday, 2015.

Bauman, Zygmunt. *Retrotopia.* Cambridge: Polity Press, 2017.

Butler, Judith. *Frames of War: When Is Life Grievable?* London: Verso, 2009.

Cornwall, Andrea. "Introduction: Masculinities Under Neoliberalism." In *Masculinities Under Neoliberalism*, edited by Andrea Cornwall, Frank G. Karioris, and Nancy Lindisfarne. London: Zed Books, 2016: 1–28.

Cottle, Ana. "'The Handmaid's Tale': A White Feminist's Dystopia." *The Establishment*, May 17, 2017. https://theestablishment.co/the-handmaids-tale-a-white-feminist-s-dystopia-80da75a40dc5. Accessed 2.8.2018.

DeLillo, Don. *White Noise.* New York: Viking, 1985.

Feagin, Joe R., and Kimberly Ducey. *Elite White Men Ruling: Who, What, When, Where, and How.* New York and London: Routledge, 2017.

Giesler, Markus. "Tesla's Chief Driver of Success: Masculinity." *Huffpost, The Blog*, July 10, 2014. https://www.huffingtonpost.com/markus-giesler/meet-the-tesla-man_b_5941716.html. Accessed 10.23.2017.

Johnson, Mat. "Margaret Atwood's *The Heart Goes Last.*" *New York Times,* September 23, 2015. https://www.nytimes.com/2015/09/27/books/review/margaret-atwoods-the-heart-goes-last.html. Accessed 2.7.2018.

Levine, Sara. "These Margaret Atwood Signs at the Women's March Will Give You the Chills." *Bustle,* January 21, 2017. https://www.bustle.com/p/these-margaret-atwood-signs-at-the-womens-march-will-give-you-the-chills-32074. Accessed 2.7.2018.

Lindisfarne, Nancy, and Johnathan Neale. "Masculinities and the Lived Experience of Neoliberalism." In *Masculinities Under Neoliberalism,* edited by Andrea Cornwall, Frank G. Karioris, and Nancy Lindisfarne. London: Zed Books, 2016: 29–50.

Margolin, Emma. "'Make America Great Again'—Who Said It First?" *NBC News,* September 9, 2016. https://www.nbcnews.com/politics/2016-election/make-america-great-again-who-said-it-first-n645716.   Accessed 10.23.2107.

Murray, Melissa. "Intimate Choices, Public Threats: Reproductive and LGBTQ Rights Under a Trump Administration." *New England Journal of Medicine* 376, No. 4 (January 26, 2017): 301–3.

Parker, Ashley. "Karen Pence Is the Vice President's 'Prayer Warrior,' Gut Check and Shield." *Washington Post,* March 28, 2017. https://www.washingtonpost.com/politics/karen-pence-is-the-vice-presidents-prayer-warrior-gut-check-and-shield/2017/03/28/3d7a26ce-0a01-11e7-8884-96e6a6713f4b_story.html. Accessed 10.23.2017.

Wacquant, Loïc. "Class, Race and Hyperincarceration in Revanchist America." *Journal of the Research Group on Socialism and Democracy* 28, No. 3 (November, 2014): n.p. http://sdonline.org/66/class-race-and-hyperincarceration-in-revanchist-america/. Accessed 2.8.2018.

INDEX

A

African Americans and racialized
blackness, 3, 11, 29–31, 34–40,
53–54, 60n22, 61n29, 62n30,
81, 89–95, 102n19, 120, 140,
148–56, 158, 166–69, 177n11,
178n14, 226, 236n8
Agamben, Giorgio, 17
Ahmed, Sara, 115
Alexander, Michelle, 236
Alexander, Victoria N., 215
Atwood, Margaret, 87
Handmaid's Tale, The, 17, 223–24,
226
Heart Goes Last, The, 17–18, 175,
223–35
Avila, Eric, 178n14

B

Babb, Valerie, 56
Baldwin, James, 11, 102n19
Barrett, James, 57n7
Bauman, Zygmunt, 230–31
Baym, Nina, 7
Beckman-Long, Brenda, 109, 113

Begley, Louis
About Schmidt, 14–15, 185–215,
228, 230
Matters of Honor, 194
Memories of a Marriage, 216n16
personal background, 14, 185
Wartime Lies, 185
Berthold, Dana, 87
Bloom, John, 168
Bonilla-Silva, Eduardo, 218n45
Boren, Zachary, 75
Bourdieu, Pierre, 4
Boym, Svetlana, 8, 113, 119, 123,
163, 231. *See also* Nostalgia,
reflective and restorative
Branca, Ralph, 168
Brodkin, Karen, 51, 194
Bruce, Lenny, 156, 160, 172
Butler, Judith, 234

C

Carroll, Charles, 94, 104n41
Cavelier, René-Robert, Sieur de La
Salle. *See* La Salle
Cazdyn, Eric, 21n25

© The Editor(s) (if applicable) and The Author(s) 2018
T. Engles, *White Male Nostalgia in Contemporary North American
Literature*, https://doi.org/10.1007/978-3-319-90460-3

Cheever, Abigail, 63n38
Christ, Birte, 63n39
Coates, Ta-Nehisi, 18n1
Columbus, Christoper, 121
Connell, R.W., 20n7
Conrad, Joseph, 203
Coontz, Stephanie, 17, 21n23
Cornwall, Andrea, 229

D
Dean, Robert, 42–43
DeLillo, Don
  Americana, 147, 160, 176n4
  Body Artist, The, 160
  Great Jones Street, 160
  Mao II, 160
  personal background, 147, 176n2
  Underworld, 9, 15–16, 147–76,
    186, 231, 232
  White Noise, 148, 166, 173, 174,
    177n8, 237n11
Doane, Ashley W., 31, 55, 59n15,
  59n21, 178n19
Driscoll, Christopher, 93
Dubek, Laura, 101n10
Ducey, Kimberly, 236n3
Dunbar-Ortiz, Roxanne, 79
Duncan, Jack, 201, 206
Duncan, Nancy, 201, 206
Duvall, John N., 148, 152
Dwyer, Owen J., 13, 113, 140

E
Edwards, Thomas R., 191
Eisenhower, Dwight D., 190
Ellison, Ralph, *Invisible Man*, 30, 31,
  58n8
Ethnicist presence, 10, 41–46
Ethnicity, 35, 57n4, 57n7

and animatedness, 53, 64n48,
  65n52
as authenticity, 44–46, 63n38
dominant hidden, 10, 26, 31, 55,
  59n15, 228
German, 190, 203, 208, 218n40
Irish, 61n27, 157
Italian, 15, 41–46, 50–53, 147,
  154–60, 176n3, 179n23
Jewish, 48–49, 51, 64, 156, 160,
  185, 188, 192–97, 212–14
Polish, 129, 201. *See also See also*
  White Anglo-Saxon Protestant
  (WASP)

F
Fanon, Frantz, 90
Farough, Steven D., 136, 200
Feagin, Joe R., 236n3
Flatley, Jonathan, 187
Forman, Murray, 179n32
Forth, Christopher, 64n40
Freud, Sigmund and Freudian inter-
  pretation, 75, 77, 98, 101n10,
  210
Friend, Tad, 190
Frye Jacobson, Mattew, 36

G
Gamble, Sarah, 143n21
Gauthier, Marni, 180n41
Gerstle, Gary, 61n29, 62n31
Giaimo, Paul, 162
Gleason, Paul, 162
Goetz, Rebecca Anne, 88
Gombrowicz, Witold, 217n35
Gonsalves, Joshua David, 54
Gourevitch, Philip, 102n21
Guglielmo, Thomas, A., 159

H

Hale, Grace Elizabeth, 144n35
Haney López, Ian, 3, 179n22
Harding, Wendy, 123, 164
Harris, Cheryl, 199
Harvey, Jennifer, 71
Heise, Thomas, 152
Hill, Henry, 157, 179n21
Hoberek, Andrew, 58n8
Hodgkin, Katherine, 132
Holliday, Carl, 192
Holway, John, 177n11
Honeywill, Ross, 11
Hoover, J. Edgar, 155, 172
Horsman, Reginald, 26
Howells, Coral Ann, 112, 127
Hutner, Gordon, 58

J

JanMohamed, Abdul R., 92, 101n33
Johnson, Allan G., 133–34
Johnson, Lisa, 143n21
Johnson, Mat, 232
Jones III, John Paul, 13, 113, 140
Jurca, Catherine, 32, 59n16

K

Kafka, Franz, 216n5
Katznelson, Ira, 60n22
Kennedy, John F., 43, 63n37
Kerouac, Jack, 44, 64n40
Kidd, Colin, 94
King, Martin Luther, Jr., 103n25
Kissinger, Henry, 195
Kovel, Joel, 4

L

La Salle, 122, 131, 143n22
Lensmire, Timothy, 217n34

Leotta, Alfio, 101n14
Lipsitz, George, 36, 101n15, 199
Long, Christian, 31
Lowenthal, David, 27, 178n20
Lugones, María C., 217n33

M

Mailer, Norman, 44, 64n40
Mansfield, Jayne, 151, 161
Martschukat, Jürgen, 58n10
Masculinity
    as rational, 39, 80
    entitled white, 188–97
    WASP masculinity as effeminate,
        42–43
    WASP masculinity as sovereign,
        197–202
Matt, Susan J., 28
Medovoi, Leerom, 152
Mills, Charles, 31
Monroe, Marilyn, 161, 227
Moore, Donnie, 168, 180n37
Moreton-Robinson, Aileen, 14
Morrison, Toni, 10, 58n9, 59n12,
        62n30, 178n18
    Africanist presence, 38, 39, 155
Mraović-O'Hare, Damjana, 153–54
Musk, Elon, 230, 236n12

N

Native Americans and indigeneity, 79,
        113, 115, 116, 123, 131–33,
        135, 138, 166
Naturalization Act (1790), 27, 36,
        179n22
Neoliberalism, 175, 223–35
Ngai, Sianne, 53, 65n48
Noon, David, 180n35
Nostalgia, 20n13
    as collective phenomenon, 75–76

commodified and operationalized, 227
for nature and wilderness, 118–24
immigrants, as mental illness of, 27
pseudo-feudal, 47–55
reflective, 8, 14, 123, 124–31, 160–64, 163
restorative, 8, 13, 113, 119
Nussbaum, Martha C., 193, 194

O
Osteen, Mark, 162
O'Toole, Garson, 20

P
Parker, Charlie, 167
Payne, Buckner H., 94, 104n40
Peck, Gregory, 25
Pence, Mike, 223, 235n1
Perkinson, James W., 93, 102n22, 103n38
Pierce, Jason E., 119, 137
Pinder, Sherrow O., 189
Porter, William Sydney (O. Henry), 215, 218n46
Presley, Elvis, 227
Purwar, Nirmal, 39, 56

R
Radstone, Susannah, 132
Reagan, Ronald, 227, 236n10, 237n13
Resaldo, Renato, 171
Robinson, Jackie, 177n11
Robinson, Sally, 6, 7, 55, 173, 177n8, 186, 212
Rodia, Sobata (Simon Rodia), 162

Roediger, David R., 57n4, 57n7, 179n23
Roy, Wendy, 110

S
Salinger, J.D., 178n16
Salván, Paula Martín, 176n7
Schwebel, Sara L., 10
Scorsese, Martin, 157
Sherwood, Jessica Holden, 192
Shields, Carol, 172
    Happenstance, 12–13, 15, 160, 165, 166, 176n4, 230
    personal background, 109, 142n7
    Stone Diaries, The, 124–27
Silver, Nate, 18n1
Sinatra, Frank, 153
Street names, raced and/or gendered, 115–18, 139, 166
Sullivan, Shannon, 76, 122, 143n23, 200, 202

T
Thandeka, 209
Thomson, Bobby, 169
Traber, Daniel S., 148, 176n5
Trinh, T. Minh-ha, 116
Trollope, Anthony, 206
Trump, Donald, 1, 2, 5, 227
    white male support for, 18n1
Twine, France Winddance, 59n17
Tygstrup, Frederik, 2, 216n4

V
van der Kolk, Bessel A., 218n42
Vincent, Jonathan, 30
Vogel, Todd, 64n41
Vrasti, Wanda, 169

W
Wacquant, Loïc, 236n8
Walker, Margaret, 104n42
Warren, Jonathan W., 59n17
Watson, Veronica T., 80
Watts Towers, the, 162
Wayne, John, 237n11
White Anglo-Saxon Protestant
    (WASP), 3, 14, 197
  as dominant hidden ethnicity, 10,
    26, 55
  history, 29, 185, 190, 198
  law firms (white shoe), 196
White male
  common dispositions, 3
  death drive, 89–99
  emotional constipation, 35–40, 81,
    170
  immaturity, 205–09
  mobility, 135–40, 143n23
  shame, 209–15
White male nostalgia
  and baseball, 16, 151–54, 167–68
  forms of, 9; commodified, 224–35;
    denying, 147–76, 231–32;
    ethnicized, 25–57; moralizing,
    69–100; possessive, 14, 78–79,
    185–215; spatialized, 79,
    109–42
White masculinity, 20n8
  and bodily containment, 15, 17,
    71–72, 98, 117, 206–08,
    218n37
  and work, 30, 34, 43, 48, 71–73,
    84, 98

White men
  as free-floating individuals, 2
  as unmarked, 4, 29, 34, 70, 80
Whiteness
  and Christianity, 81–89, 93–96,
    102n22, 104239
  and socio-spatial epistemology, 113,
    132–40, 164, 202–05, 230
  as disembodied, 35–40, 43, 62n30,
    118
  as ever expanding, 34, 59n17
  as purity, 81–89, 137, 171
  as unmarked, 36, 56, 58n9, 133,
    144n35, 172
  relational assertion of, 77, 80, 81,
    85, 102n17, 104n38, 123,
    148, 201
Whitman, Walt, 137, 139, 161
Wilson, Sloan
  All the Best People, 26, 37, 193
  Man in the Gray Flannel Suit, The,
    3, 7, 9, 10, 25–57, 139, 172
  personal background, 3, 26, 60
  What Shall We Wear to This Party?,
    60
Wright, Richard
  "Between the World and Me", 91,
    102n17
  Black Boy, 90
  personal background, 69
  Savage Holiday, 9, 10–12, 18, 26,
    156, 210, 228, 232